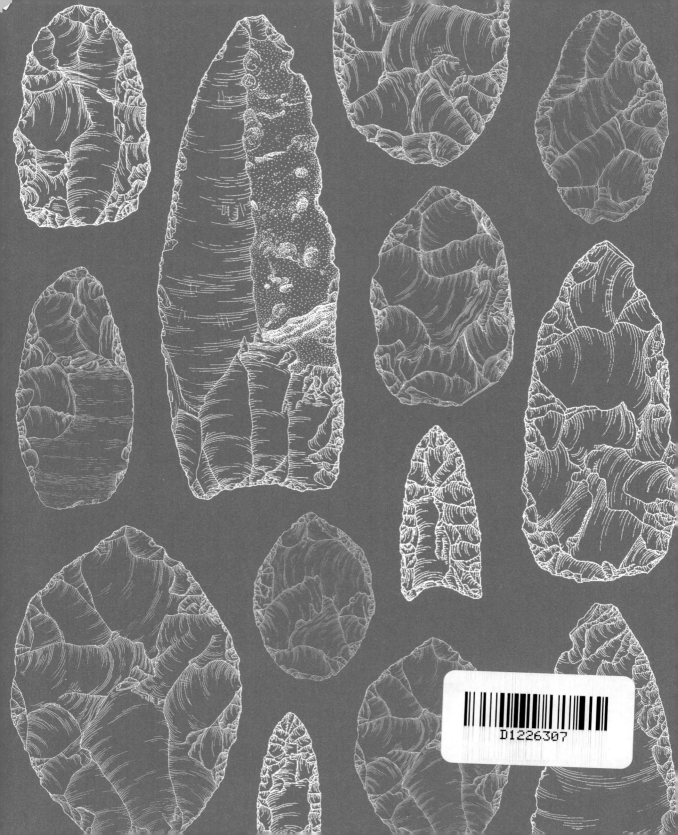

IN SEARCH OF
ICE AGE
AMERICANS

IN SEARCH OF
ICE AGE
AMERICANS

By Kenneth B. Tankersley
Foreword by Douglas Preston

Gibbs Smith, Publisher
Salt Lake City

First Edition
06 05 04 03 02   5 4 3 2 1

Text © 2002 by Kenneth B. Tankersley
Foreword © 2002 by Douglas Preston

Illustrations © 2002 by:
Anne M. Chojnacki: 220, 224
Robert G. Larson: 176
Sarah Moore: 110 all, 111, 112 all, 113 all, 114, 115
Kenneth B. Tankersley: 8, 54, 207

Photographs © 2002 by:
Anonymous: 59, 66, 183
Peter Bostrom: 79, 82 lower, 83 all, 84, 85 all, 86, 87 all, 88 all, 89, 90, 91 upper, 92,
    93, 94, 95, 96, 97, 107, 163, 164, 165, 166 all, 169 lower, 170 lower, 171, 172, 174
    upper, 200
Courtesy of the Denver Museum of Natural History: 65
James Dunbar: 167, 168 upper, 176 upper
Gary Emerson: 162 lower
Russell Graham: 82 upper, 168 lower
L. Adrien Hannus: 76, 99
C. Vance Haynes: 100, 133
Yaroslav V. Kuzmin: 196, 198, 199
R. Bruce McMillan and Jeffrey Saunders: 161
Kenneth B. Tankersley: 81 all, 91 lower, 118, 127, 128, 129, 130, 137, 139, 142, 144,
    147, 162 upper, 169 upper, 170 upper, 173, 174 lower, 175 all, 191, 192, 195

Published by
Gibbs Smith, Publisher
P.O. Box 667
Layton, Utah 84041

Orders: (1-800) 748-5439
www.gibbs-smith.com

Edited by Monica Weeks and Holly Venable
Designed by FORTHGEAR, Inc.
Printed and bound in Hong Kong

Library of Congress Cataloging-in-Publication Data

Tankersley, Kenneth B., 1955-
In search of Ice Age Americans / Kenneth B. Tankersley;
foreword by Douglas Preston — 1st ed.   p.   cm.

ISBN 1-58685-021-0
1. Clovis culture. 2. Paleo-Indians—North America.
3. North America—Antiquities. I. Title.
E99.C832 T36 2002

970.01—dc21

                                    2001005401

To Clovis, without you this book would not have been possible.

CONTENTS

FOREWORD
CLOVIS HUNTERS

The foreword is by the internationally distinguished author Douglas Preston, who has written extensively about the Americas' past in books such as Dinosaurs in the Attic, Cities of Gold, Talking to the Ground, The Royal Road, *and* Jennie. *He is best known for his archaeological suspense mysteries such as* The Relic, Riptide, Reliquary, *and* Thunderhead, *and his contributions to motion pictures, television, and* The New Yorker, National Geographic, Natural History, Smithsonian, *and* Harper's *magazines. Preston is no stranger to archaeology. Indeed, he is a research associate at the Laboratory of Anthropology in Santa Fe and a board member of the School of American Research. In the foreword, Preston provides the reader with a superb summary of the people, events, and current issues discussed in the book.*

Sometime during the last Ice Age, a seemingly trivial event took place, one that would change human history forever: a human being first set foot in the New World. We do not know where this person came from, or why, or where the first footfall landed on the New World. Unlike the first man to walk on the moon, the unknown pioneer who made this giant step for mankind was probably not aware of doing anything significant at all, perhaps just taking one more weary stride in a long tramp across the frozen tundra, searching for game. But in that moment, a Garden of Eden of vastness and splendor fell to our species. It would be the last large inhabitable area of earth to be occupied by human beings. Not until we colonize the stars will an event of comparable significance take place.

American archaeologists have long been fascinated—even obsessed—with this transcendental moment. What would it have been like for those first Americans to burst into this unspoiled land teeming with animals that had never before seen a human being? What would it have been like to top that rise and see, spread out below, a verdant valley carpeted with game, ripe for the taking? To many American archaeologists, this moment possesses an almost religious significance since it was the beginning of everything—the milestone that opened the door to thousands of years of cultural differentiation across the New World, a vast proliferation of languages, and the rise of great civilizations and tiny tribes alike. This was the moment that would culminate, after many devious and complex byways, in an explosion of humanity in all its rich diversity—from the great temples of the Aztecs to the naked Carib Indians who first greeted Columbus on the sands of Hispaniola.

There is a great deal of controversy about who these first Americans were and where they came from. The standard theory is that they were the immediate ancestors of the Clovis people—the mammoth hunters of North America. This is by no means a settled question. The debate about whether or not Clovis was here first—and who the Clovis people actually were—is as spirited today as it was when the first distinctive Clovis points were unearthed with mammoth bones in the early 1930s in eastern New Mexico. Despite intense research, the question of who these first Americans were remains one of the greatest archaeological mysteries of all time. Recent tantalizing evidence that the Clovis hunters might have been a Caucasoid people, who may have even originated in Europe, has only deepened the interest—and heated the controversy.

Archaeology is perhaps the most public of the sciences. Passionate debate in physics, chemistry, psychology, astronomy, and most of the other sciences usually takes place far from the public eye, in specialty journals, conferences, and the halls of academe. Archaeology has always been different. When Heinrich Schliemann announced he had discovered the city of Troy, it astonished the world. When the tomb of Tutankhamen saw first light, it made headlines around the globe. More than half a century after Piltdown Man was proven to be a hoax, books and articles are still being published speculating as to who perpetrated this most puzzling of frauds. Stonehenge, Easter Island, the pyramids, the lines on the Nazca Plains, the ruins of Chaco—these mysterious archaeological sites are known to millions. Archaeology is one of the few sciences with a huge amateur following—and where, in fact, amateurs have made contributions of real significance.

The very profession was largely founded by amateurs and aficionados. Thomas Jefferson himself directed what was probably the first real archaeological excavation in America, near his Monticello estate. He also published a book that caused a storm of protest among the religious by suggesting that the Indians must have been in North America "an immense course of time" to explain the vast number of languages, cultures, and physical types that Jefferson saw in America. The debate over who the First Americans were and when they arrived dates back to the very founding of the Republic. As Anglo settlement pushed westward and encountered such wonders as the mounds of Ohio and, later, the colossal ruins in Chaco Canyon, New Mexico, the question continued to hold a peculiar fascination to Americans. Where did these people come from, and when? As a result, the latter half of the nineteenth century saw an explosion of amateur interest in American archaeology. Most of the core archaeological (and anthropological) collections in America were amassed during this time—largely by nonprofessionals—from the Heye collection, now the center of the Smithsonian's new Museum of the American Indian, to the vast collections at the American Museum of Natural History in New York and the Field Museum in Chicago.

This long history of amateur interest has left professional archaeologists today in something of a bind. They have never been able to capture the profession entirely for themselves and shoo out the amateurs, as some would clearly like to do. Amateurs continue to collect, buy, and sell artifacts, despite the increasingly vehement objections of some archaeologists who decry the very notion that artifacts should have a monetary value. In my view, this is an illegitimate objection. It is certainly true that the high value of artifacts has led to the destruction of sites for profit, particularly in places with weak or corrupt governmental oversight, as in South America and Cambodia. Looting of sites is a critical problem in the world. But to demand a world in which objects of beauty and rarity have no monetary value is to demand a world that will never be. It would be far better for professional archaeologists to ask how amateurs and collectors can continue to help the profession, rather than to scold them for not keeping to an unreasonable standard of conduct that is contrary to the way of the world in general. In no scientific field have amateurs and collectors contributed as much of value as in archaeology. Looting will never be controlled by trying to squash the market in legitimate artifacts—but it can be curbed by educating collectors and dealers, protecting sites, prosecuting looting, and alleviating poverty in the Third World where much of the looting occurs. Finally, professional archaeologists themselves are not free of sin: many have been responsible for the destruction of important sites by excavating them and then failing to publish the results. Eventually their notes become mislaid, the artifacts dispersed, or their provenience confused— and the site is as effectively lost as if it had been bulldozed by a pothunter.

It is impossible to imagine what the history of archaeology would have been like without the contributions of amateurs, from Thomas Jefferson on down. In October of 1999, a conference in Santa Fe, entitled "Clovis and Beyond," was attended by fourteen hundred people and became one of the seminal conferences in the history of American archaeology—and it was sponsored and financed by Forrest Fenn, an amateur collector. Most of the original Clovis sites were discovered by amateurs, as was the first Folsom site; indeed, the majority of the great prehistoric sites in America were brought to the attention of archaeologists by amateurs: collectors, ranchers, cowboys, Native Americans, and aficionados of various kinds.

At no time has popular interest in archaeology been higher than it is today. We live, as the Chinese proverb goes, in interesting times. We are, without doubt, on the cusp of tremendous new discoveries. The search for the First Americans has captured the public's interest like no other scientific detective story of our time. And it is a search that we all, in one way or another, can participate in by following the news from our armchairs, volunteering at museums, or even working with such organizations as Earthwatch, which recruits paying volunteers to help archaeologists excavate sites.

The theory that the Clovis mammoth hunters were the First Americans has held now for almost seventy years. But it is being assaulted as never before. There have always been archaeologists who have claimed that their particular site proves that other humans arrived in North America long before the Clovis. Most of these early site claims, however, have serious problems with them, either in the quality of the archaeology or uncertainties in the dating. Some of the earliest claims, such as Sandia Cave, have been shown to be the result of incompetence and possibly even fraud. The best candidate for a genuine pre-Clovis site is the Monte Verde site in southern Chile, which was superbly excavated by a team led by Tom Dillehay and carefully dated to several thousand years before Clovis. Some of the dates at Monte Verde go back as much as thirty-three thousand years. Studies of modern Native American languages, teeth shapes, and DNA also point to a pre-Clovis entry of human beings into the New World—again, in the twenty- to thirty-thousand-years range. But the case is not proven. The paradigm has not quite shifted. The question as to whether the Clovis hunters were truly the First Americans remains open. We do know one thing: if there were other human beings in the New World before Clovis, we have found precious little evidence of their passing. They must have been mighty few and far between or else they restricted themselves to using bone and wood tools, which have largely perished.

The greatest discoveries lie ahead. In the next fifty years, better dating methods and field techniques, and a raft of highly advanced technological tools such as DNA testing and isotope analysis will likely solve this most enduring of archaeologist enigmas. We *will* know who first set foot in the Americas, where they came from, and when.

In the nineteenth century, many American archaeologists believed, almost as a matter of faith, in the deep antiquity of humans in the New World. They believed that America must have had a Paleolithic Age—an Old Stone Age—just as Europe did. Archaeologists unearthed crude tools that to them proved man had been in America for tens of thousands of years. The cruder the tool, the older it had to be. But as the century drew to a close, several archaeologists and physical anthropologists launched a reaction against these flimsy claims of antiquity. They pointed out that one could only date a tool with reference to its geological context; in other words, the artifact was usually the same age as the layer of soil in which it was found. Just because a stone axe or point was roughly fashioned did not mean it was old. (We now know that the notion of crudeness signifying antiquity is a foolish idea. The truth is, in fact, just the opposite: the earlier peoples in America, the Clovis and other

Paleo-Indians, made the very *finest* stone tools and points.)

By the close of the nineteenth century, the antiquity of human beings in the New World rose to become one of the truly burning scientific questions of the time, as it has become again today. Time and again, respectable archaeologists and quacks alike had announced triumphantly that they had discovered one site or another "proving" the Indians had been in the New World for tens and even hundreds of thousands of years. Each time, this same small group of skeptics, centered on the Smithsonian Institution, investigated the claim and showed it to be the product of wishful thinking, sloppy fieldwork, incompetence, or even outright fraud. The battle between the skeptics and the true believers reached a climax in the beginning of this century—a debate that was abruptly silenced by a stunning discovery.

One of the leaders of the skeptics was a man named Ales Hrdlicka, curator of the Division of Physical Anthropology at the Smithsonian Institution. He was a towering figure in the field, a severe, exacting man, a European of the old school who went into the field impeccably dressed with high starched collar, black frock coat, hat, and cravat. Photographs show an unsmiling man of rigid posture and stern mien with a leonine shock of hair combed back. Hrdlicka undertook a crusade to debunk the bad science of the archaeologists and amateurs who were advancing these claims of deep antiquity. The very heavy involvement of amateurs and quasi-professionals in the field, while positive in many ways, had also delayed the introduction of rigorous field methods and a high standard of proof. As a result, Hrdlicka found much bad science to debunk. Hrdlicka, for his part, relished the role of spoiler. He held that the Indians had arrived in the New World no earlier than 1,000 B.C. As a physical anthropologist he based his opinion on skull morphology: the Native American skull type appeared modern, utterly unlike the Neanderthal skull type, and Native Americans were clearly of Asiatic ancestry. Thus they could not have been in America very long.

Whenever a new discovery was made, Hrdlicka often swept down upon the site like a vulture on a kill, tearing apart the archaeologist's methodology, denouncing the geological interpretations, and contradicting any enthusiastic declarations of antiquity. He was usually right. He was so powerful that he could, and did, ruin careers. By 1925 some of Hrdlicka's attacks had taken on a personal tone, and the atmosphere was such that one archaeologist wrote that it would be best "to lie low for the present." So many hasty and ill-considered claims had been made that it gave the search for the earliest Americans a bad odor.

Hrdlicka's attacks brought a long-overdue rigor into the field of archaeology, but at the expense of delaying, probably by several decades, the realization that humans had been in the New World far longer than his cut-off point of 1,000 B.C. It is ironic that, in the end, the amateurs turned out to be right for all the wrong reasons, while the professional was wrong for all the right reasons. The story of how Hrdlicka was proved wrong is a most interesting one.

While this controversy raged in the halls of academe, the curious chain of events that led to the discovery of the earliest Americans had already started on the high plains of eastern New Mexico. In August 1908, a terrific localized storm struck Johnson Mesa in the northeast corner of the state near the Colorado line, dropping thirteen inches of rain. The water rushed off the mesa and barreled through a network of remote gullies and arroyos to finally merge into a savage flash flood that tore through the valley of the dry Cimarron River and struck the town of Folsom, demolishing the town and killing seventeen people.

A month after the disaster, the foreman of the Crowfoot Ranch, George McJunkin, was riding his fencelines along the foot of Johnson Mesa when he encountered a problem. The storm had cut a ten-foot gully in the bottom of Wild Horse Arroyo, leaving a gap under the fence through which cattle might escape. While pondering how to fix the fence, he noticed some freshly exposed bones at the very bottom of the arroyo.

Curious, he got off his horse, climbed down into the gully, and pried loose a few bones with his fencing pliers. McJunkin was something of a collector, so he tied them behind his saddle and brought them back to the ranch house, where he added them to his mantelpiece "museum." They took up residence next to other things he had found—rocks, arrowheads, potsherds, and an ancient Indian skull. Later, when McJunkin passed by Wild Horse Arroyo, he would often pry out another bone or two and put them into the collection.

McJunkin was no ordinary cowboy. He was an avid reader of scientific books and encyclopedias. He had learned enough to realize that the bones must have come from an extinct animal. Although they looked like bison bones, they were much larger. He figured the bones must be very old because they were thirteen feet below the surface and were heavy, having been partly mineralized. He felt that the "bone pit," as he called it, might be important and should be reported.

McJunkin first wrote to a man in Las Vegas, New Mexico, who he heard knew about bones, but he could not persuade the man to visit the remote site. He also gave detailed instructions to a man named Carl Schwachheim, a blacksmith in the nearby town of Raton, who collected bones. Schwachheim was interested, but he never had the time to make the two-day horseback ride to the remote bone pit, thirty miles away. McJunkin also described the bone pit to Fred Howarth, the local banker in Raton, who had once dug up a woolly mammoth skeleton. But Howarth was also averse to the idea of a two-day trip. Years went by while the bone pit slumbered in obscurity.

We know very little about George McJunkin. He had been born a slave on a ranch in Midway, Texas, in 1851. His name then was simply George. His father, whom we know only by the nickname Shoeboy, had bought his own freedom and was saving up to buy the freedom of his son when Union soldiers arrived at the ranch to tell them the Civil War was over and that the slaves had been set free.

George spent three more years on the ranch. At seventeen, he got a job on a cattle drive to Dodge City, Kansas, and adopted the surname of his former owner, John McJunkin. He worked cattle for various outfits, finally ending up in the valley of the dry Cimarron River in northeastern New Mexico. He fell in love with the Cimarron Valley. Because New Mexico had sided with the Union during the war, and because it had a racially mixed population of Hispanics, Anglos, and Indians, an African American man was more readily accepted as an equal.

One of the ranchers he worked for asked McJunkin to train his two sons to ride and rope. In exchange, the boys taught McJunkin how to read from their schoolbooks. He became a voracious reader and developed a deep interest in science. By the time McJunkin became foreman of the Crowfoot Ranch, he was considered to be one of the top cowboys in the county, and he had a number of white cowboys working underneath him. He was particularly noted for his ability to punch (castrate) cattle as cleanly as a surgeon, without causing excessive blood loss or infections, a skill he learned from a doctor for whom he had once worked. McJunkin also taught himself to use a compass and transit. White landowners called on him to survey land and mediate boundary disputes—and submitted to his expert judgment. When horse races took place, his honesty was held in such high repute that he was asked to hold the betting pool. He also spoke fluent Spanish and sometimes acted as a bridge between the Hispanic and Anglo communities. When McJunkin encountered prejudice, his cowboy friends backed him up. A story is told about McJunkin and a friend named Gay Mellon, who decided one day to have a fancy lunch at the Eklund Hotel in Clayton, New Mexico. When they were told that the hotel's policy did not allow Negroes to be served in the dining room, Mellon pointed his long-barrelled Colt .45 at the manager's heart and said, "Your policy has just been changed."

McJunkin rigged his saddle with two scabbards: in the left he carried his rifle, and in the right, his telescope—with which he kept track of cattle by day and studied the stars by night. In his room at the ranch house he kept a small but treasured library of old encyclopedias, books about geology and surveying, and a well-worn Bible.

Despite all his letters and conversations, nothing came of McJunkin's efforts to interest someone in the bone pit. The years passed, McJunkin grew old, and the Crowfoot Ranch was sold. He moved out of the main ranch house to an isolated line cabin on the ranch. Not long afterwards, lightning struck the cabin and it burned to the ground. McJunkin lost everything: fossils, telescope, books, and the bones from Wild Horse Arroyo. McJunkin became ill and moved into a room at the Folsom Hotel. Eventually he could not get out of bed and is said to have sustained himself on raw bootleg whisky sipped through a rubber tube his friends rigged up for him. Near the end, McJunkin's friends took turns sitting at his bedside, telling stories and reading him passages from the Old Testament. One man recalled later that every person in that room had been "taught about horses and cattle, about roping, about reading brands, by McJunkin." On January 21, 1922, McJunkin asked to hear the passage from Deuteronomy about the Promised Land. Then he said, "I'm going where all good niggers go," and died.

Four months after McJunkin's death, Carl Schwachheim and Fred Howarth finally decided to visit McJunkin's bone pit. Howarth, the banker, had purchased a motorcar, and suddenly the arduous two-day horseback trip became a pleasant afternoon's drive. Schwachheim and Howarth found the bone pit just where McJunkin had described it, and they filled a feed bag with bones. That evening, the two men went through several books trying to figure out what kind of animal the bones were from. They decided that they must be from an extinct elk or bison, but as Raton was far from a museum or university, four more years passed before they had the opportunity to show the bones to a scientist.

In January 1926, Howarth had to deliver some cattle to a stockyard in Denver. He hired Schwachheim to look after the cattle on the train trip, and in Denver the two men carried the sack of bones over to the Colorado Museum of Natural History (now the Denver Museum). They were ushered into the office of Jesse D. Figgins, the museum's director, and unwittingly stepped into the center of the great controversy of when humans had first entered the New World.

J. D. Figgins was one of Ales Hrdlicka's bitterest enemies. He had endured a scathing attack from Hrdlicka over a site he had excavated in Texas. (Figgins later wrote a letter to a colleague that he was "suffering" to prove Hrdlicka wrong.) When Figgins saw the bones from McJunkin's bone pit that Schwachheim and Howarth dumped on his desk, it seems that he saw a way to accomplish his goal. The key, as Figgins and others knew, was to find a prehistoric artifact unmistakably *in situ* with the bones of an extinct Ice Age (Pleistocene Age) animal. Any deposit of ancient animal bones was therefore worth looking at. Figgins recognized these bones as being from an extinct Pleistocene bison, now called *Bison antiquus figginsi*. He apparently suspected from the first that the bone pit might be a prehistoric kill site and might offer just the proof he had been looking for to take down the arrogant Hrdlicka. At worst, he would end up with a nice bison skeleton that he could mount and display at his museum, something he was desirous of doing anyway.

In the summer of 1926, Figgins organized an excavation of the pit, hiring his son, Frank Figgins, and Carl Schwachheim to direct the work. They uncovered skeleton after skeleton, mostly articulated, all from a species of giant bison that had been extinct for ten thousand years. On July 10, one of the diggers found a peculiar spear point with the bones—a superbly knapped point with a distinctive longitudinal flake, or flute, struck off down the middle. It was so beautifully made that it hardly seemed possible it was ten thousand years old. Unfortunately, the diggers had removed it from its resting place before it could be properly analyzed *in situ*. Figgins cautioned his crew to watch for more artifacts but under no circumstances to remove them. Despite careful searching, no more points were found that summer.

Jesse Figgins published a report that fall suggesting that these prehistoric bison had been killed by human hunters. He later wrote that it was a "deliberate attempt to arouse Dr. H. and stir up all the venom that there is in him." Hrdlicka, however, was far too sophisticated to take the bait. He had a courteous meeting with Figgins and told him that if his diggers found any more points, to please leave them in place and wire museums and scientists to come so that the discovery could be independently inspected and corroborated.

On August 29, 1927, Carl Schwachheim made the discovery that would ring changes in history: he found one of the distinctive spear points embedded in matrix between the ribs of a bison skeleton. Figgins ordered the artifact left in place and covered up. It couldn't have come at a more opportune time. At Pecos, New Mexico, a few hundred miles away, a scientific conference was taking place, attended by two of the country's leading archaeologists, Frank H. H. Roberts of the Smithsonian and Alfred Vincent Kidder, the archaeologist who had established the entire cultural sequence for the Anasazi Indians. Figgins fired off telegrams to Pecos and to scientists around the country: *ANOTHER ARROWHEAD FOUND WITH BISON REMAINS AT FOLSOM NEW MEXICO HAVE INVITED HRDLICKA TO MAKE INVESTIGATION. J D FIGGINS.*

Roberts and Kidder showed up to look at the point, along with famed paleontologist and geologist Barnum Brown of the American Museum of Natural History. (Brown still holds the record for finding more dinosaur bones than any man, living or dead.) The covering was removed, and Brown carefully cleared the dirt from one side of the point without dislodging it. It was a fluted point just like the other, unquestionably in situ, sitting between the ribs of a bison. The three scientists gazed at each other with wild surmise. Here was the long-sought proof that human beings were in the New World during the Ice Age. (At the time, the antiquity of the Ice Age itself was unknown and would remain so until the advent of carbon dating, but it was believed to have ended at least ten thousand years ago—pushing Hrdlicka's limit back at least seven thousand years.) These early bison hunters were named Folsom, after the town nearest the dig.

So entrenched was the opposition, however, that when Brown, Roberts, and Kidder reported on the discovery at the next American Anthropological Association meeting, they were greeted with an uneasy skepticism. Not even the editors of *Scientific American* were immune to the climate of intimidation fostered by Hrdlicka. A year later, when one of the archaeologists published a report in *Scientific American* on the Folsom discovery, the magazine printed a boxed statement at the beginning of the article stating that "the editor disclaims all responsibility" for "claims concerning the proof of the antiquity of man in America." Further painstaking excavations by a joint American Museum/Colorado Museum expedition at the bone pit, which uncovered more points, finally convinced the world that this mass of bison skeletons was in fact a prehistoric kill site. Hrdlicka wisely refrained from a frontal attack on the veracity of the site—something he could not do with Roberts, Brown, and Kidder all supporting it. Nevertheless, the grumpy old warlord of American archaeology went to his grave without admitting that he had been wrong.

Not one contemporary scientific publication about the Folsom discovery mentioned George McJunkin. The first reports all gave Howarth and Schwachheim full credit for discovering the bone pit. Although the legend of George McJunkin did not die, by the 1960s many archaeologists assumed that the persistent story of the ex-slave turned cowboy-scientist who discovered the famous bone pit was no more than a colorful myth. A Paleo-Indian archaeologist named George Agogino became curious about the persistent tale. He went to the tiny town of Folsom, and in a series of interviews with local ranchers, cowboys, and townspeople, pieced together the remarkable story of George McJunkin. Indeed, he found that one of the largest gravestones in the Folsom cemetery belonged to McJunkin—placed there by a grateful friend. Half a century after his death, McJunkin was still held in high regard by the citizens of Folsom, who knew nothing about the scientific revolution McJunkin had caused, yet still remembered with great affection the remarkable black cowboy with the telescope, bones, and scientific books.

We can now form a clear picture of what happened at Wild Horse Arroyo some ten thousand years ago. The early Folsom hunters evidently drove a bison herd to the head of a boxed valley and got them milling about in confusion. Then they heaved spears into them and backed off, waiting to see which died. Most of the skeletons were left still articulated, meaning the animals hadn't been butchered. As a result, the Folsom hunters left behind many of their spear points still embedded in the flesh. The tailbones of the some of the skeletons were missing, proof that some of the animals had been skinned, since, as buffalo hunters say, "the tail goes with the hide."

The bone pit discovery finally broke the Ice Age barrier. Now archaeologists knew what to look for, and they no longer had to fear being ridiculed and attacked for making a claim of antiquity. The discovery of the Folsom complex opened up vast new vistas for scientific research. Suddenly, archaeologists had many more thousands of years of human history to account for. The extremely high quality of the Folsom points (some of the knapping is so fine that it is visible only with a microscope) strongly suggested that there must have been a hunting people who preceded the Folsom in the New World. They must have been the end product of a long evolution since the distinctive fluting seen on the Folsom point had never been seen on any Old

World point. The search was on for the precursors of the Folsom.

That mysterious older culture—the ancestors of the Folsom—came to light only a few years later. Again, it was an amateur who made the first discovery.

As a young boy, James Ridgely Whiteman used to wander among the sand hills of Blackwater Draw near Clovis, New Mexico, picking up arrowheads and bones of animals exposed by the wind. In 1929, Whiteman found a curious spear point in a blowout next to some charcoal and mammoth teeth. Like the Folsom points, this point was fluted—that is, it had long flakes struck longitudinally from its base—although it was much longer and heavier than the typical Folsom point. Whiteman was only nineteen, but he knew enough to realize the find was important and sent the point to the Smithsonian with a letter stating he had found it alongside some mammoth bones.

The Smithsonian sent back an archaeologist to investigate. Whiteman, now eighty-seven years old and still living near Clovis, remembered taking the archaeologist to Blackwater Draw and showing him the charcoal and bones. The man, Whiteman told me scornfully, "looked the area over and decided it was *too unimportant* to work on."

Although Whiteman did not know it at the time, he had made an extremely important discovery: he had uncovered the first evidence of the great mammoth hunters of North America now known as the Clovis people. Like McJunkin, Whiteman, who is part Native American, was never given adequate credit for his find.

Two years later, the state of New Mexico started digging gravel from Blackwater Draw to build the road between Portales and Clovis. Using horse-drawn scrapers, they soon began unearthing huge bones and projectile points in the gravel bars. The bones caused a sensation, and some of them were carted to Portales and propped up in the window of Ed J. Neer's store, a prominent establishment specializing in furniture, undertaking, and drugs. The *Portales Valley News* reported, "centuries ago monsters roamed the prairies where Portales now stands and one can visualize these strange animals after looking at the bones now being uncovered."

In the fall of 1932, Dr. Edgar B. Howard of the Philadelphia Academy of Natural Sciences heard about the bone discoveries and rushed to New Mexico to visit Blackwater Draw. He excitedly telegraphed back east: *Extensive bone deposit at new site. . . . Some evidence of hearths along edges.* He arranged to begin preliminary excavations the following summer. His crew (which included Whiteman as one of the diggers) found large fluted spear points, just like the one Whiteman sent to the Smithsonian, scattered around and about mammoth skeletons, and arranged in such a way that it was clear they had once been embedded inside the animal. At first Howard called them "generalized Folsoms," because of the similarity in fluting; later they became known as Clovis. It was stunning proof that humans had hunted these great animals in North America. Further excavations in 1936–37, supervised by John Cotter of the University of Pennsylvania Museum, revealed a series of Paleo-Indian camps and kill sites at what had once been a shallow lake where humans had ambushed mammoths and other prehistoric animals. They found a hearth with partially burned mammoth bones in it, surrounded by flakes and broken knives—a good indication that the Clovis people had been sitting around the fire, roasting and carving off chunks of mammoth meat. Other bones found at the site included dire wolf, the terrifying short-faced bear, camel, prehistoric horse, bison, sabertooth tiger, and giant sloth. One of the dire wolves had died with a Clovis point apparently lodged in its jaw—an intriguing fact suggesting that either the humans were hunting wolves or vice versa. Directly above the Clovis level, they found a layer of Folsom points associated with extinct bison bones—a strong indication that the Clovis culture had evolved into the Folsom culture.

Later excavations at the site (now officially called Blackwater Draw Locality Number One) exposed an astonishing cultural sequence, beginning with thirteen-thousand-year-old Clovis and running through Folsom, Portales Complex, Archaic Indian, and even Pueblo Indian. A measure of the site's importance can be seen by the roster of famous archaeologists who worked there, including C. Vance Haynes, the prominent geochronologist at the University of Arizona; Marie Wormington, author of the classic *Prehistoric Indians of the Southwest;* Dennis Stanford, now chairman of the Smithsonian Institution's Department of Anthropology; David Meltzer, a leading Paleo-Indian archeologist and historian; and George Agogino, who discovered the famed Hell Gap site and founded the Anthropology Department at Eastern New Mexico University. These scientists and many others piled up a record of extraordinary finds at Blackwater Draw, which included more than a dozen mammoths with embedded Clovis points, bison similarly peppered with Folsom points, and important Archaic Indian campsites. They also unearthed something quite unexpected: a thirteen-thousand-year-old well, the oldest in the New World, apparently dug by the Clovis when the water level dropped during a drought. At the bottom lay five turtle shells that had been hardened by fire and probably used as dipping cups for water. Excavations also revealed a spiritual dimension to the lives of the Clovis people: some of the ancient spring channels at Blackwater Draw were loaded with artifacts and bones, which appear to have been offerings to the water.

During this time, Blackwater Draw had the misfortune of becoming one of the largest gravel mines in New Mexico. While the gravel operation exposed many of the archaeological treasures, it also destroyed them. For years archaeologists worked under extremely frustrating conditions, trying to excavate as much of the site as they could before it was eaten up by heavy machinery, mechanical draglines, blasting, and dredging. The owner of the mineral lease, Sam Saunders, made a laudable effort to work with the archaeologists, but he came under increasing financial pressure from the state and private contractors to supply huge quantities of cheap gravel for a boom of postwar road building. Sometimes groups of local volunteers from Clovis and Portales were rounded up for emergency salvage efforts, and they worked frantically —almost under the blades and buckets of the excavating equipment. As time went on, the gravel business fell into debt, and there were conflicts with the archaeologists. As a result, much of the site and its lode of priceless artifacts and bones were chewed up and spread on roads across eastern New Mexico; many driveways in Portales, it is said, still contain fragments of mammoth bones. "I sure wish," Whiteman told me, "that I had all the points that went into building those roads."

During this time, archaeologists made many efforts to preserve the site, but their requests fell on the deaf ears of obtuse New Mexico state officials. As early as 1940, a report recommended that the locality be preserved as a museum, noting that "there is probably no other fossil bed in the country which lends itself so perfectly to *in situ* demonstration showing prehistoric animals and human artifacts together." In the mid-1960s, Governor Jack M. Campbell finally stepped in, coaxed some money out of the legislature to buy the site, and the huge gravel operation ceased. By then, millions of cubic yards of material had been removed and the archaeological deposits virtually obliterated, with the exception of one patch of mammoth bones and the Clovis well. These are still visible today and make for a fascinating visit, although they are but a ghost of the place's former glory. In 1966, Blackwater Draw was listed on the National Register of Historic Places.

One of the great mysteries of the site—and a powerful indication that Clovis may indeed have been the first Americans—is that the thirteen-thousand-year human occupation of Blackwater Draw seems to stop dead at the Clovis level. Prehistoric bones were found in great abundance below the Clovis level, indicating it was a rich area long before then, but there were no signs of human occupation. Robson Bonnichsen, director of the Center for the Study of the First Americans at Oregon State University, has an answer to this: he speculates that there were artifact bearing levels at Blackwater Draw below Clovis. These people, he thinks, may have made their tools out of flaked and shaped bone rather than stone. Those delicate and hard-to-recognize bone tools may have all ended up in the gravel crushers.

Just as with the Folsom discovery, the discovery of Clovis at Blackwater Draw stimulated a wave of discoveries of Clovis sites all across North America—discoveries that continue today. Only one thing is still missing: the people themselves. Despite intensive searching, no human remains of Clovis (or Folsom) have ever been found, except some crumbling bones from the Montana burial that are presently useless for scientific analysis. One of the archaeologists who worked at Blackwater Draw, George Agogino, told me that a gravel operator at Blackwater Draw accidentally uncovered a complete skeleton out of the Clovis layer, but because he had damaged it and was worried about losing his job, he quietly turned it back under the dirt—a tragic loss for archaeology.

Today, Blackwater Draw can be found just off the Clovis-Portales Highway, under the magnificent open skies of the Llano Estacado. It is an arid place, a quiet grassy scar in the landscape surrounded by gentle mounds of overburden and dotted with young cottonwoods. A small but excellent site museum greets the visitor. Below, set into the side of the old gravel pit, a metal building protects the last remaining cluster of mammoth bones. Nearby, a small A-frame shelters the Clovis well.

Standing at the site, it is not hard to conjure up in one's mind the landscape of thirteen millennia ago. The archaeological record suggests the Clovis at Blackwater Draw were a prosperous people living in a good land. Back then, the draw would have been verdant, a sea of deep waving grasses around a shimmering sheet of water. Some trees would have dotted the grasslands, creating a landscape not unlike East Africa. It would have been a lively place, echoing with the shouts of children and the sharp clicking sounds of hunters flaking out new tools. Once in a while, when the Clovis caught a mammoth at the water, the draw would fill with the enraged bellows of the dying animal, speared again and again by its nimble human predators; then the smoke of campfires would ascend to the sky and mingle with the smells of roasting meat—and the feast would begin at Blackwater Draw.

Interest in the Clovis people—and in the question of the first Americans—subsided for some time after the Clovis discoveries at Blackwater Draw. But five years ago, a chance discovery thrust this question back into the public mind. On July 28, 1996, in mid-afternoon, two college students were watching a hydroplane race on the Columbia River in Kennewick, Washington, when they decided to take a shortcut along the river's edge. While wading through the shallows, one of them stubbed his toe on a human skull partly buried in the sand. They picked it up and, thinking it might be that of a murder victim, hid it in some bushes and called the sheriff's department.

The County Coroner was called in, and the police gave him the skull in a plastic bucket. In the late afternoon, the coroner called James Chatters, a forensic anthropologist and owner of a local consulting firm called Applied Paleoscience. Chatters had often helped the police identify skeletons and sort out murder victims from prehistoric Indian burials.

"When I looked down at the skull," Chatters told me later, "right off the bat it appeared to have a very large number of Caucasoid features"—in particular, a long, narrow braincase, narrow face, and receding cheekbones. But after Chatters took it out of the bucket and laid it on his worktable, he began to see some unusual traits. The teeth were worn flat, a common characteristic of prehistoric Indian skulls, and the color of the bone indicated it was fairly old, perhaps 150 to 200 years—earlier than permanent European settlement of the Columbia River. On the other hand, the individual was much taller than most prehistoric Native Americans were. His skull sutures had fused, indicating he was past middle age—positively ancient for prehistoric Indians, who normally had a shorter lifespan. The man was in exceptional health for a prehistoric Indian of middle age: he had, for example, all of his teeth and no cavities.

As dusk fell, Chatters and the coroner went out to the site to see if they could find the rest of the skeleton. There, working in the dying light, they found more bones lying around on the surface of the sand and mud in about two feet of water. The skeleton was remarkably complete: only a few tiny hand, wrist, and foot bones were missing, along with the sternum. The bones had evidently fallen out of a bank during recent flooding of the Columbia River.

The following day, they spread the bones out in Chatters's laboratory. In forensic anthropology the first order of business is to determine sex, age, and race. In this case, determining the latter point was particularly important because, if the skeleton turned out to be Native American, it fell under a federal law called the Native American Graves Protection and Repatriation Act (NAGPRA). NAGPRA passed in 1990, requires the government—in this case, the Army Corps of Engineers, which controls that stretch of the Columbia River—to ascertain if a skeleton is related to a living Indian tribe and then "repatriate" it.

Chatters determined that the skeleton was male, Caucasoid, from an individual between forty and fifty-five years old, about five feet nine inches tall. (In physical anthropology the term "Caucasoid" does not necessarily mean "white" or European; it is basically a descriptive term applied to certain biological features. The term "Caucasian" is a culturally defined, racial category quite different from Caucasoid.) "I thought maybe we had an early pioneer or fur trapper," he said. As he was cleaning the pelvis, he noticed a grey object imbedded in the bone, which had partially healed and fused around it. He took it to be x-rayed, but the object did not show up, meaning it was made of something other than metal. So he requested a CAT scan. To his surprise, the scan revealed the object to be part of a willow-leaf-shaped spear point, which had been thrust into the bone and broken off. It strongly resembled a Cascade projectile point, an Archaic Indian style in use from around nine thousand to forty-five hundred years ago.

By the end of the week, Chatters sent the left fifth metacarpal bone, a tiny bone that attaches the pinkie to the hand, to the University of California at Riverside. He soon received back a telephone call from the radiocarbon lab, reporting the bone was between ninety-three hundred and ninety-six hundred years old. And that was when he knew that all hell was going to break loose.

Almost immediately afterward, the Army Corps of Engineers demanded that all study of the bones cease and ordered the skeleton to be put in sheriff's lockup. Based on the carbon date, the Corps had decided the skeleton was Native American and that it fell under the NAGPRA law. The Confederated Tribes of the Umatilla Reservation, leading a coalition of five tribes, formally claimed the skeleton under NAGPRA, and the Corps had almost immediately decided to "repatriate" it. The Indians stated that they were going to bury the bones where scientists would never find them again. A group of leading anthropologists sued the government for the right to study the bones before they were turned over to the tribes. The bones of

Kennewick Man have been mired in legal crossfire ever since. Publications around the world have reported on the controversy, and there have been almost a dozen television documentaries on it.

The Kennewick Man discovery—and the examination of half a dozen skeletons of similar age—added to a small but growing body of evidence that at least one early group of inhabitants in the New World might have been a Caucasoid people from Europe. This group may have been the Clovis people, or their immediate ancestors, of which Kennewick Man might have been a descendent. Other evidence suggested a link between Europe and Clovis. A study of Clovis knapping techniques by archaeologist Bruce Bradley showed their sophisticated techniques to be almost identical to that of points made by the mammoth-hunting Solutrean people of France and Spain. This was not, he feels, a case of convergent evolution since the techniques are too complex and refined to have been happened upon independently. Dennis Stanford, the director of the Smithsonian's Department of Anthropology, recently advanced the idea that the immediate ancestors of the Clovis may have even migrated directly from Europe to America in small skin boats during the height of the last Ice Age while the North Atlantic was frozen from France to Nova Scotia. He suggests they might have followed the edge of the ice, which would have afforded good marine hunting as well as unlimited freshwater for a long journey. And, in fact, recent studies of Native American mitochondrial DNA have identified a genetic marker termed X that originates in Europe.

These first Americans may have been genetically swamped and possibly even displaced about nine thousand years ago by a large wave of Asiatic emigrant stock who walked from Siberia to Alaska. In other words, the most recent discoveries hint that the first Americans might have been Caucasoid "Europeans" who were later displaced by the ancestors of the American Indians. To call this theory controversial would be an understatement.

The evidence for a European origin of Clovis theory is fragmentary and contradictory. This is science in the making: messy, confusing, at times full of passionate intensity, at others lacking all conviction. Critical research remains to be done and many studies are still unpublished. The theory may turn out to be completely false. At some point, a Clovis skeleton in good condition will be found in clear association with Clovis tools and weapons. When this happens—if the NAGPRA law allows it—

DNA analysis will probably solve the riddle of the Clovis origins and may even answer the greatest mystery of all: who were the first Americans?

Even if the Clovis are displaced as the first Americans by an earlier group, they will always remain an exceptionally interesting people. They were perhaps the most successful prehistoric peoples in North America. No prehistoric culture discovered since has covered more territory than the Clovis. Their distinctive tools and points have been found almost everywhere in North America, which was ice-free in the late Pleistocene era, from Florida to Washington and from Canada to Mexico. The Clovis were among the greatest human hunters to walk the planet. They were among the first human beings to develop weaponry that allowed them to go one-on-one against big dangerous game. Their favored prey was the Columbian mammoth, the largest land animal our species ever hunted. It stood up to thirteen feet at the shoulder, weighed between eight and nine tons, and could run perhaps twenty-five or thirty miles an hour. It was fifty percent heavier than the African elephant, which is today an extremely dangerous animal to hunt even with a high-caliber rifle. Like the modern elephant, the mammoth was probably intelligent. A provoked mammoth very likely fought like an elephant as well. To be a Clovis hunter caught by a mammoth would not have been pretty. The mammoth would have gored and slashed at its assailant with its tusks, trampled, crushed, and battered using its head, and picked up what was left, flailing it about until the pieces flew apart.

The Clovis hunters probably stalked mammoths with two particularly lethal weapons. The first, a thrusting spear, was for close-in work. The second may have been an atlatl—a spear launched with a throwing stick. (The bow and arrow weren't invented until thousands of years later.) In either case, both required the hunter to be dangerously close to the animal. The Clovis compensated for this by developing a particular type of projectile point, beautifully designed to kill a mammoth. It was a long, tapered, viciously sharp spear point flaked from stone, strong enough to resist breaking against the hide. When thrown or thrust into the mammoth, it tore a big hole in the tissue and caused heavy blood loss; it was long, so that every time the mammoth took a step after being hit, the point would saw and slice away in the flesh, causing more damage with every movement the animal made.

We do not know exactly how the Clovis hunted mammoths. They probably refrained from attacking a family group or a powerful bull—that would have been suicide. They may have waited until a younger, less-experienced animal strayed from its family group, hit it with a few atlatls, and followed it until it died. Alternatively, they may have killed mammoths by sneaking up beside them while they were slowed down in water or muck, and shoving spear after spear through the rib cage into the vital organs. Most Clovis kill sites have been found near shallow lakes like those at Blackwater Draw, where mammoths presumably watered. Either way, a mammoth took a lot of killing: one skeleton found in southern Arizona had eight Clovis points in its body, and it was one that probably got away.

This view of the fearless Clovis hunter has been challenged by some archaeologists who think the Clovis were more opportunistic scavengers than bold hunters. In their view, the Clovis primarily cornered sick or mired mammoths at waterholes and killed them. Sick and dying elephants often become overheated and retreat into water in a desperate effort to cool off, and many Clovis sites—such as Blackwater Draw—have been found near such waterholes. The Clovis may have even scavenged the dead carcasses of mammoths. One archaeologist joked that maybe each generation of Clovis killed one mammoth and then spent the rest of their lives bragging about it. They hypothesize instead that the Clovis people got most of their nutrition from hunting small game and gathering plants. It was, they say, too dangerous for a small band of hunters to go after an elephant that might kill several of their fittest individuals, devastating the survival chances of the band. The meat just wasn't worth the risk.

The facts, in my view, do not support this theory. Shortly after the Clovis appeared, for example, mammoths and mastodons swiftly departed the scene, becoming extinct only a few thousand years later. The timing seems suspicious. While it may have been a coincidence—solely the result of climactic change—it seems quite likely the Clovis helped them along to extinction. Most of the Clovis sites found so far contain a lot of mammoth bones and not a huge quantity of other bones, indicating they did eat a great deal of mammoth meat, at least at those sites. If there are other Clovis campsites where they ate other animals in quantity, these campsites have not been found. A number of caches of Clovis tools and weapons have been discovered. These caches of tools feature almost exclusively long, deadly spear points (and a few rare examples of detachable foreshafts) perfect for killing mammoths but unsuitable for other game. Other cache tools include large blades and heavy knives that seem also to have been designed for skinning and butchering a mammoth. Few, if any, tools have been found in these caches that seem appropriate for hunting and butchering smaller game such as bison, deer, rabbits, or birds. Archaeologists have found several mammoth skeletons peppered with Clovis points in which the animal appears to have gotten away, only to die a natural death later; so at least some of the mammoths attacked by the Clovis were healthy enough to escape.

As the population of prehistoric elephants became extinct, the Clovis people were forced to change their prey, their hunting techniques, and their stone technology. In so doing they became the Folsom people, who switched largely to hunting prehistoric bison. The Folsom people continued to make fluted points but on a smaller scale, as the smaller caliber point had more penetrative power on a bison.

Like most hunters, the Clovis dearly loved their weapons. We know this because they went to great lengths to obtain the most gorgeous, semiprecious stones suitable for flaking into points: translucent agate, chert, smoky quartz, red jasper, black obsidian. They traveled or traded for hundreds of miles to obtain beautiful stones. These stones were not just pretty to look at; when knapped they formed keen edges and glossy flake scars that were almost silky to the touch. To make pleasing flake patterns on their points, the weapons producers used a technique that the French call *outre passe*, or overshot flaking. In this exceedingly difficult technique, the edge of the stone is struck in such a way that a long flake, shaped like a scimitar, travels all the way across the face of the spear point. Sometimes the Clovis knapped the stone on the diagonal for further decorative effect. Clovis points today are both very attractive and very rare.

One sign of the growing interest in the First Americans has been the explosion of interest in flint knapping and, in particular, re-creating the Clovis point and other finely made Paleo-Indian points, which are considered to be the apotheosis of the flint-knapper's art. There are more than thirty "knap-ins" around the country every year, some attended by hundreds of people from all walks of life. One recent Missouri knap-in required twenty pickup truckloads of rock. There are probably more than five thousand knappers now working around the country, turning out an estimated one-and-a-half million stone points and tools every year. A recent article in the journal *American Antiquity* called this "a twentieth-century stone age." Many archaeologists are terrified that the flood of new artifacts is contaminating the archaeological record; already, museum collections are believed to be rife with fakes. On the other hand, some of the finest knappers have been able to reverse engineer the Clovis and other complex Paleo-Indian points, making a valuable contribution to archaeology. A good Clovis replica might sell for two hundred dollars, but a superb original point could be worth ten, twenty, or even thirty thousand dollars.

One of the foremost collectors of Clovis projectile points in the United States is a Texan named Forrest Fenn. Now in his sixties, Fenn, a former Air Force pilot who was shot down over Laos during the Vietnam War, lives in Santa Fe in a large house hidden behind adobe walls. Wagon ruts from the Santa Fe Trail run across his backyard. In the early 1970s, Fenn started the first major art gallery in Santa Fe; he was the dealer who established Santa Fe as an international art market. Fenn sold the gallery in 1988 and has since spent most of his time publishing books and collecting Paleo-American points.

Fenn's collections are displayed around his office—a fossil skull of a giant short-faced cave bear, a mummified and wrapped falcon from Egypt, old Indian pots, beaded moccasins, arrowheads, peace pipes, tomahawks, a cast of the Kennewick Man skull. The real treasures, though, are hidden in a walk-in vault in the back of a nearby closet, where he keeps his Paleo-Indian point collection. His Clovis assemblage is the greatest in the world outside the Smithsonian Institution. Eventually, Fenn hopes they will form the centerpiece of an Ice Age museum that he and a group of collectors plan to establish in Santa Fe—another example of an amateur collector making a valuable contribution to archaeology.

I have spent many hours in Fenn's house, admiring his collection of Clovis points. No one who has actually handled a good Clovis point can ever think of it as a mere tool or a utilitarian object again. When you hold a fine Clovis projectile point—five inches long, leaflike, cool, deadly, balanced, luminous—you know that you are holding something that reaches far beyond the utilitarian into a higher realm of aesthetics. Each point is an object made with not only enormous skill but also with love, simplicity, and something almost akin to religious faith. These stunning projectile points were the embodiment of the Clovis way of life—objects of tremendous pride, the centerpiece of a most dangerous but essential activity: the hunting of the mammoth. In the end, it is the beautiful and deadly Clovis point itself that speaks to me most profoundly about who these ancient hunters were.

—Douglas Preston

PREFACE

For almost a half millennium, books have been written about the search for America's earliest human history, but few, if any, have told the true stories behind the most-significant, breakthrough discoveries. American citizens such as a frontiersman, a former slave, a cowboy, a farmer, a teenager, and even a U.S. President, made them. Indeed, America's most significant archaeological finds were not made by professional archaeologists from prestigious Ivy League universities, but by self-educated laypeople—amateurs, collectors, and the interested public. This book is about their contributions to the advancement of our knowledge of America's most ancient past. It is also a book about archaeological discovery and the passion that drives people in their relentless pursuit of the truth.

"A Day in the Life," chapter 1, is the story of a fall day in northeastern Wyoming, in the year 11,000 B.C. It grew out of a dinner conversation in the Santa Fe home of art expert Forrest Fenn, when Gibbs Smith turned to me and asked, "Could you tell us what you think a day in the life of an average Ice Age American would have been like?" Using facts from recent archaeological discoveries, ethnographic analogies, and my own personal biases, I began to weave a tale about a band of mammoth hunters, their families, and their relationship with the environment. Afterward, Gibbs said, "That is the kind of introduction that I would like you to write for the book." While this chapter is entirely fictional, I believe that it is as close to the roles of individual people that the archeological record will presently allow.

"Frontier Archaeology," chapter 2, is a history of the search for the First Americans during the eighteenth century. It describes early European encounters with American Indians, and the stories they told about their ancestors, which actually may contain an oral record of the last Ice Age, a time when mammoths, mastodons, and other now-extinct, giant animals roamed the earth. Chapter 2 tells of the archaeological contributions of backwoodsmen like Christopher Gist, known to most historians as

George Washington's guide, the person who showed Daniel Boone the way to Kentucky, and the grandfather of *Sikwo-yi* (Sequoyah), inventor of the Cherokee alphabet. It recounts the early excavations of William Henry Harrison and George Rogers Clark, and it reveals how the founding fathers of the United States, Benjamin Franklin and Thomas Jefferson, searched for clues about the earliest Americans amidst economic trouble, political upheaval, and war.

"European Influences," chapter 3, continues the history of the search for the First Americans into the nineteenth century, and explains how it was both stimulated and stifled by archaeological finds overseas. With the unequivocal discovery of Ice Age relics in Europe, people searched the American countryside for comparable remains. Because America has its own unique cultural history, scientists failed to recognize truly ancient artifacts when they were found. At the same time, more recent artifacts were accepted as ancient because they fit a scientific stereotype, a preconceived notion of what America's earliest archaeological record was supposed to look like. In the absence of early human remains, some scientists even suggested that people had not been in America for more than a few thousand years.

"Cowboys and Collectors," chapter 4, continues the history of the search for Ice Age sites into the twentieth century. It is a story about the real heroes of American archaeology. It reveals how an African American cowboy, a self-taught geologist and former slave, forever revolutionized the way we look at America's earliest past. Chapter 4 tells how an Irish farmer conducted the first survey of Ice Age American artifacts, long before the scientific community recognized their antiquity. It shows how a teenager refused to give up his belief that he had found a truly ancient site, despite the fact that a professional paleontologist from the Smithsonian had told him that he had found nothing of significance. Each of these people became a hero of the past because, despite all the odds, their discoveries led to a quantum leap in our knowledge of Ice Age America. Chapter 4 also tells how some professional archaeologists misbehaved when they were confronted with data that was contrary to their lifelong view of the past.

"Clovis Culture," chapter 5, is a summary of what is currently known about America's oldest recognized Ice Age culture. It not only describes the kinds of archaeological sites and artifacts that have been discovered, chapter 5 provides an interpretation of the Ice Age climate, environments, and resources. It explains, on the basis of the most current archaeological finds, ethnographic records, and experimentation, how Clovis people made a living, hunting wild animals and gathering wild plant foods, as well as providing a glimpse into their social structure and belief systems.

"The Crook County Clovis Cache," chapter 6, "The Trail to Crook County," chapter 7, and "The Sunrise Mine," chapter 8, chronicle a modern-day archaeological adventure, the search for one of America's most rare Ice Age sites. It is a nonfictional detective story that shows how tantalizing clues obtained from collector interviews, archival records, and mountains of maps were used to pinpoint the exact location of a treasure of Ice Age tools and weapons, buried in northeastern Wyoming some 13,000 years ago. Chapter 6 gives a historical perspective of how Ice Age cache sites have been serendipitously discovered. Chapter 7 provides the logic and deductive reasoning process behind a progressive archaeological investigation. It extends into chapter 8, giving a glimpse of the physical experience, the emotional ups and downs, and the conversations of fieldwork, from the cockpit of a plane landing on an isolated Wyoming runway, to a four-wheel drive truck roaming across the unspoiled grassland of the High Plains, to the exploration of an ancient mine in a western ghost town.

Chapter 9, "Thieves of Time," is about the people who deliberately set out to rob us of the truth about the past. Throughout the twentieth century, federal and state legislation was passed that protects archaeological sites from the wanton destruction that results from people who dig them for profit. With the long-term protection of public lands, many looters have turned to the production of fraudulent artifacts and sites. These people range from unscrupulous flint knappers, artifact collectors, and art dealers, to Machiavellian archaeologists, museum curators, and university professors. Unless their deeds are detected, unsuspecting students and professional archaeologists document the fakes as authentic artifacts and forever contaminate our record of the past. Chapter 9 provides two modern examples and shows the remarkable similarities between them and the infamous Piltdown hoax.

"How Old Is Clovis?" chapter 10, tells the story of another hero of American archaeology, an amateur, Willard Libby, and his lifelong dream to accurately date the past. Faced with the career busting, lampooning criticism of his peers, Libby persevered and, in 1960, received the Nobel Prize in chemistry for the development of radiocarbon dating. Although it is not a perfect measure of time, it is today the single best method of dating America's Ice Age.

"Were Clovis the First Americans?" chapter 11, answers this question from a historical perspective. Although we can now say, without a reasonable doubt, that Clovis does not represent the first group of people in America, our answer to who were the First Americans is, in many ways, no different than the explanation given almost a half a millennium ago. Chapter 11 provides a historical perspective to the problem and brings it up to the latest breaking discoveries from linguistics and genetics. Rather than new finds from the field, our answers may be found in DNA and the languages of American Indians. Chapter 11 also explains the nature of scientific inquiry as it is applied to modern archaeological field and laboratory investigations.

Chapter 12, "Routes of Entry," looks at how people may have first entered America during the Ice Age. Regardless of who the First Americans were and when they arrived, there are a limited number of routes of entry—overland or by sea, from the Far East or Western Europe. Although an overland route from Siberia has been the most popular explanation since the sixteenth century, other possibilities are discussed from the perspective of archaeology, economic anthropology, and human geography.

"Ice Age Cave Explorers," chapter 13, examines one of the greatest mysteries of American archaeology. If people entered caves around the world during the last Ice Age, and both people and caves were present in America at that time, then why is there no archaeological evidence of this activity? This question remained an archaeological enigma until an amateur archaeologist discovered Sheriden Cave, a deeply buried Ice Age American site in northwestern Ohio. The cave not only sheds new light on Ice Age Americans, Sheriden provides new clues to climate change and the demise of the megamammals.

Chapter 14, "Clovis and Beyond," is a behind-the-scenes story of the planning and execution of a fieldtrip for the greatest Ice Age American conference of the twentieth century. The narrative is set at San Lazaro Pueblo, the site of the "Clovis and Beyond" fieldtrip and one of the largest Anasazi and ancestral Pueblo ruins in America. Chapter 14 reveals the discussions, passion, and visions of the conference planners. It is also a tour guide of the San Lazaro Pueblo, combining archaeological interpretation with historic and ethnographic facts. The book ends with an excerpt from Ray Bradbury's *The Martian Chronicles*. Aside from being my favorite novel, I find the parallel between the fictional colonization of Mars and factual colonization of America uncanny.

On a final note, throughout the book I use the term *Ice Age* to refer to the geological epoch known as the Pleistocene, a period of time between two million and eleven thousand years ago. I use the term *Ice Age Americans* to refer to all of the people and cultures that lived in America during the Pleistocene.

—Kenneth B. Tankersley

ACKNOWLEDGEMENTS

I am extremely grateful to Douglas Preston for taking time out of his busy international schedule to write the foreword. Doug is a true gentleman and a scholar, not to mention a great archaeologist. I want to thank Gibbs Smith for providing me with the opportunity to write this book, and for his inspiration and guidance, often given to me during hikes across an artifact-strewn desert. Madge Baird and Glenn Law did a superb job of organizing and doing the final edit of this book. I am eternally grateful to Forrest Fenn who taught me the importance of educating the public and writing books that can be read by all Americans, from children to adults. I would also like to thank Forrest for reminding me that without amateurs and collectors, there would be no American archaeology. Charmay Allred not only provided me with warm hospitality, fine food, and shelter during my extended visits to Santa Fe, New Mexico, she introduced me to contemporary southwestern culture. Charmay also spent countless hours reading and editing earlier drafts of the chapters. Jack Holland and my brothers, Kevin and Steve, accompanied me on numerous expeditions to Ice Age sites across America, often putting them in harm's way. I am indebted to C. Vance Haynes, George C. Frison, and Patty Jo Watson for the inspirational time that they spent with me in the field, and for the motivating campfire discussions with David Hurst-Thomas at San Lazaro Pueblo. I will never forget the endless hours that Patrick J. Munson and Cheryl Ann Munson spent working with me, side-by-side, deep underground. Alice Trateba provided me with the essential clues that I needed to relocate the Crook County Clovis Cache site. Joseph L. Cramer provided information about the Ice Age atlatl. Barry L. Isaac taught me that economy is the key to human adaptation and, ultimately, survival. His many nightlong one-on-one seminars on livelihood were invaluable. I want to thank the faculty of the Departments of Anthropology at the University of Cincinnati and Indiana University, and the Quaternary Research Program at the Illinois State Museum for giving me the tools that I needed to investigate the past. I am especially grateful to

James Kellar, R. Bruce McMillan, Bonnie Styles, Russ Graham, Jeffrey Saunders, Eric Grimm, Terry Martin, and Mike Wiant. Thanks also to Brian G. Redmond and N'omi Greber, Department of Archaeology, Cleveland Museum of Natural History; Adrein Hannus, Department of Art and Archaeology, Augustana College; Marjorie Stewart, SUNY at Brockport; and Pete Bostrom and the Lithic Casting Lab for providing invaluable support. The Clovis and Beyond conference was made possible with the help of Robson Bonnichsen, Dennis Stanford, Gentry Steele, Jo Ann Harris, Mike Kammerer, Kris Kammerer, Peggy Fenn, Betsy Mecom, Mark Mullins, Marisa Lile, Kelly Sparks, Jean VanCamp, and the Eugene V. and Clare E. Thaw Charitable Trust. Field and laboratory research for portions of this book was made possible with funding from the National Science Foundation (Grant SBR9707984) and the Cleveland Museum of Natural History. Finally, I could not have written this book without the encouragement of my wife Jenny and the ever-warm presence of my cat, Clovis.

A Day in the Life

It is late September and there's already a bite of cold in the early morning air. A burst of northwesterly wind pushes waves across the tops of auburn-colored prairie grass. A family of mammoths is foraging on sedge and willow leaves as they follow the dry mud-cracked streambed in search of water. An old matriarch, like her mother before her, is leading the herd to a source of water, just as she has done hundreds of times before. She is taking them slowly across the broad flat plains to a spring-fed pond at the head of a coulee in the western hills. Raising the dexterous tip of her trunk, she detects faint traces of moisture in the air, a reinforcing gesture to the other mammoths that indeed they are on the right path to water.

The herd is being watched by a small band of Clovis hunters lying flat in the tall grass, just below the crest of a sandstone-capped ridge. They have been following the mammoths for weeks, waiting for the perfect time and place to ambush them. It is too dangerous, perhaps even fatal, to attack the herd on the open prairie. Their grandfathers taught them that it is best to ambush mammoths at a watering hole where they can surround, cull, and kill their prey quickly and efficiently.

Hours later, the old cow leads the mammoths up the streambed and into the coulee where the damp sand sticks to their footpads. There, they find the willows a little greener and the flies more abundant, both indications that water is near. Thirst is the driving force behind the pace and upward movement of the herd.

Out of sight and downwind, a procession of old men, women, and children fills the valley, creating a human corral behind the advancing herd. Everyone in the band is helping in the hunt because mammoths are the most important of all creatures. Long ago, the White Mammoth Cow Woman taught their grandfathers that these animals are sacred, and that they come from the place where the Great Spirit lives. The White Mammoth Cow Maiden told them that the mammoth is their mother, that if they respect her, she will nourish them with the essentials of life. Mammoths symbolize the universe because everything needed for their survival is contained within them—food, shelter, clothing, tools, and weapons.

Following the herd's movements from their ridge-top overlook, the young men move into position on either side of the coulee. As the mammoths progress toward the pool of water, the Clovis hunters descend the hill with weapons in hand, slipping through the grass on their stomachs, using their fingertips and toes to advance. Their stealthy movements are muffled by the sound of wind rushing through the branches of spruce trees surrounding the black, boggy ground of the spring-fed pond.

The sky is cloudless and the sun's rays feel good on the backs of the young hunters. Though well hidden from the approaching mammoths, they are under the watchful eye of a porcupine clinging to an overhanging branch. As the day warms, frogs belch out their calls, lizards poise atop glacial boulders, and a snapping turtle pokes its head out of the water for a quick look and a deep breath. Tracks in the dark mud, urine-stained rocks, and a pile of soft fur-filled scats are telltale signs that a pack of dire wolves is lurking nearby.

The time is perfect to hunt mammoths because it has been dry for a long time. To drink the water, the herd will have to walk deep into the muddy ground surrounding the spring-fed pool. There, they will be vulnerable because their movements will be restricted.

The ground vibrates as the mammoths move toward the spring. When the wind changes direction, it brings the strong musty smell of sweaty wool mixed with the decaying stench of the mire. The sounds of snapping branches and crunching gravel grow louder, clearer, and more distinctive. Now the mammoths are close enough for the hunters to hear the rhythmic sounds of stiff bristle-covered tails swooping through the air, swatting at the dense swarms of large biting flies that surround the herd.

The animals appear one by one, using their robust, widely curved tusks to push their way through the trees and the tough thick vegetation bordering the spring. Their small hair-covered ears twitch and flap at the irritating mosquitoes buzzing around them. The Clovis hunters can see that the hairy humps on their backs are swollen with fat-rich meat.

As the mammoths move toward the water, the old cow lets out a prolonged sigh of relief, emanating from the swollen sinuses in her forehead and bellowing out her stout mucus-filled trunk. The great weight of her body drives her legs deep into the muck as she approaches the pool. Her young calf tries to follow at her side, but struggles to keep his balance in the seemingly bottomless ooze. Fearing that her calf will collapse and become hopelessly mired, the aged cow uses her trunk and tusks to shove him forward onto more stable ground.

The Clovis hunters seize their opportunity. With weapons at their sides, they rise from their natural blinds of tree-falls and boulders, less than ten feet away. Then, with the snap of their wrists, they launch stone-tipped darts at the old cow quickly, accurately, and with deadly force. Thump, thump, thump! Thump, thump! Thump! Six of the projectiles hit their target, penetrating the mammoth's thick wool-covered hide. One of the hunters approaches the cow's blind side, waiting for her left front leg to move forward and expose the tissue over her heart.

Despite the six wooden shafts protruding from her sides, the protective instincts of the old cow trigger her swift actions to shield her calf, trumpet danger, and retreat to the rest of the herd. A hunter runs forward with his lance and, with a sudden thrust, impales the cow's body cavity. The stone-tip tears through her soft unprotected stomach and penetrates her left lung. With her eyes open wide and glazed over with pain, the mammoth lifts and twists her head violently.

Another hunter dashes forward and forces his stone-tipped spear into the back of the mammoth's neck near the base of her skull. It is a mortal wound that causes the cow's body to collapse on top of her calf, pressing its small body into the suffocating muck. More hunters rush in and, with needlepointed bone- and ivory-tipped spears, they repeatedly stab the fallen mammoth. Her body shakes in seizure, her molars grind, and her front and back legs stretch and stiffen until they become still. The old cow's pale pink tongue goes limp and slowly emerges from the side of her mouth as blood flows freely from her wounds, drenching her black woolen coat. The sulfuric smell of the mire is replaced with the coppery smell of blood and torn flesh. The rest of the herd moves away from the hunters as a single unit, grouped tightly together for safety and the protection of their young.

The hunters hold their weapons high above their heads and, together, they release primal screams of triumph. It is a signal to the rest of the band that a mammoth has been slain and it is time to join them in the celebration. Four old men emerge from the brush, carrying a large, heavy, ground sloth skin on their shoulders. Kneeling down in front of the corpse of the old cow, they unroll the hide over the blood-soaked, muddy ground. The bony plates in the thick sloth skin provide firm, sure footing on the quaking boggy earth.

The hunter who inflicted the lethal wound stands above the skyward eye of the old cow, watching the last spark of life disappear from her dilating pupil. He kneels down on one knee, says a prayer of thanks to the dead animal's spirit for the food she is about to give them, and tells her that she will live on in the lifeblood of his people. He opens the medicine bag hanging around his neck and pulls out a pinch of chaparral, offering it up to the four sacred directions, mother earth, father sky, and to the mammoth whose life he has taken.

After the ritual prayer, the Clovis hunter pulls his lance out of the belly of the dead cow. Expressing a look of amazement, he discovers that the finely flaked stone spear tip is still sharp and intact. It has penetrated the bellies of twelve mammoths without breaking. Considering it his lucky spear, he carefully leans the lance against the trunk of a nearby spruce tree while he assists the others who are gathering for the butchering process.

One of the hunters is pulling the tail of the dead mammoth with all of his might, while another grabs two handfuls of belly hair, tugging the skin taut. A third man, with a sharp flake of pink quartzite, cuts through the thick gray hide and exposes the white bloodless layers of fat across the entire length of the mammoth's belly. They cut the hide clean from the fat and pull it back over the carcass. Returning to the tail, they make another slice, cutting deep beneath the deposits of fat and into the bloody red- and white-mottled flesh. With the next cut, they disembowel the cow—the inflated, balloon-like stomach and intestines spill out onto the sloth hide.

The Clovis hunters pull the heavy pile of guts clear of the carcass and crawl deep into the cavernous body cavity toward the exposed liver. They cut away the large lobes of the meaty tissue and emerge blood-covered with the wet meat in their hands. One by one, each hunter tilts his head back and, with both hands, lifts the massive fleshy organ over his face and lowers it to his mouth. Sinking his teeth into the end of the floppy, bloody tissue, he tears away a mouthful of meat and passes it on to the next hunter. The fresh liver is chewy, warm, and wet, easily sliding down their throats.

After the hunters have eaten their fill, the rest of the band is invited to join in the feast. It gives the hunters great pleasure and prestige to pass out thick slices of fresh red meat to young and old alike. No one is allowed to go hungry, and all of them eat well into the night, until they feel their stomachs are going to burst open.

Dancing around the campfire, the men reenact the kill, taking the roles of the hunters and the hunted. One young man stretches his arms past his mouth, imitating the curved tusks of a mammoth. He jumps up and turns around in circles about the sparking flames of the fire, pretending to be the great cow trying to shake the darts from her side during her final death throes. Another man jumps forward, acting as if he is about to thrust his spear into the mammoth's belly. A third man jumps over the fire with a make-believe spear and pretends to stab the mammoth in the back of the neck. The man playing the role of the mammoth falls flat on the ground next to the crackling fire. It is a wonderful performance that is enjoyed by all. The women, old men, and children cheer, and afterward they dance and sing the night away, giving tribute to the White Mammoth Cow Woman who has bestowed upon them this great feast. The sounds of the celebration and the sight of firelight cause the distant pack of hungry dire wolves to bay at the moon.

The next morning, the men begin to gather on a dry sandy area above the kill site where they have brought beautifully colored stones that they have carried with them more than a hundred miles. Sitting in a circle with their legs crossed, the men remove cylindrical ivory hammers from their toolkits. Each knapper firmly holds his stone in one hand and a billet in the other. Pop, pop! Ping! Ting! The stones ring out as they are rhythmically struck, and large flakes fall from the handheld stones. With each strike of their hammers and with amazing artistic skill, the knappers begin to shape and thin the brittle stones into teardrop shapes.

The knapping is momentarily interrupted when a group of women step into the circle, bending over their husbands, fathers, and brothers, and pick up the largest, sharpest, and sturdiest flakes they can find. They are looking for good butchering tools, ones that can cut through thick layers of fat and muscle tissue. Little girls at their mothers' side bend over and select small flakes that they will use to butcher an imaginary mammoth. After selecting a handful of cutting tools, the women and their daughters leave for the kill site. The boys are running around them with miniature darts and spears, shouting and screaming, acting as if they are ambushing a herd of mammoths.

The women find the mammoth carcass stiff and cold, but the flesh is easy to cut. Their flake knives glide easily through the meat as they cut it into long strips, then place it in the sun to dry. During the process of butchering, they expose stone-dart points deep in the mammoth's flesh. A few of the points have broken into sharp fragments and have cut their way through the mammoth's muscle tissue.

While the meat is being prepared for transport and storage, an older man hacks away at one of the great tusks with a large angular stone chopper. His grandson selects the best flakes of ivory to make beads, buttons, and sewing needles. At the other end of the mammoth, the boy's father is pounding on an exposed, lower back leg with a heavy granite cobble.

Thwack! Snap! Crack! The leg bone breaks open and exposes the cheesy pink marrow inside. Hearing the bone give way, the children playing in the area run toward the butcher knowing that a tasty treat is at hand. With his index finger and thumb, he pulls out chunks of marrow and gives them to the children, rubbing the greasy residue into their shiny black hair as they collect their snack. With all of the marrow removed, he uses a smaller stone to knap the bone, removing one large, sharp flake after another to make ideal butchering tools with razor sharp edges that cut as well as stone. He puts the longer, thicker flakes in his toolkit to be used another day for making tools and weapons.

Some of the young women are preparing strips of mammoth meat in small earthen ovens where they are sandwiching the meat between layers of wet, green rush at the bottom of a shallow pit, then covering them with hot coals. While the meat slowly cooks, one woman uses a stone flake to strip long lengths of spruce root into flexible fiber. Pinching one end with her fingers, she rubs the other between the palm of her hand and the top of her thigh, twisting the fiber into a pliable cord. Bit by bit, she splices and ties the ends, creating a series of chevron patterns, then shapes them into a woven bag to carry the meat.

The older women are cleaning the mammoth's intestines so they can be cut, tied off, and used to carry water. The stomach tissue is also being cleaned so it can be used to store meat in the cold waters of the pool. The freshly cut strips of meat now cover the grassy ground as far as the eye can see. It will be impossible to eat all of the meat before it spoils, and there are not enough people to carry the meat to their next camp, so they will have to carefully store it at the bottom of the pond where the wolves and bears cannot rob them of the rewards of their hunt.

On the nearby hillside, a shaman and his apprentice are walking beneath a sandstone outcrop, prospecting for red ochre. They are searching for a place where the Great Spirit shed her blood, a symbol of the sacred circle of life. The shaman knows that if they are going to find the red earth, it will be near the base of a cliff. On the bench ahead of them, the prairie grass is sparse and the ground is pink in color, a stark contrast to the beige-colored soil on the surrounding slope. Picking up a couple of old bleached bones from the hillside, the shaman and his apprentice dig into the dense dirt and expose a rich vein of blood-red earth. The apprentice unwraps a well-worn deerskin, and the shaman begins to scoop the sacred mineral from the ground.

After filling the small hide container with red ochre, the shaman removes a hoard of hefty weapons and tools from a woven pouch worn at his side. They are manufactured from mammoth ribs and exquisitely patterned stone diagonally wrapped in a golden-colored sinew that glistens in the sun. The shaman disrobes, removing his breechcloth and moccasins, exposing his naked body to the elements. Lifting the toolkit with both hands, he turns, faces west, and offers up a prayer of thanks. Then turning very slowly to the north, he offers up the same prayer. In the same manner, he turns to the east and then to the south. After completing the round, he raises the toolkit to the sky and then points it at the earth, praying constantly.

After the rite, the shaman and his apprentice bury the toolkit in the red ochre and wait for a messenger from the Great Spirit. The sun is momentarily blocked by the shadow of an enormous soaring bird; it is one of the condors circling in the thermals over the dead mammoth. It is a sign that it is time to go.

The days pass into months and the months pass into years, the toolkit remains undisturbed and unclaimed, safely cached in the red ochre. Then, one summer morning, the tranquil sounds of the prairie are silenced by the loud howls and shrieks of a great yellow mass moving down the coulee toward the bench. The sweet smells of pine and Little Bluestem are replaced with dense bursts of acidic, throat-choking smoke. The ground vibrates as the blade of the bulldozer bounces off of the sandstone bedrock and across the top of the bench, exposing the cache for the first time in thirteen thousand years.

FRONTIER ARCHAEOLOGY

The search for Ice Age American sites is an exciting tale that is centuries old.

At the beginning of the eighteenth century, the western frontier of America was the land beyond the Alleghenies, the Ohio River Valley, and a place called "Kentuckie." To the European explorers, this land was wild and full of adventure and unsolved mysteries. Many of those who entered this country found their way to Big Bone Lick, a place where milky blue springwater bubbled to the surface with the smell of rotten eggs. It was a place where the ground was littered with the bones of long dead behemoths, the likes of which had never been seen anywhere else in the world. And, it was a place that held clues to America's most remote past.

In 1729, the commander of Fort Niagara, Captain Charles Lemoyne de Longueil, provided military support for a French mapping expedition from Lake Ontario to the headwaters of the Ohio. With the assistance of Indian guides, Longueil and his provincial American troops made their way downstream to a trail that had been blazed by migrating herds of bison. The well-worn path that was two wagons wide went through forests of tulip poplars, buckeyes, shagbark hickory, beech, oak, elm, chestnut, locust, sugar maple, and willow. The woods were immense but with no undergrowth.

Eventually the trace led them to a broad green valley filled with deer, elk, and bison in a pasture of grass and sedge. They found the animals aggressively licking bare patches of black, quaking, boggy ground around foul-smelling springs. Isolated dead trees with gray barkless trunks were decorated with colorfully painted symbols. The Indian guides told Longueil that their people had come to this place since time immemorial because this land was not only an important hunting ground for many tribes but also a place of healing. The water of Big Bone Lick was medicinal for people and animals alike because it provided their bodies with much-needed salt and sulfur that aided their digestive systems.

As Longueil examined the area around the springs, he found the giant leg bones, jaws, and ivory tusks of an extinct, elephant-like creature. Politically, this was an important discovery because ancient elephant bones and a primitive stone tool had been found in England thirty-nine years earlier. When he asked about the bones, the Indian guides told him that their ancestors had hunted and killed the great animals. Longueil's find was later recorded on Jacques Nicolas Bellin's 1744 map of what was then the land between New France and "Louisiane." It referred to Big Bone Lick as *Endroit ou on a trouve des os d'Elephant* en 1729—"the place where they found elephant bones in 1729."

As alliances strengthened between the French and Indians, Canadian fur trappers began to make regular canoe trips down the Ohio, and the entrepreneurial English Indian traders were quick to follow. One such individual was Robert Smith, who set up an Indian trading post just outside of the Twigtwee village, about fifteen miles north of Big Bone Lick. In 1744, Smith was able to verify Longueil's earlier discoveries when he found numerous mastodon bones, including a rib eleven feet long, a skull six feet wide, and tusks of ivory that weighed more than one man could carry. In 1751, Smith reported his findings to Colonel Christopher Gist, an employee of the Ohio Land Company of Virginia. Gist went to the Lick and collected a mastodon tooth that weighed more than four pounds. He later gave this specimen to Benjamin Franklin and the American Philosophical Society, the first scholarly society in America. The tooth and stories about Big Bone Lick made members of the Society hunger for more information about the mastodon and this unique site.

Growing discontentment with the French and Indians resulted in skirmishes along the Ohio River. While these acts of aggression made it impossible to excavate at the Lick, they did not stop people from visiting the site. In the autumn months of the French and Indian War (1754–1763), the Shawnee came to Big Bone Lick to boil salt, as did many Indian traders and backwoodsmen such as Daniel Boone, Simon Kenton, and John Finley. Salt was crucial to life on the frontier, especially after blockades cut off shipments from the West Indies. It took about seventy-five gallons of spring water to produce about one gallon of salt. Sitting around their boiling pots of saltwater, the Shawnee told stories of how the "Old Ones" had once hunted the great beasts whose bones were now bleached white by the sun and salty ground. The ancient mastodon bones were so abundant and large that they were often used as camp furniture. Ribs were used for tent poles and vertebrae for seats. In 1756, Mary

Ingles was brought to the Lick as a captive of the Shawnee. Years later, after her heroic escape, Ingles recalled a Frenchman in their company "sitting on one of the big bones cracking walnuts."

After the war, Benjamin Franklin and the American Philosophical Society were anxious to obtain a collection from Big Bone Lick. In 1765, they sponsored Colonel George Croghan, an Indian agent of the Pennsylvania Colony, to lead a small expedition from Fort Pitt to the Lick, where they found mastodon bones and tusks exposed in a cut bank at a depth of between five and six feet. Croghan collected one of the tusks and a sample of bones, but, unfortunately, these specimens were lost a week later when the expedition was captured by a group of Kickapoo and Mascoutin.

A year after the attack, Croghan signed new peace treaties with the Indians of the Ohio River Valley and immediately organized another expedition to Big Bone Lick. This time, with military support and a party of Indian guides, Croghan was able to collect a sample of mastodon bones, teeth, and tusks from the muddy ground around the salt springs. In 1767, following instructions from Benjamin Franklin, he brought the specimens to New York and separated them into two boxes for shipping to England. Croghan sent one box (containing molars and a lower jaw) to Lord Shelbourne, minister to the American colonies, and the other (containing a vertebra, four molars, and four tusks) to Benjamin Franklin. Franklin was in London at the time, acting as a colonial agent trying to prevent the passage of the Stamp Act.

When Franklin presented the tusks and teeth to the Royal Society of London, he suggested to Society members that the specimens belonged to an elephant-like creature that lived at a time when the climate was different from the present. Leonardo da Vinci had suggested more than two-and-a-half centuries earlier that such climatic changes were possible. Although Franklin was puzzled as to why so many animals died at the same location, he maintained that they died out before the arrival of the American Indian. His presentation was of great interest to members of the Society because of the 1690 discovery in London of an ancient artifact with bones of an extinct form of elephant known as a mammoth. George Louis de Clerc de Buffon, a naturalist examining the specimens, stated that he could see definite similarities between the Big Bone Lick sample and examples of mammoths from both Ireland and Asia.

William Hunter, a celebrated anatomist, disagreed with Franklin and Buffon, arguing that the shape and structure of the bones were quite different from those of the elephant. He used the form of the molars to make the case that the American mastodon was actually a great carnivore, a formidable predator, and probably a devourer of human flesh. Hunter believed that it was much more likely that the Indian tribes united out of fear for their lives, setting aside their animosities until their common enemy, the mastodon, was hunted into extinction. Then, in defense of his position, Franklin sent one of the molars from Big Bone Lick to the great explorer, Abbe Chappe, for comparison with the molars of frozen mammoths in Siberia.

Upon Franklin's return from England, he recommended that the American Philosophical Society acquire a complete mastodon skeleton from Big Bone Lick. On May 12, 1774, Governor Thomas Jefferson awarded Big Bone Lick and several thousand surrounding acres to Colonel William Christian as a military grant for his service in the war between Great Britain and France. Thirteen months later Christian sold the Lick to David Ross, but Ross could not take physical possession until August 1, 1808. This break gave the American Philosophical Society and Jefferson ample time to conduct excavations at the Lick, where Ross was allowed to establish a commercial salt works.

Jefferson, who often is referred to as the father of American archaeology, was fascinated with both mastodons and the Ice Age Americans. Unlike Franklin, Jefferson was convinced that people lived in the Americas at the same time mastodons were living at Big Bone Lick. His reasoning was based, in part, on an oral tradition of Delaware Indians, which he had recorded firsthand. During the American Revolution, Jefferson had met with a group of Delaware warriors and asked them, "What happened to the great animal whose bones were found at the salt licks on the Ohio?" A chief in the group stood up and said,

> In ancient times a herd of these tremendous animals came to the Big Bone Licks, and began a universal destruction of the bear, deer, elks, buffaloes, and other animals which had been created for the use of the Indians; that the Great Man above, looking down and seeing this, was so enraged that he seized his lightning, descended on the earth, seated himself on a neighboring mountain, on a rock of which his seat and the print of his feet, and hurled his bolts among them till the whole were slaughtered, except the big bull who, presenting his forehead to the shafts, shook them off as they fell; but missing one at length, it wounded

him in the side; whereon, springing round, he bounded over the Ohio,
over the Wabash, the Illinois, and finally over the great lakes, where he
is living at this day.

Because suggestions of contemporaneity between people and mastodons are not unique in the oral traditions of American Indians, some anthropologists believe that these stories represent a faint but actual memory of the time when mastodons lived in the Americas.

In 1785, Jefferson examined mastodon bones from Big Bone Lick on display at Charles Willson Peale's Philadelphia Museum, the first museum in America. The sight of actual specimens from the Lick so heightened Jefferson's desire to learn more about mastodons and the Ice Age Americans that, in 1795, he instructed General William Henry Harrison to go to Big Bone Lick and make a collection of mastodon bones for him and the American Philosophical Society. Harrison went to the site and conducted a massive excavation of the ground around the springs, but regrettably, the collection was lost when the boat transporting the bones overturned in the Ohio River just below Pittsburgh.

Disappointed by the loss, Jefferson sought the services of French General Colland, who had conducted excavations at Big Bone Lick about the same time as Harrison. When Colland's collection was turned over to Jefferson in 1797 as a token of thanks to the French government, Jefferson sent a sample of the bones to Baron Georges Dagobert Cuvier. In a paper presented to members of the National Institute of France, Cuvier used the specimens from Big Bone Lick as evidence that the earth had undergone a series of catastrophes that corresponded to the biblical days of creation, with Noah's flood being the most recent.

The mastodon bones, teeth, and tusks collected by Colland looked modern because the enamel on the teeth was still bright and polished. That fact and the folklore of the Delaware implied to Jefferson that the possibility of finding living mastodons farther west was quite real. He was so enthusiastic about this prospect that in 1803 he instructed Meriwether Lewis and William Clark to search for these animals during their exploration of the Louisiana Territory. Jefferson thought that mastodons would be important in the Indian trade. (*See photograph on p. 82.*)

Jefferson was not the only one interested in mastodons. Word quickly spread that private collectors and museums were willing to pay top dollar for bones from Big Bone Lick. One collection from the Lick sold for $5,000. Then, in 1804, William Goforth, a poor medical doctor and collector from Cincinnati, began to excavate extensively around the saline springs and seeps. Within a year, he recovered almost five tons of bones. Deplorably, Thomas Ashe, a British con artist, swindled him out of the bones in 1806. Ashe displayed Goforth's collection in museums throughout England and later made an immense fortune by selling the bones to both the Royal College of Surgeons and private collectors in Scotland and Ireland.

By 1806, Jefferson was not only President of the United States but also President of the American Philosophical Society. Since Lewis and Clark had failed to find the mastodon alive in the Far West, it was beginning to look as if the bones in Kentucky were much older than Jefferson previously had suspected. Writing on Jefferson's behalf for the Society, Casper Wistar requested that William Goforth procure a complete collection of mastodon bones from Big Bone Lick. Goforth replied to President Jefferson directly, writing that in addition to the remains of mastodon, he had found the bones of a single paw, similar to a bear's foot except that it "nearly filled a flour barrel." Unbeknown to Goforth, he was describing the remains of the giant ground sloth, an extinct animal with which Jefferson was quite familiar. Goforth also wrote that the large bones occurred on the surface of a layer of salt water and gravel at a depth of eleven feet, and below layers of stiff blue clay containing bones of smaller, more-modern animals such as deer, elk, bison, and bear. He felt that the larger animals had been preyed upon because their remains were not found articulated.

Jefferson was ecstatic when he received Goforth's letter in the winter of 1807. At that time, he was debriefing Captain William Clark at the White House, so he asked Clark to stop at Big Bone Lick as he passed through the area on his way back west, employ Goforth and local laborers, and supervise an excavation of the site. Jefferson promised Clark and the American Philosophical Society that he personally would cover all expenses. Clark, who was promoted to general, was joined by his brother, General George Rogers Clark, in the Big Bone Lick expedition.

The Clark brothers and Goforth excavated at the Lick during the summer of 1807. As they moved an enormous amount of dirt from around the springs, they amassed an extensive collection of mastodon bones, teeth, and tusks, as well as numerous stone tools and weapons. Three of these artifacts were the flaked-stone tips of ancient spears, known today as Clovis points.

Clovis points excavated from Big Bone Lick, Kentucky, by George Rogers Clark, William Clark, and William Goforth during the 1807 expedition funded by Thomas Jefferson.

Goforth and the Clark brothers had found the first absolutely positive evidence of the Ice Age Americans, possibly in direct association with the remains of one or more extinct animals, including the mastodon. Unfortunately, the significance of this discovery went unrecognized for almost two hundred years.

In 1808, Jefferson placed three hundred bones from Big Bone Lick on display in a large room at the White House. They included a nearly complete mastodon skull, four complete lower jaws, and four tusks, one of which was about ten feet long. He sent duplicate specimens to the National Institute of France in Paris. After he left office, Jefferson donated a musk ox skull from the collection to the American Philosophical Society and moved the rest of the collection to his home, Monticello. Although the musk ox skull is still curated by the Academy of Natural Sciences in

Philadelphia, most of the Monticello collection was destroyed in Jefferson's later years when he fell on hard financial times and the bones were ground into a fine powder to use for fertilizer.

Because the focus of President Jefferson's excavations was the collection of mastodon bones, Goforth was able to keep all of the artifacts recovered during the dig. In 1817, Goforth's artifact collection was left to his medical successor, Daniel Drake, who then donated it to the Western Museum of Cincinnati, Ohio, in 1818. The collection was later purchased by Thomas Cleany in the late 1850s and donated to the Cincinnati Art Museum in 1887. Today, it is curated at the Cincinnati Museum of Natural History.

EUROPEAN
INFLUENCES

CHAPTER 3

The quest for the Ice Age Americans was encouraged by an important new discovery in Europe when Jacques Boucher de Perthes, a customs officer and avocational archaeologist, found flaked-stone tools in direct association with mammoth bones in the ancient gravel of the Somme River near Abbeville in northern France. The pear-shaped artifacts were almost identical to the ones John Conyers, a pharmacist, had found among mammoth bones in a London gravel pit in 1690. Geologist Paul Desnoyers attributed the gravel to the Ice Age, a time when massive glaciers covered significant portions of both Europe and the Americas. In 1829, he called that period of time the "Quaternary."

Boucher de Perthes's discovery suggested that people must have lived at the same time as the mammoth, during the Ice Age. He published his findings in 1836 and displayed the artifacts and bones at professional meetings, scientific expositions, and museums throughout Europe. Christian Thomsen, director of the Museum of Northern Antiquities in Copenhagen, Denmark, wanted to display artifacts like those discovered by Boucher de Perthes and Conyers in an exhibit on the development of technology. He decided to separate the exhibit into three periods of human history based on the materials most commonly used in the production of tools. Although there was no measurement of time, the artifacts were arranged in the gallery from the assumed oldest to youngest: Stone Age, Bronze Age, and Iron Age. The term "Stone Age" was used to represent a time when people hunted mammoths.

The concept of a Stone Age attracted the attention of Albert Koch, a collector and owner of a private museum in St. Louis, Missouri. In the autumn of 1838, Koch began to search for evidence of an American Stone Age in western Missouri. The fervor of his search was driven, in part, by the hope of finding enough bones to assemble a complete mastodon skeleton. His first serious excavation was at a spring site near the Bourbeuse River, about eighty miles west of his museum, where, in the

56

sediments around the spring, he found a large number of blackened mastodon bones, large rocks, and stone tools. Koch passionately believed that the rocks had been used as weapons to kill the mastodons, and the stone tools and blackened appearance of the bones were evidence that the animals had been butchered, cooked, and eaten.

In 1839, Koch began excavations at a sulfur-water spring a few miles south of St. Louis, today known as the Kimmswick site. He recovered a number of mastodon bones, including a complete skull, and a few flaked-stone artifacts. Not completely satisfied with his finds, Koch decided to move his excavations westward to a spring site near the Pomme de Terre River in the Osage country. There, in 1840, Koch found two flaked-stone spear tips and enough bones to construct a complete mastodon skeleton. Because one of the spear points was found beneath and in direct contact with a leg bone, Koch believed that he had found the first unquestionable evidence of the Ice Age Americans. He suggested that the physical connection of the weapon tip with the remains of the mastodon was "conclusive evidence, perhaps more than in any other case, that they were of an equal, if not older, date than the bones themselves."

Although the direct association of flaked-stone weapons with mastodon bones found at the Kimmswick site was verified almost a century and a half later, at the time of Koch's excavations, his claims were widely disputed. Part of the problem was that most people, including many members of the scientific community, considered the notion of a Stone Age to be heresy. Among them was the British geologist Charles Lyell, often referred to as the father of geology.

Lyell believed that Quaternary sediments actually represented two distinctive epochs of time—the Pleistocene and the Recent. In 1839, he used the term Pleistocene to describe layers of earth that contained evidence of the Ice Age and the remains of large extinct animals such as the mammoth, while he used the term Recent to refer to sediments containing the bones of modern animals, stone tools, and human remains. Lyell believed that in both Europe and America recent geological processes had fortuitously mixed the bones of extinct animals and stone artifacts. In 1841, he traveled to Big Bone Lick, Kentucky, to see the site that had been celebrated for more than one hundred years for its unique Ice Age history. However, after examining the Lick and the surrounding geology, Lyell still could find no evidence for an American Stone Age.

In 1859, Charles Darwin published his landmark book *On the Origin of Species by Means of Natural Selection Or the Preservation of Favoured Races in the Struggle for Life,* writings inspired by Charles Lyell's book, *Principles of Geology,* which suggested the earth has undergone continuous transformations. If this were true, Darwin argued, all living organisms must also have undergone continuous change. While Darwin's book is often referred to as the first one on human evolution, it neither contains the term evolution nor uses humans as an example of an evolved species. The word "evolved" was the last word in his book, and only one sentence in the conclusion refers to humans: "Light will be thrown on the origin of man and his history." The implication, however, was obvious, and everybody got it. After reading the book, Charles Lyell publicly announced that he had been wrong about the recent geological history of people. His admission opened the door and many minds to exciting new possibilities in the search for the Ice Age Americans.

In 1862, the same year as the Civil War Battle of Manassas at Bull Run, George Gibbs published the first field guide on American archaeology, titled *Instructions for Archaeological Investigations in the United States.* It alluded to the possibility, if not the probability, that Stone Age artifacts could be found in the Americas. To many readers, this meant that the artifacts of the Ice Age Americans should look like the bouchers collected in Europe. Bouchers, named after Jacques Boucher de Perthes, were teardrop-shaped, flaked-stone tools with sharp edges and pointed tips. Rather than searching for more examples of the distinctive, truly Ice Age American–made, flaked-stone spear points recovered during the Jefferson expedition at Big Bone Lick or Koch's excavation at the Kimmswick site, archaeologists and other professional scientists searched for bouchers.

Nathaniel Shaler, director of the Geological Survey of Kentucky, had read the work of Gibbs and decided to reexamine Big Bone Lick during the summer of 1868. By then, the bone-bearing deposits had been greatly depleted by nearly a century and a half of excavation and the construction of nearby salt works, vacation resorts, and a fort. Shaler found the Lick to be a ghost of its former fame. Primeval forests no longer surrounded the salty bog. An earthen fort that once flew the successive flags of pioneering French, British, and American militias was now unrecognizable. The once-thriving salt works of Dan Ross were now in ruins, overgrown with thick brush and weeds. Health spas, springwater resorts, and a grand hotel that had attracted tourists from around the world just forty years earlier were deserted and rapidly falling into decay. Instead of mastodon bones, Shaler found the ground littered with the remains of bison that once filled the valley. The bison had been exterminated for almost seventy years, and their bones were "as close as the stones of a pavement" in the muddy ground.

An early-twentieth-century archaeological expedition at Big Bone Lick, Kentucky.

Not surprisingly, Shaler was unable to find Stone Age artifacts among the remains of the extinct animals. While he did not favor a great antiquity for people at Big Bone Lick, he cautiously wrote that "it is not yet time to form a final opinion on this point." Shaler believed that climatic change at the end of the Ice Age rather than human hunting was responsible for the demise of the mastodon and other extinct species. Although a local collector found another stone spear point similar to the ones discovered during the Jefferson expedition, after Shaler's excavation the significance of this discovery was overlooked for another seventy years.

Shaler was working under the assumption that direct positive evidence of the Ice Age Americans would be found in the form of a boucher. This seemed to be the case in 1875 when Dr. Charles Conrad Abbott announced that he had discovered Stone

Age artifacts in glacial gravel near Trenton, New Jersey. Shaler examined the find spot and concluded that it was, indeed, glacial outwash. The boucher-like artifacts were given the name "paleoliths." To Shaler, they looked like Stone Age artifacts, exactly what he expected to find at Big Bone Lick if people were present at the same time as the mastodons. In the following years, more paleoliths were uncovered at a number of sites in eastern North America.

Dr. Charles L. Metz, who was digging with Frederic Ward Putnam of the Peabody Museum, found a paleolith at a depth of eight feet in glacial gravel during his 1885 excavation of the early historic Madisonville village and cemetery located along the Little Miami River in southwestern Ohio, about twenty-five miles north-east of Big Bone Lick. Upstream near the town of Loveland, Metz also discovered a second paleolith about thirty feet below the surface and in close proximity to mastodon bones.

By the 1890s, examples of paleoliths excavated from glacial deposits were commonplace. For instance, by 1888, Abbott alone had found four hundred, sixty of which had been collected from the depths of glacial gravel. In his 1892 book *Man and the Glacial Period*, Frederick Wright, a professor at the Oberlin Theological Seminary, illustrated exemplary paleoliths and their find spots. In addition to record-ing the discoveries of Abbott and Metz, Wright described artifact finds from Indiana, Minnesota, and a gravel pit in Newcomerstown, Ohio. He suggested that the Newcomerstown specimen was an artifact that "resembles in so many ways the typical implements found by Boucher de Perthes, at Abbeville, that except for the difference in the material from which it is made, it would be impossible to distin-guish it from them."

Wright's book engendered a debate about the Ice Age Americans that is still being fought today in both spirit and tone on many academic fronts. William Henry Holmes, an archaeologist trained in geology who was working for both the Smithsonian Institution and the Bureau of American Ethnology (BAE), believed that Wright's paleoliths were nothing more than the manufacture rejects of recent stone tool and weaponry production. Because Holmes's reexamination of the find spots failed to produce a single artifact in undisturbed glacial gravels, he argued that the paleoliths were, at most, a few thousand years old. Holmes reiterated Lyell's earlier criticisms, suggesting that the artifacts had found their way into the glacial gravels through natural geological processes such as slumping, overturning trees, and decaying roots. He also argued that the European artifacts that Wright used for comparison with the paleoliths were equally defective.

As the debate quickly became a nasty, mean-spirited war of words, the professional integrity and honesty of archaeologists on both sides were brought into question. Wright dismissed Holmes's criticisms by stating that the top professionals in the country had amply documented his findings. Among the scientists in support of Wright were Dr. Charles Abbott, Professor Lucien Carr, Dr. Charles Metz, Professor Frederick Putnam, Professor Nathaniel Shaler, and Professor J. D. Whitney. Wright was willing to acknowledge that overturning trees and decay of their roots could disturb artifacts at a depth of three or four feet but not as deep as fifteen or twenty feet. He went on to accuse Holmes of falsifying drawings of the artifacts and their locations.

Fuel was added to the fiery debate when Czechoslovakia-born Ales Hrdlicka was brought to the Smithsonian Institution in 1903. Like most European-trained physical anthropologists of the day, Hrdlicka's specialty was the shape of the human skull. By the turn of the twentieth century, it was apparent in Europe that bouchers were hand-axes made by an earlier and physically more primitive human form. In Germany, hand-axes had been found in caves and glacial gravels along with thick, human-like skulls possessing low, sloping foreheads and heavy, protruding brow ridges. As Charles Lyell illustrated in his 1863 book, *The Geological Evidences of the Antiquity of Man with Remarks on Theories of the Origin of Species by Variation*, the skulls were larger than those of chimpanzees but smaller than those of modern humans.

European archaeologists responded to the discovery of subhuman fossils by incorporating them into a new subdivision of Thomsen's Stone Age—"Paleolithic," or Old Stone Age, and the "Neolithic," or New Stone Age. The term Paleolithic was used exclusively with extinct Ice Age animals and primitive human forms, and the Neolithic was associated with modern animals and anatomically modern humans.

Hrdlicka's position on the Ice Age Americans was quite simple. If people were living during the Ice Age along with extinct species such as the mastodon, then there should be some evidence of human skeletal remains with primitive cranial features. Armed with this single-minded view of prehistory, Hrdlicka systematically refuted all assertions of human antiquity in both North and South America. Regardless of how old they looked, he declared that all human skeletal material found in the Western Hemisphere was anatomically modern based on the shape of the skulls. His criticisms of new claims of American antiquity were vicious, relentless, and ostracizing. As he got older, Hrdlicka's writings became rigid authoritarian dogma, and the deliberate exploration for the Ice Age Americans came to a standstill. No one individual did more to stifle Ice Age American research than Ales Hrdlicka. And so it remained for almost half a century.

Like most fiercely fought academic debates, both sides were partly right and both were partly wrong. Wright was correct about the antiquity of people in the Americas, but he was right for the wrong reason. Paleoliths were not the same age as the European hand-axes; many were much more recent artifacts. Holmes was correct in pointing out that stone tools are not necessarily old just because they look primitive. Lyell's cautions were also warranted because all archaeological sites are subjected to some degree of change from natural geological processes such as plant growth, burrowing animals, wind, water, gravity, freeze-thaw, and even earthquakes and volcanoes. Hrdlicka, too, had been correct about the older-looking human bones from the Americas when he maintained that the degree of fossilization has nothing to do with a bone's age. Truly ancient bone can appear pristine under the right geological conditions, while modern bone can be mineralized in a matter of years. Hrdlicka and Holmes, however, were completely wrong in their assumption that anatomically modern people were not contemporaries of the mammoth, mastodon, and other extinct species of the Ice Age.

The debate among Wright, Holmes, and Hrdlicka was eventually brought to an end and the search for the Ice Age Americans was renewed—not by a world-famous archaeologist, geologist, or philosopher, but by a couple of cowboys. Like most of the great discoveries in science, the first recognized and accepted evidence of the Ice Age Americans was made through pure and simple serendipity.

COWBOYS &
COLLECTORS

When the long hot summer of 1908 came to an end with the catastrophic explosion of a large thunderhead, more than ten inches of rain poured from the clouds and onto the desert pavement near Folsom, New Mexico. After the coulees flashed with turbulent floodwater, the arroyos had been cut deeper and wider. To George McJunkin, an African American cowboy and foreman of the Crowfoot Ranch, a flash flood meant fence repair.

While riding the fence line northeast of the ranch headquarters, McJunkin found a gaping ditch eroded beneath a section of barbed wire in Wild Horse Arroyo. At the bottom of the gully, more than ten feet below, he spotted large bones protruding from the sun-baked clay and gravel. McJunkin had an innate curiosity about natural history, was well read, and avidly collected rocks, minerals, fossils, and artifacts. He scrambled into the ravine and dug out a couple of the bones with a pair of pliers, tied them to the back of his saddle, and took them home to add to his collection. He later named the site "the Bone Pit" because bones were always weathering out from the gully. Although McJunkin did not recognize them as belonging to an extinct species of bison identified many years earlier at Big Bone Lick, he reasoned that the bones must be old because they were buried deeply in the ground. As a self-taught surveyor, McJunkin recorded the exact spot of his discovery. He spread the word to local collectors, including banker Fred Howarth and blacksmith Carl Schwachheim, both of Raton, New Mexico. Neither of them, nor anyone else for that matter, was willing to make the thirty-mile journey on horseback with McJunkin to see the bone pit.

A year or two after McJunkin's discovery of extinct bison bones near Folsom, New Mexico, Irish farmer Thomas Patrick Kiley became interested in what he called "grooved arrowheads." His Uncle Barney had sold a steam engine plow to a Mr. Keck of Mount Pulaski, Illinois, who was using the plow to pull stumps and clear the ground between Clinton and Salt Creeks when it began to rain. The ground softened

George McJunkin discovered the Folsom site.

and eventually the plow could not move in the mud, so Keck decided to take advantage of the rainfall and spend the rest of the day hunting arrowheads, his favorite pastime. When a Catholic priest stopped by on his way to visit the sick wife of a tile cutter, Keck showed the priest about twenty-five or thirty points. The priest was surprised to see that eight of them were grooved, unlike any he had seen before, and Keck told him that he had another at home.

When Kiley, who was fascinated by the rare and unusual, heard the story, he had to see the grooved arrowheads for himself. It did not matter whether it was Missouri mules, productive oil wells, or grooved arrowheads, Kiley liked to keep detailed records of their occurrence. He discovered that Keck had about one grooved arrowhead for every one hundred that was not, and that they varied in size from two to more than six inches in length. From that day on, Kiley examined numerous artifact collections from DeWitt County, Illinois, in search of the unique grooved arrowheads.

Thomas Patrick Kiley conducted the first Ice Age American artifact survey.

When Kiley found someone with a specimen, he usually recorded in a notebook the name of the owner, the length of the point, its color, when and where it was found, and, frequently, the circumstances associated with the discovery. The following notations are examples of the information in Kiley's records:

> *Edgar Baum found two on Old Mill Hill, 1916. One is 2 1/4 inches long and gray in color. The other is red/brown and 3 3/4 inches long. Both points were found in a road ditch after a hard rain. He lived in Decatur.*

Dave Alers found three just over the line in Piatt County, east of Weldon. One is white/blue in color, 3 1/2 inches long. The other two are halves, both white in color, and were found with a tooth as big as your fist in Little Creek sand bar, April 3, 1921.

It is quite likely that the tooth "as big as your fist" that Kiley referred to was a mastodon molar. The grooved arrowheads were the same type of artifact that had been discovered during the nineteenth century with mastodon remains at both Big Bone Lick and the Kimmswick site. Years later, Ed Crain, an oilman from Texas, told Kiley that he had found nine grooved points around Midland, but he was surprised to see them in Illinois.

Kiley's ledger, which represents the oldest and longest survey of Ice Age American artifacts, documents 332 examples in DeWitt County, Illinois, 138 of which have exact locations for their find spots. Ironically, Kiley did not collect artifacts. Although he did note in his ledger that his wife had found a grooved arrowhead at the bottom of a pond on their farm, Kiley did not own a single example. It seems clear from his notes that he did not realize that he had recorded objects manufactured by Ice Age Americans. He was simply interested in the presence of these unique flaked-stone artifacts in the area surrounding his farm.

In the spring of 1922, a few months after the passing of George McJunkin, Carl Schwachheim and Fred Howarth visited the bone pit. They found it exactly where McJunkin said they would, eight miles west of Folsom near the head of Wild Horse Arroyo, a dry tributary of the Cimarron River. They filled a feedbag full of bones, which they took back to Raton, New Mexico, where they compared them with pictures in their fossil books. They were able to narrow them down to one of two possibilities—an extinct Pleistocene species of moose/elk or bison. They realized that a vertebrate paleontologist would be needed to make a more accurate identification, although at that time there were only a handful of Pleistocene bone specialists in the country, the closest in Denver, Colorado.

Four years later, Schwachheim and Howarth had an opportunity to visit the Colorado Museum of Natural History, where they met with the museum's director, Jesse D. Figgins, who was also a vertebrate paleontologist. He identified the bones in the feedbag as an extinct species of Pleistocene bison. Because artifacts were also found in the area, he believed that the bone pit might be an Ice Age American site. To Ales Hrdlicka, such thinking was bad science, but Figgins was not afraid of Hrdlicka. Since he already had felt Hrdlicka's wrath for his work on an Ice Age American site in Texas, from that point on Figgins was obsessed about proving the cantankerous old curmudgeon wrong.

Under Figgins's direction, the Colorado Museum of Natural History funded a paleontological expedition to the McJunkin bone pit. In the summer of 1926, under the direction of Figgins's son, Frank, and Schwachheim, the dig began. The excavators followed the contours of bones exposed in the gully, removing the sediment above and alongside the bones, a procedure that meant undercutting layers of clay, silt, and gravel between four and thirteen feet thick that hung overhead. The clay content and dry air made deep excavations possible, and they gradually exposed one nearly complete skeleton after another, side by side.

There was no question about it—Jesse Figgins's identification had been correct; the bones belonged to an extinct species of Pleistocene bison. Figgins also was correct about the potential of the site to produce evidence of Ice Age Americans when two flaked-stone weapon tips were found in clay removed from around the bones. Then on July 14, 1926, Frank Figgins exposed a fragment of the second specimen still in place in the Pleistocene clay along with the ribs of an extinct bison. The artifact was thin, delicate, and finely flaked with a concave base, ear-like projections, and a groove-like flake removed from both sides. Unquestionably human made, it was what Thomas Kiley had called a grooved arrowhead sixteen years earlier. It also was similar to the artifacts recovered by Albert Koch at the Kimmswick site in 1839, and to those found during Thomas Jefferson's 1807 expedition at Big Bone Lick.

Following his father's instructions, Frank removed a sediment block containing the bones and the artifact for shipment back to the museum. Jesse Figgins was determined to use the artifact to show that Hrdlicka had been wrong about American prehistory because Figgins had undeniable proof that the artifact was manufactured during the Ice Age.

Harold J. Cook, curator of paleontology, was no stranger to proclamations about the Ice Age Americans. In 1925, he wrote an article, "Definite Evidence of Human Artifacts in the American Pleistocene," for the prestigious journal *Science*. In 1926, Cook set the stage with his *Scientific American* article, "The Antiquity of Man in

America: Who Were the Ice Age Americans? Whence Came They?" It was a stark contrast to Hrdlicka's confident and convincing paper, "The Race and Antiquity of the American Indian: There is No Valid Evidence That the Indian Has Long Been in the New World," published the same year in the same magazine.

Predictably, Hrdlicka insisted that the artifacts had washed into the deeper levels of the bone pit from above. Hrdlicka even questioned Figgins's honesty because he did not show the find to his colleagues, thus implying that Figgins had committed fraud. On December 17, 1926, fellow paleontologist Oliver Hay wrote a letter to Figgins stating that the artifacts alone would never convince Hrdlicka or his supporters. Hay suggested that Figgins had to establish "the age of the deposit, either from fossils or from the geology of the region"; otherwise, Hrdlicka would always be justified in saying that the artifacts were recent intrusions. Figgins was tenacious and refused to give up, so he decided to have a museum crew return to the bone pit and expand the excavations the following summer. In light of Hrdlicka's brutal accusations, he instructed Schwachheim and his son, Frank, to halt the digging if another artifact was found in place among the bones.

During the summer of 1927, four more of the characteristic artifacts were found at the site. Then, on August 29, when Schwachheim exposed a fifth specimen among the ribs of a bison, he followed Figgins's orders and left the artifact imbedded in the clay. When Figgins received word of the discovery, he immediately contacted the leading archaeological institutions in the country, asking them to send their foremost experts to inspect the find. On August 31, Figgins wrote Schwachheim to "cover carefully and securely and await further instructions. Have telegraphed several scientists inviting them to examine the point in position."

Dr. Barnum Brown, a paleontologist at the American Museum of Natural History, and Dr. Frank H. H. Roberts, an archaeologist at the Smithsonian Institution, were the first outside scientists to see the artifact in place. Dr. A. V. Kidder, an archaeologist at the Robert S. Peabody Foundation for Archaeology, arrived two days later. Brown was given permission to remove some of the sediment encasing the artifact. As one of the sides was carefully exposed and it became apparent that it was yet another example of the grooved artifacts, the three visiting scholars were convinced that Figgins had, indeed, discovered incontrovertible evidence of the Ice Age Americans. They presented their conclusions at the annual meeting of the American Anthropological Society, while Figgins announced the discovery to the public in an essay, "The Antiquity of Man in America," published in *Natural History.* In the article, Figgins renamed the bone pit the Folsom site after the nearby town and applied the term "Folsom points" to the distinctive flaked-stone artifacts.

In the summer of 1928, excavations resumed as a joint venture between the Colorado and American Museums of Natural History. As during the previous summers, more Folsom points were found among skeletons of the extinct bison. Experts in archaeology, paleontology, and geology were once again invited to examine the artifacts in place. Three years of fieldwork had revealed nineteen Folsom points among the bones of twenty-three extinct bison. Harold Cook, who showed on the basis of geology that both the artifacts and bison were Pleistocene in age, published his findings in a *Scientific American* article, "Glacial Age Man in New Mexico." It was also evident to most archaeologists that the artifacts were weapons used by the Ice Age Americans to kill big game during the Ice Age. McJunkin's bone pit had become the single most important American archaeological discovery.

Even when presented with evidence of the Ice Age Americans that was beyond a reasonable doubt, Hrdlicka refused to accept it. He became an embittered old man who would shuffle into one professional meeting after another to explain in his characteristically toned-down, Old World accent that Figgins's artifacts and bison may very well be the same age, but the animals must have survived into modern times. He would try to convince anyone who would listen to him that the archaeology of America was nothing but a recent phenomenon. For the first time in his career, Hrdlicka was fighting a battle that he could not win. Meanwhile, discoveries of Ice Age American sites continued to be made in the Southwest.

On the eve of the Great Depression, James Ridgely Whiteman, a young Native American cowboy working on the Southern Plains near the Pecos River of New Mexico, wrote in a letter to Alexander Wetmore, assistant secretary of the Smithsonian Institution, that he had found "warheads" among the bones of extinct elephants near the town of Clovis, New Mexico. Like the rest of the country, Whiteman had read of the great archaeological discovery near Folsom and recognized that the warheads he had found were quite similar to the points found at the Folsom site.

By 1929, the Folsom site had put every vertebrate paleontologist in the country on alert that Pleistocene fossil sites may contain artifacts of the Ice Age Americans. With that possibility, the Smithsonian sent one of their paleontologists, Charles

Gilmore, to examine Whiteman's site. That spring Gilmore met Whiteman in the town of Clovis, from where they drove about fourteen miles south to Blackwater Draw, a place where the winds of the Dust Bowl had created a large blowout and one of the places where Whiteman had found a Folsom point and fossil bison bones scattered across the surface. Gilmore was able to find a mammoth tooth but no artifacts, so he was anxious to get back on the road, assuming that the trip to Whiteman's site had been a wild goose chase. After all, what were the chances that a cowboy—and a teenager at that—would find another Folsom site?

Gilmore told Whiteman that there was nothing at the site to merit a professional excavation, so Whiteman's time with a real-life representative of the Smithsonian Institution lasted no more than an hour. He was devastated and could barely hold back the tears as Gilmore drove him back to Clovis, where he was left dazed and confused. Whiteman knew that he had found Folsom artifacts together with fossil bones. He also knew that there were more artifacts and bones to be found at the site, but it would take more than an hour to find them. Now, no one would believe him— or so he thought.

Unbeknown to Whiteman, Edgar Billings Howard, a retired army officer and soft-spoken gentleman of the Old South, had been searching caves in the Chihuahuan Desert and foothills of the Guadalupe Mountains for evidence of the Ice Age Americans. Howard was working as an archaeologist for the University of Pennsylvania Museum when A. W. Anderson, a newspaperman, and George O. Roberts, an artifact collector, visited him in August 1932 at the close of his excavation at Burnet Cave. When Anderson and Roberts told Howard about Whiteman's discoveries in the blowouts at Blackwater Draw, Howard decided to see the site himself.

Unlike Gilmore, Howard was able to confirm the presence of artifacts among the bones of extinct animals. After Howard examined the site, Anderson introduced him to Whiteman, who told him that there was no doubt in his mind that Blackwater Draw was a most significant site and should be excavated as soon as possible. When Howard also asked Whiteman if he could borrow some of his artifacts to compare them with points from Burnet Cave and the Folsom site, Whiteman was more than happy to comply. In fact, he was overjoyed that a professional scientist would take him seriously after his humiliating encounter with Gilmore. Howard promised Whiteman that he would return the following summer to begin a formal excavation.

That fall, the New Mexico Highway Department dug a gravel pit in the basin between Clovis and Portales, close to the spot where Whiteman had found the Folsom points and mammoth bones. As heavy equipment ripped right through a Pleistocene bone bed, mammoth, horse, and bison bones were scattered everywhere. When Howard was contacted at the University of Pennsylvania Museum about the incident, he quickly returned to New Mexico to secure permission to examine the property during the following summer.

When Howard returned and hired Whiteman to assist him with the 1933 summer fieldwork, their first objective was to conduct a survey of exposures along the low sloping terraces of Blackwater Draw. The most productive areas were along the margins of the gravel pit where layers of bison and mammoth bones were easily accessible. Within a few weeks, they had found flaked-stone artifacts among mammoth bones. Like Figgins, Howard invited scientists from the top institutions in both the U.S. and Europe to examine the association of bones and artifacts. They concluded that the young Native American cowboy Ridgely Whiteman had indeed discovered a site that contained direct positive evidence that during the Ice Age people were in the Americas at the same time as the mammoth.

Excavations at Blackwater Draw continued summer after summer. By 1936, however, the dig was producing more questions than answers because a wide variety of flaked-stone weapons had been found among the bones of extinct Pleistocene animals. Some of the artifacts were virtually identical to those from the Folsom site, but others were quite different. A number of them had grooves that were much shorter than those on Folsom points, and most of such specimens were long, thick, and crudely flaked. There were even a few points that looked like miniature versions of the larger varieties. To further complicate the issue, other sites with artifacts displaying similar ranges of variation were being excavated in Colorado, Texas, and Nebraska.

The archaeological community scrambled to figure out the meaning of the similarities and differences among the flaked-stone artifacts. In 1936, when Henry Shetrone, director of the Ohio State Archaeological and Historical Society and Museum, proposed the term "fluted" for flaked-stone weaponry with groove-like flakes or channels, archaeologists and collectors quickly adopted the name, which is still used today to describe all such artifacts from Alaska to the tip of South America. But, what should the people who made the artifacts be called?

In 1940, Frank H. H. Roberts introduced the term "Paleo-Indian" to describe people who lived in North America during the Ice Age. Although the term Paleo-Indian quickly caught on, it became a multipurpose catchall word used to describe Ice Age American sites, artifacts, and methods of survival. Today, there is still no unanimity on how it should be used, not even on how it should be spelled—Paleo-Indian, Palaeo-Indian, Palaeoindian, or Paleoindian. However, it was becoming apparent that the Ice Age Americans included more than one group of people, so some means of separation was necessary.

On May 21, 1941, Edgar B. Howard wrote to Kenneth M. Chapman of the Laboratory of Anthropology in Santa Fe, New Mexico, about holding a meeting to unravel the Folsom problem. Chapman was excited about the meeting and helped Howard with its organization. They encouraged people to bring representative artifacts from their collections to help promote an open discussion about their meaning. On September 3 and 4, when more than sixty professional archaeologists and avocationals met in Santa Fe, they examined and discussed the artifacts exhibited by those in attendance. Working together in an open, informal, hands-on forum, professionals and collectors were able to establish a clearer understanding of the Ice Age Americans. The participants decided that the term "Folsom" would be retained for fluted points from the type-site, the place where they were first discovered, but "Clovis" would be used for the artifacts discovered at Blackwater Draw.

Having solved the problem of the name game, the next big question was to determine exactly how old the Clovis and Folsom sites were. Could they be the same age? At the time of the Santa Fe meeting, it was safely assumed, on the basis of physical geology and paleontology, that Clovis and Folsom artifacts dated to the last Ice Age, so they were somewhere between ten thousand and thirteen thousand years old. Many archaeologists reasoned that if Clovis and Folsom points were present together in the same layer at the same site, then they must be the same age.

In 1949, Elias H. Sellards and Glen L. Evans from the Texas Memorial Museum found an exposure at Blackwater Draw where Clovis points and mammoth bones occurred in a layer that was below one containing Folsom points and bison bones. Before the advent of radiocarbon dating, this stratigraphic superposition provided the first unquestionable relative age for Clovis as being one that is older than Folsom. Thus, the real importance of Blackwater Draw was neither site size nor artifact quantity; rather, it was the site's role of providing a crucial temporal and environmental context for the Clovis culture. Blackwater Draw remains the single best site that proves beyond a reasonable doubt that Clovis is older than Folsom.

Since Whiteman's discovery of Blackwater Draw, the number and kinds of Clovis artifacts discovered have increased dramatically. Cutting and scraping tools and split-bone and ivory tools have been discovered, in addition to fluted points, stone hammers, large blades, and blade cores. Split-bone and ivory tools include shaft wrenches, billets, awls, punches, beads, and beveled crosshatched-base compound points and foreshafts. Less formal bone and ivory artifacts consist of expedient and carefully shaped rib segments with rounded and polished ends, scrapers, fleshers, flakers, and inscribed objects.

Although many archaeologists have placed a special emphasis on Clovis points, the split-bone tool industry may have been of greater importance. At Blackwater Draw, split-bone artifacts are more abundant than any specific flaked-stone tool type, with the exception of side scrapers. Clovis fluted points were considered significant because they had been picked up on the surface at various places across North America, from coast to coast. While there are noticeable geographic differences in Clovis point styles, the range of variation from a single site often is as diverse as variations between sites.

It also soon became apparent that fluted points were not the only distinctive Clovis artifacts found outside of Blackwater Draw. Projectile points and foreshafts manufactured from split-bone and ivory were found in mammoth-bearing deposits in central Alaska, southeastern Saskatchewan, southern Oregon, and northern Florida. Like at Blackwater Draw, a Pleistocene age was proposed for the artifacts because the ivory and bone had been worked while it was still fresh and resilient, and mammoths and mastodons had been extinct since the end of the Ice Age, more than ten thousand years ago.

Today, Clovis is widely recognized as a clearly defined Ice Age culture in American archaeology. The distinctive nature of the Clovis culture is found in the techniques of weapon and tool production. While Clovis artifacts vary greatly in shape and size, they are remarkably similar in their method of manufacture. Thus, technology provides an archaeological fingerprint for the Clovis culture.

CLOVIS CULTURE

Clovis people were hunters and gatherers who lived during the Ice Age and carried with them a tool kit of Old World derivation. Their archaeological remains and group mobility were unlike those of modern hunter-gatherers because Clovis bands probably moved their camps many times a year. The groups were typically small, consisting of twenty to fifty people. Band organization was egalitarian, which means that there were no formal leaders and no social ranking or classes. Except for differences of age, sex, and personal qualities, individuals were considered equals.

Because there were few Clovis hunter-gatherer bands in the Americas, their archaeological sites are small and scattered across the landscape. They created a variety of sites, including big-game kill and scavenging sites, stone quarries, workshops, base camps, short-term camps, burials, caches, and a seemingly infinite

The Lange-Ferguson Clovis mammoth kill site.

number of areas of more limited activity. Unlike later sites, the remains of Clovis camps contain no evidence of permanent housing and little refuse or features such as pits and fireplaces. Hunting sites occur where Clovis people could ambush game at the margins of bogs, ponds, slow-moving streams, river confluences, shallow fords, major game trails, and mineral springs. The larger campsites appear where there are outcrops of large masses of high-quality stone for tool making. Such sites often were reused year after year. Nearly all of the Clovis sites are in areas where game could have been obtained, processed, or monitored.

During the Ice Age, although America's climate was cooler than it is today, it was extremely erratic and subject to rapid and profound changes. Most of the country was covered in an ever-changing mosaic of vegetation. Some areas were patches of open grasslands, while others were dense hardwood forests. Ice Age animals, referred to as "megamammals"—such as mammoths, mastodons, bison, giant ground sloths, camels, moose-elk, horse, musk ox, giant beavers, tapirs, and peccaries—roamed the countryside along with modern game such as caribou, elk, deer, antelope, turkeys, rabbits, turtles, and snakes.

As the climate changed, so did the distribution of plants and animals. Since environmental change was constant, the geographic extent and abundance of trees and grasses changed continuously because every species has its own individual tolerance of climatic change. It is unlikely that vegetation stability existed anywhere in America during the Ice Age. Concurrent with changes in vegetation, animal communities were reorganized, their ranges shifted, and some thirty species of megamammals became extinct. The question of why they became extinct remains unanswered. Were these animals unable to respond to the rapidly changing environment, were they hunted into extinction, or was it a combination of both pressures?

Clovis hunter-gatherers responded to these environmental changes in several ways. They shifted their hunting grounds from open areas with low relief to the more rugged, closed terrain of the mountains. This shift accompanied a significant change in food getting, from specialized big-game hunting to more generalized foraging in which smaller animals became a more important source of protein. Many of these changes in livelihood were associated with the disappearance of the megamammals. Unlike big game, which often is concentrated in herds, small food animals such as deer, turkeys, and rabbits are more dispersed. Access to evenly spread small game does not require people to move as often or far as does the hunt for megamammals. Thus, environmental change eventually brought Clovis hunters into every region of North America.

Clovis people used a distinctive tool kit that was well adapted for the hunting and processing of big game in near-arctic environments. This tool kit, which originated somewhere in Eurasia during the Pleistocene epoch, changed little as the ancestors of Clovis hunters entered America and gradually spread southward. There are recognizable similarities between the tool kits of Clovis hunters in places as far separated as the Pacific and Atlantic coasts, since megamammals were found across the continent.

Specialized hunting requires high mobility by the hunters. Because large game animals migrate seasonally, Clovis hunters had to be at least as mobile as the animals they hunted, but not so aggressive that they rode the tails of the migrating prey. A good measure of Clovis mobility is their flaked-stone weapons, which are often found hundreds of miles from where they were made. The individuals who used them likely manufactured most of their own weapons and tools.

The Clovis tool kit included a variety of stone, bone, ivory, and antler implements in addition to items of wood, hide, and fiber from plants and animals. Clovis technology was portable; the entire assemblage could be carried in an attaché-like pouch. A tool kit's compact size and light weight are exactly what we would expect of nomadic Clovis bands who might pick up their possessions and move camp several times each year, if not each season.

Flaked-stone knives and scrapers, which are the most common tools, were made from long blades struck from specially prepared, multifaceted cores and preforms from the early stages of weapon manufacture. Knives and scrapers were necessary for butchering game, processing hide and sinew, and creating cordage from plant fibers.

Clovis tools were also used to make other tools. The sharp broken corner of a stone knife or a small spur protruding from the side of a scraper was used to cut long slivers of bone, ivory, or antler, which were made into awls and sewing needles. Archaeologists call this the "groove and splinter" technique. Awls and sewing needles were essential for the manufacture of baggage, netting, clothing, and shelter, items that may have been made from plants, animals, or both; regardless, they were portable and disposable.

The key to survival was probably what Edgar B. Howard in 1943 first called "the Clovis fluted point." There is no question that Clovis points were used as weapons. What remains unclear is whether they were thrust as spears, thrown as javelins, propelled as darts, or even shot as arrows. It is safe to assume that the larger and heavier the stone tip, the shorter the range of the weapon. The largest Clovis points were undoubtedly used as the tips of thrusting and throwing spears, and the smaller ones would have made ideal dart tips propelled by a throwing board or "atlatl." Although miniature Clovis points would have been perfect arrowheads, we have no direct positive evidence that the Ice Age Americans had the bow and arrow. However, we do know that the bow and arrow were present in the Old World during the Ice Age, thousands of years before Clovis people were in the Americas.

A Clovis point from the Lange-Ferguson mammoth kill site.

Whether or not Clovis hunters threw or thrust spears or used darts and the atlatl would have depended upon the opportunity presented by the game and the effectiveness of the weapon. Thrust and thrown spears are most effective when they are used at close range on confined prey. Atlatl darts can be launched from either the side of the body or over the shoulder. An atlatl dart is an accurate and deadly weapon when launched with a snap of the wrist from the side, but only at a distance of seven to eight feet. While an over-the-shoulder throw significantly increases the dart's range, it loses accuracy, speed, and penetration power. Also, long distance throws require more release time and space. However the dart was thrown, hunting with an atlatl would have been done in open environments.

The effectiveness of Clovis points would have been enhanced if they had tipped a compound harpoon-like lance. Foreshafts nearly identical to those used in whale hunting by certain Inuit groups have been found on Clovis sites across North America. Like the Inuit harpoon foreshafts, the ends are beveled and incised in a crosshatched pattern to help hold the stone point in its haft. The bevel of the foreshaft is also about the same width as the flutes on the base of the Clovis points. Once hafted, the ears of the Clovis point would protrude from the binding and create barbs similar to those of Inuit ivory and bone harpoons. After the projectile pierces the flesh, the shaft can be withdrawn, leaving the Clovis point-tipped foreshaft deeply embedded in the body of the prey. The compound nature of the spear allows the hunter to rearm his weapon quickly with another foreshaft and point and to drive the lance repeatedly into the animal until it dies.

George Frison's experimental archaeology in Africa proved that a finished Clovis spear point is a well-designed piece of flaked-stone weaponry that is capable of repeated, predictable, and dependable use in killing big game. As part of a culling operation, Frison used replicas of Clovis weaponry to inflict lethal wounds on African elephants in Hwange National Park in Zimbabwe. His experiments on mature elephants, both living and dead, showed that Clovis spear points have a sharp tip for initial piercing and sharp blade edges to cut a hole to allow deep penetration of the projectile, the haft bindings, and the shaft. Frison further demonstrated that the Clovis spear point was the first piece of flaked-stone weaponry in the world that was designed well enough to provide a single hunter with a dependable and predictable means of pursuing and killing an elephant on a one-to-one basis.

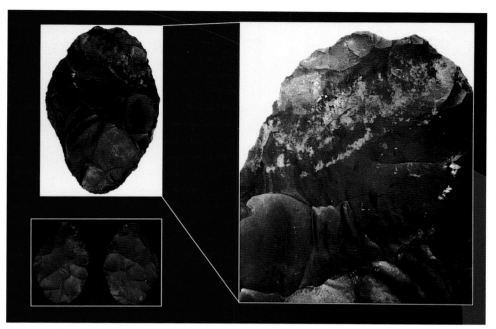

A large Clovis biface with a diagonal pattern of red ochre, from the Crook County Clovis Cache.

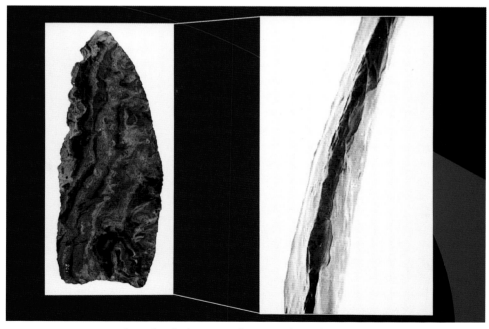

A Clovis knife showing edge wear, from the Crook County Clovis Cache.

The bones, teeth, and tusk of a mastodon.

A mastodon molar is a "tooth as big as your fist," as Thomas Kiley put it.

Examples of what Thomas Kiley called "grooved arrowheads."

A Clovis mammoth-bone chopping tool excavated by Dr. Adrien Hannus.

A Clovis flaked mammoth bone excavated by Dr. Adrien Hannus.

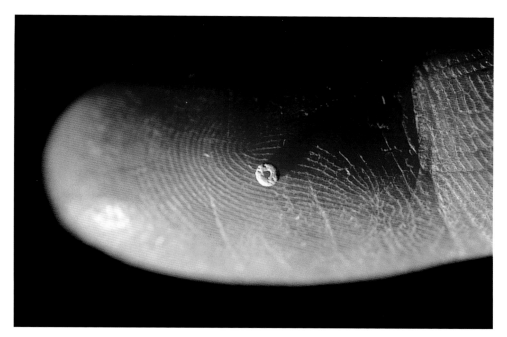

A Folsom bead.

A mammoth bone tool.

A Folsom bison bone tool.

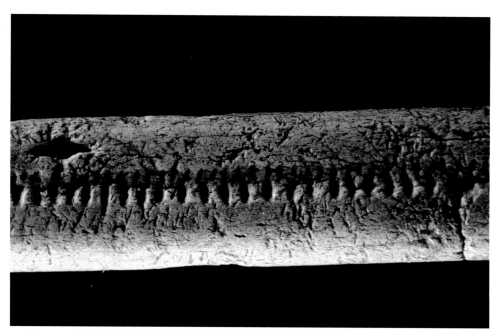

An artistically engraved mammoth rib.

Clovis cores and blades.

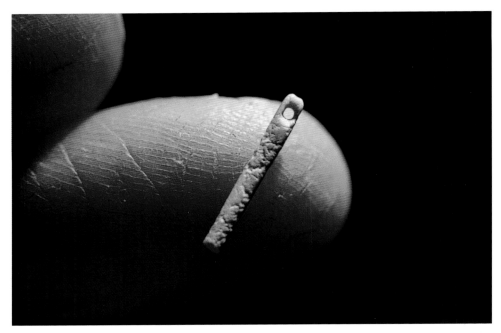

An Ice Age sewing needle.

A large early-stage Clovis biface, from the Fenn Cache.

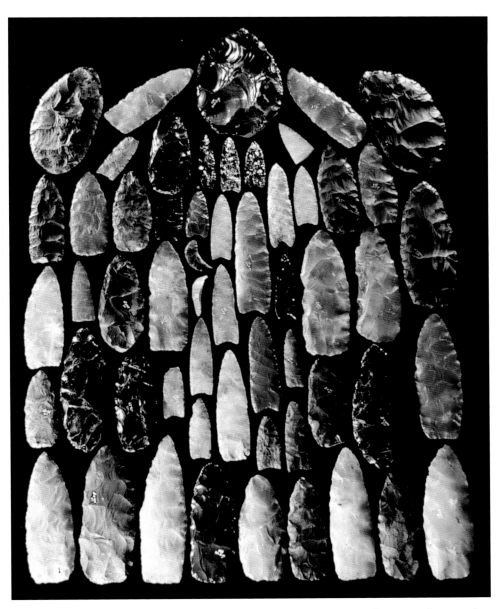

The Fenn Clovis Cache.

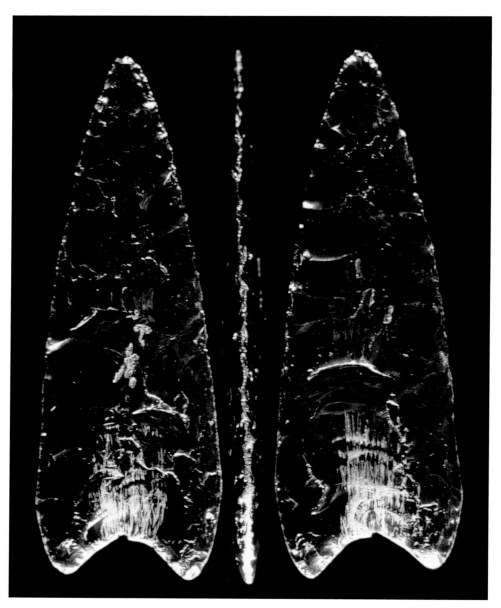

An obsidian Clovis point, from the Fenn Cache.

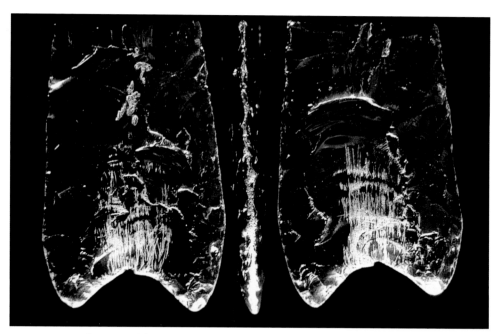

A close-up of the haft element of an obsidian Clovis point, from the Fenn Cache.

The red ochre deposit where the Crook County Clovis Cache was buried.

A Clovis point manufactured from smokey quartz, from the Fenn Cache.

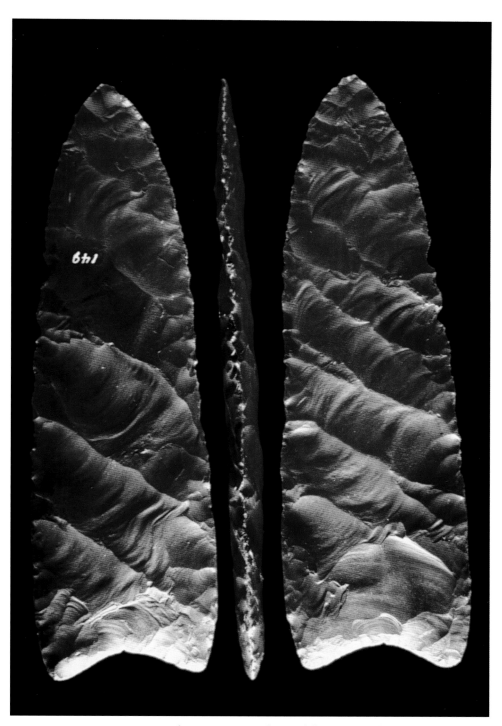

A Clovis point manufactured from jasper, from the Fenn Cache.

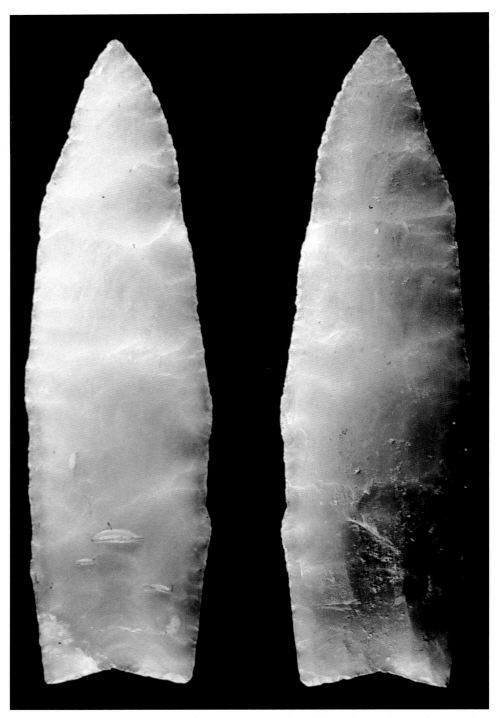

An incomplete Clovis point, from the Richey-Roberts Clovis Cache.

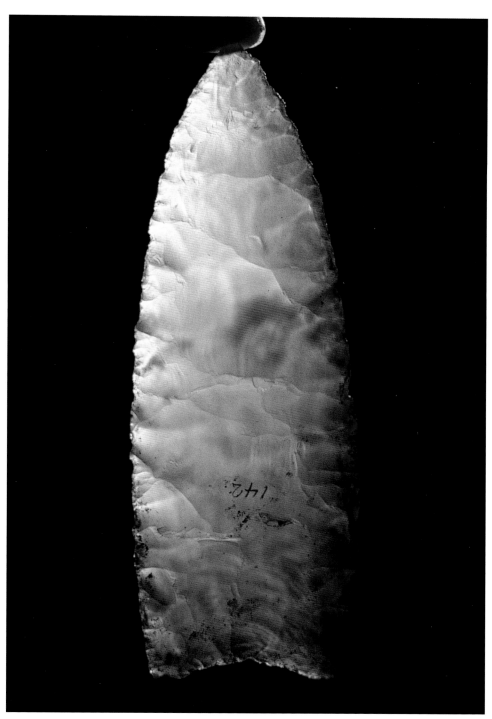

A finished Clovis point with a diagonal pattern of red ochre, from the Fenn Cache.

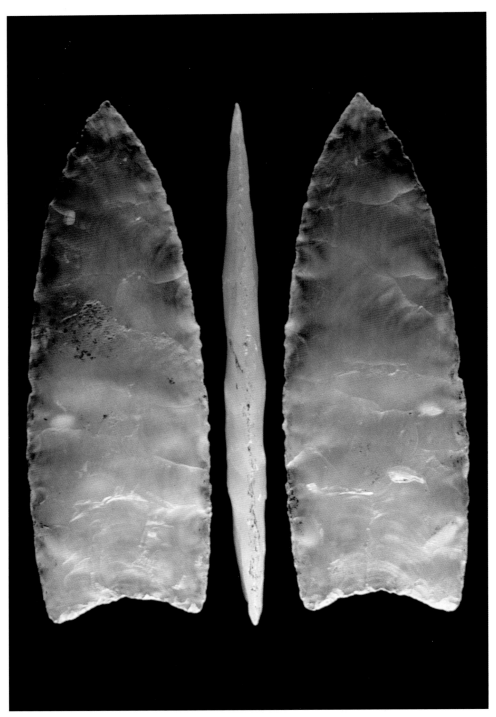

A finished Clovis point with a diagonal pattern of red ochre, from the Fenn Cache.

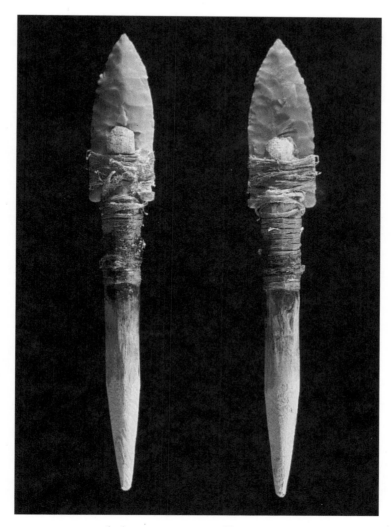

An experimental Clovis spear point used by George C. Frison to deeply
penetrate the body of an African elephant.

Clovis people may have made their weaponry even more effective by connecting
the lance to the foreshaft with a strong cord, using it in a manner similar to the
method used by the Bambuti elephant hunters of the Ituri region of West Africa prior
to World War II. The Bambuti killed elephants with long harpoon-like lances. Their
spearhead, with its foreshaft fishhook-like barbs, formed a single unit that fit loosely
into the hollowed end of a wooden spear and was attached with several coils of strong

cord. They approached the elephant from the rear, thrust the compound lance into the soft unprotected belly, and immediately ran for cover. The elephant, enraged with pain, ran away. The great impact of the elephant's massive footpads hitting the ground jarred the lance, eventually detaching the shaft from the barbed spearhead still embedded deeply in the animal's abdomen. As the animal ran, the shaft, still attached to the spearhead by long coils of cord, trailed it. As the shaft would get entangled among the trees and shrubs, the elephant would tug and tug and eventually plunge forward with all of its might to free itself. With great force, the elephant would pull free and the barbed spearhead would come out along with the animal's stomach and intestines. Then the elephant would stagger about until it collapsed from a loss of blood.

Whatever strategy Clovis hunters used, the Clovis point was clearly designed to kill large game efficiently. Although it took extra time and raw material to make Clovis weaponry, the returns, measured in meat protein, were high.

Beyond points, knives, and scrapers, Clovis groups had several basic knapping tools, including two types of hammer: a hard, hand-sized round stone and a thick, dense, cylindrical billet of ivory, antler, bone, or wood. The stone hammers were used to remove broad, short, wide flakes from high-quality tool stones such as flint, jasper, agate, chalcedony, chert, quartzite, rhyolite, crystalline quartz, and obsidian. Billets produced long, thin, narrow flakes. Sharpened antler and bone were used to remove small flakes and create sharp cutting edges on tools and weapons. Like the rest of the tool kit, knapping tools were discarded as they wore out.

Clovis hunters were after big game. Throughout America, Clovis points have been found among the remains of many species of large animals, including mammoth, mastodon, bison, horse, camel, tapir, ground sloth, bear, musk ox, peccary, big horn sheep, caribou, elk, antelope, and deer. Remains of smaller terrestrial and aquatic animals such as rabbits, turtles, and fish, along with nuts, berries, and other plant foods that have been found on Clovis campsites, would have been a source of backup and emergency foods.

Few archaeologists today view Clovis people as strictly big game hunters. While the artifacts that have been preserved suggest a livelihood consisting of big game hunting exclusively, some archaeologists believe that Clovis people had a mixed foraging strategy in which megamammals played an important but not dominant role. In addition to hunting a variety of animals, Clovis groups incorporated carbo-hydrate-rich plant foods into their diet to counterbalance the nutritional stress and fat depletion that most animals experience during the lean months of winter. Clovis people had access to a wider range of food resources than were available to later populations.

Clovis kill sites are not common. Many of them are deeply buried in river terraces and sinkhole caves where they are often exposed whenever there is a change in erosion patterns or, accidentally, during deep mining. Many Clovis kill sites in the Southwest were exposed after devegetation and a significant drop in the water table promoted extensive weathering and erosion.

The Lange-Ferguson Clovis mammoth kill site.

Naco, located in southern Arizona near the Mexico border, is perhaps one of the most mysterious of the Clovis kill sites. In 1950, when Marc and Fred Navarette found a couple of Clovis points and mammoth bones weathering from an arroyo bank in the San Pedro Valley, they went to Tucson and showed the materials to Emil

W. Haury of the Arizona State Museum. If verified, Haury knew that Naco would be the fourth-known buried Clovis site.

When Haury began excavations at Naco in 1952, remarkably he found five Clovis points among the bones of a single mammoth, all within a square yard. One of the points was found near the base of the skull, another rested against a neck vertebra, a third was lying near the left scapula, and two were stuck between ribs. Eight Clovis points were found altogether—two initially by the Navarettes, five in Haury's excavation, and another upstream in the arroyo. The Naco mammoth had four times as many points associated with it as have been found with any other mammoth. Stylistically, the points displayed a wide range of variation, the diversity suggesting that multiple hunters, perhaps as many as eight, were responsible for killing the mammoth.

Mammoth tracks at the Murray Springs site in the
San Pedro Valley of southern Arizona.

The absence of butchering tools may imply that the Naco mammoth was the one that got away from Clovis hunters. However, it is equally possible that they were lost to erosion along with the hind end of the mammoth. Naco is one of four mammoth kill sites in the San Pedro Valley. The others include Murray Springs, Lehner, and Escapule. Interestingly, some of the flakes recovered at the nearby Murray Springs site match the tool stone used to manufacture one of the Naco Clovis points.

Clovis sites are recognized on the basis of their distinctive tools and weapons, particularly the fluted points. Worn flake ridges on some of these artifacts suggest that they were carried together side by side in a bag or pouch. Use-wear studies on the scrapers and knives show that animal skins and plant fibers were obtained and processed, possibly to make sacks, clothing, shelters, or traps.

Clovis groups did not live in isolation. Contact between groups occupying neighboring areas would have been necessary to maintain an open exchange of information, raw material, and mating partners. Archaeologically, our only indication of social interaction is the presence of artifacts manufactured from exotic tool stone. Although Clovis hunters likely collected all of their tool stone locally, the bulk of the exotic materials was probably obtained through exchange networks. Clovis points manufactured from exotic stone are often found in areas such as springs, where big game would have been abundant and predictable. This pattern suggests that inter-group contact and social interaction took place in hunting areas.

While we can use distinctive stone as a rough measure of social interaction, we know absolutely nothing about the populations that were directly involved in the exchange systems. The limited number of artifacts spread across the American landscape suggests that Clovis populations were sparse and scattered. That we do not have any direct demographic data may be the result of Clovis mortuary practices. It is possible that Clovis people cremated their dead or left them to decompose on the ground.

While rarely found, Clovis burials tend to contain only one or two individuals. Post-Clovis burials are so abundant and concentrated in single locations that they can almost be classified as cemeteries, a change that suggests both an increase in the frequency of burials and in their archaeological visibility. This trend may be related to an increase in population, a decrease in mobility, or both.

Where Clovis graves have been discovered, they usually consist of a badly decomposed skeleton covered in red ochre and accompanied by a cache of exquisitely made tools and weapons. These burial goods, which represent a single tool kit, may have been the dead person's possessions.

Not all caches are associated with mortuary activity. Caches of mammoth and mastodon meat and tool kits manufactured from exotic rocks and minerals were buried for future retrieval at strategic locations in order to reduce the risks associated with the survival of a highly mobile population. Such artifact caches often included tools and weaponry in virtually every stage of manufacture. Not surprisingly, caches are the rarest of all Clovis sites. Like hidden treasures, they contain materials that were precious to Clovis people, such as red ochre and some of the highest quality and most exquisite tool stone in the Americas, often obtained hundreds of miles from the cache site.

THE CROOK COUNTY CLOVIS CACHE

Crook County, located in the extreme northeastern corner of Wyoming, is an amazing place from both historical and geological perspectives. Part of the High Plains, it includes the western side of the Black Hills and the eastern side of the Powder River Basin, with bold prominent features on the landscape such as Devils Tower, the Missouri Buttes, Sundance, Inyan Kara, and the Bear Lodge Mountains.

In the not-too-distant past, great masses of migrating bison could have been seen stretching from one horizon to the next. Even today, Crook County's Thunder Basin National Grassland supports one of the largest populations of bison in the country as well as immense herds of pronghorn antelope and a seemingly endless number of deer. Not surprisingly, it was an important hunting ground of the Lakota.

Not until after the Louisiana Purchase of 1804 did American explorers and fur traders enter Crook County for the first time; by 1850, traffic from the east dramatically increased with the establishment of the Oregon Trail. Tensions mounted between the Lakota and the migrating emigrants. To ensure the safety of the settlers, the United States signed a treaty in 1851 giving the Lakota all of the land east of the Rockies to Kansas, and between the North Platte and Arkansas Rivers, with Crook County at the center, "as long as the grass shall grow, the waters flow, and the winds blow."

In 1863, John M. Bozeman cut a trail through the center of the 1851 Lakota treaty land to Virginia City, Montana. The steady stream of prospectors pouring into the area on their way to the Montana goldfields resulted in a war with the Lakota nation that ended in 1868, when the United States signed a peace treaty with Chief Red Cloud giving the Lakota a great reservation that comprised seven states, again with Crook County at the center. However, the treaty was broken six years later when General George Armstrong Custer's expedition into the Black Hills discovered gold. Once again, conflict with prospectors was a catalyst for warfare that ultimately led to the infamous Battle of Greasy Grass along the Little Big Horn River in Montana. The county is named after General George Crook, who finally ended the Indian Wars in 1877, a year after Custer's defeat.

Crook County was transformed almost overnight as the gold rushes and Indian Wars of the nineteenth century were replaced with the oil booms and political scandals of the twentieth century. Calamity Jane, Wild Bill Hickok, and Butch Cassidy and the Sundance Kid were replaced by the likes of Albert Fall, Harry Sinclair, and Edward Dohney. Peace Makers and Winchesters were replaced with drilling derricks and pump-jacks as oil and gas became the new tools of America's industrial revolution.

The exploration for oil and gas brought Harold Erickson to Crook County in the summer of 1963. He was a member of a seismic survey crew working in the northern part of the county known as the checkerboard area because the Bureau of Land Management and private ranchers managed alternating plots of land. Because Erickson was also a collector, he spent much of his free time looking for artifacts.

Erickson's subsurface mapping project took him into an area overlooking a broad coulee where a dam had been built near the head of a small spring at the bottom of the valley. In the process of dam construction, a road had been bulldozed from the bench top down into the coulee, passing under a low sandstone bluff six to eight feet high. Knowing that artifacts had been found in the area, Erickson decided to use his lunch break to examine the freshly bulldozed surface. Following the road down the hillside, he noticed a dramatic change in soil color near the bluff and about five feet below the surface. It was an area of very red earth roughly four feet wide, six inches thick, and thinning out to nothing on either end.

When Erickson picked up a broken survey stake and began breaking up the red sediment, he struck stone almost immediately. Although the compact nature of the deposit slowed his digging, Erickson was able to eventually expose a large oval-shaped, flaked-stone artifact. After pulling it out of the ground, he could see the edge of another artifact in the hole. Since the lunch hour was almost over and the surrounding red earth was too firm to remove with the survey stake, Erickson decided to return to the site after work.

That evening, Erickson came back to the artifact find spot with a shovel and tire iron in hand. He used the shovel to remove the soft overlying soil and the tire iron to excavate the artifact from the red lens. In the course of digging, he discovered that there were actually six more of the big flaked-stone artifacts in the red layer as well as two broken bone objects that looked like "tent pegs as big as your finger and a foot long." The bone artifacts were likely bevel-based, split-bone foreshafts or points broken in place by the heavy earth-moving equipment.

When Erickson returned to the site the following evening with a better set of hand tools, he dug through the red lens but there were no more artifacts to be found. Before leaving, he examined the red earth that the bulldozer had pushed over the edge of the road. Digging through the clumps of disturbed sediment, he found another sizable biface and a small Clovis point. Although he did not recognize it at the time, Erickson had discovered a cache of Clovis bifaces, the third of only two known at the time. He never returned to the site and kept its location a closely guarded secret.

The first and perhaps the most spectacular of the Clovis caches was found in 1902 somewhere in the vicinity of southwestern Wyoming, southeastern Idaho, and northeastern Utah. The exact details of the spot were lost through the generations that followed. Known today as the Fenn Cache, it includes fifty-six masterfully worked Clovis weapons and tools in virtually every stage of manufacture. While the artifacts vary greatly in shape and size, they are remarkably similar in the way the stone was flaked and shaped, displaying large flake scars produced by striking the stone with a soft but dense hammer of ivory or antler. The consistency and distinctiveness of the flaking is an archaeological fingerprint of Clovis technology. The flaking pattern of these most effective weapons was produced by a unique set of steps that guaranteed a minimal loss of high-quality stone.

The variety of the stone is another important dimension of the Fenn Cache artifacts, which were manufactured from obsidian, chert, jasper, quartz crystal, and agate, and often obtained hundreds of miles from the cache site. Regardless of whether they were acquired directly from the source areas, exchanged, or traded, these stones were hand-carried a great distance across a diverse landscape.

Most of the weapons and tools in the Fenn Cache have a thin coating of red ochre. Its occurrence in conjunction with quartz crystal spear points may provide insights into Clovis beliefs since crystals and red ochre have long been recognized as important components of the rituals and ceremonies of hunting bands. They are usually associated with hunting magic, reproduction, birth, and death.

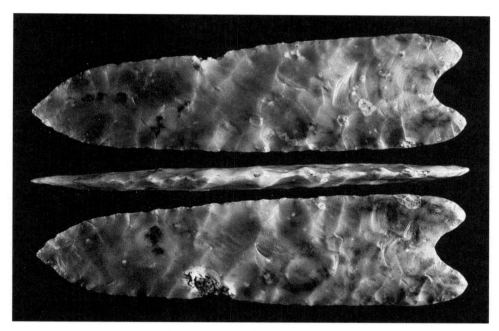

A Clovis point manufactured from chalcedony from the Fenn Cache.

In the fall of 1961, W. D. Simon found a second cache on the Big Camas Prairie of southern Idaho. When the cache was exposed a few inches below the surface by a road scraper, Simon reported the discovery to Earl H. Swanson and B. Robert Butler of the Idaho State University Museum. The Simon Cache includes about thirty-three large, flaked-stone artifacts. Like the Fenn Cache, the Simon Cache consists of large Clovis points—both finished and in various stages of manufacture—with beautifully colored, high-quality tool stone, quartz crystal bifaces, and red ochre staining.

Another possible cache from what is known as the Anzick site was discovered in 1968 near the town of Wilsal in southwestern Montana. More than a hundred Clovis artifacts were uncovered when a construction crew cleared the remains of a small collapsed rock shelter situated at the base of a cliff on a bend of Flathead Creek near its confluence with the Shields River. The fragmentary remains of at least two young children were found along with large Clovis points—both finished and in various stages of manufacture—coated with red ochre, and six bevel-based, cross-hatched, split-bone artifacts. Clovis age radiocarbon dates obtained on some of the human bone suggest that the rock shelter was a Clovis mortuary site. However, because the earth-moving equipment destroyed most of the site, we will never be certain whether the artifacts were part of a separate cache or grave goods associated with the human remains.

Ten years later, Orval Drake and a group of fellow artifact collectors discovered a Clovis cache while they were surface-hunting in a plowed field near the South Platte River of northern Colorado. The artifacts include thirteen finished Clovis points, a chert hammer stone, and numerous fragments of ivory. All of the points are quite similar in shape, flaking pattern, and exotic stone. Most of them were manufactured from a brilliantly patterned, high-quality chert from Texas known as alibates. The tips are sharpened to a point as if they were ready to be used. Although the Drake Cache is unusual because it lacks preforms and red ochre, the artifacts are stylistically comparable to the finished Clovis points in the Simon Cache.

In the spring of 1987, Moises Aguirre discovered a cache while hand-digging an irrigation ditch in the Richey-Roberts apple orchard near East Wenatchee in central Washington. The cache was found when Aguirre shoveled thirty inches into the rich volcanic soil and exposed a concentration of eighteen flaked-stone artifacts. After examining the specimens, Russell Congdon, a local avocational archaeologist, correctly identified them as weapons and tools manufactured by Clovis hunters.

In April 1988, a team of renowned Ice Age American archaeologists—including Peter J. Mehringer of Washington State University, Mel Aikens of the University of Oregon, George C. Frison of the University of Wyoming, C. Vance Haynes of the University of Arizona, and Dennis Stanford of the Smithsonian Institution— examined the site and confirmed that it was indeed a Clovis cache. Volcanic ash in the underlying sediments placed the age of the cache at the end of the Pleistocene, ten thousand years ago. After readings from ground-penetrating radar pinpointed a concentration of additional artifacts, excavation in the area produced more weapons and tools, including some of the largest Clovis point preforms ever found. They were artistically flaked from exquisitely translucent pieces of chalcedony. News of the discovery was made public, and photos of the eye-catching artifacts appeared in *National Geographic* and *Discover* magazines.

Two years later, R. Michael Gramly, of the Buffalo Museum of Science, and a group of avocational archaeologists resumed excavations at the Richey-Roberts Cache site, where they uncovered more of the amazing Clovis points and preforms, tiny bits of red ochre, and thirteen robust, bevel-based, crosshatched, split-bone artifacts manufactured from mammoth or mastodon ribs. Two of them were decorated with incised zipper-like designs. In all, this remarkable cache includes fifty-seven Clovis artifacts.

With the widely publicized discovery of the Richey-Roberts Cache, rumors began to circulate among artifact collectors that an unreported cache discovered in Wyoming back in the early 1960s contained a Clovis point as big as the ones found in Washington. In 1997, John N. Byrd chronicled the story of the Crook County Cache in several popular articles, but the exact location of the spot seemed to have vanished with the passing of Harold Erickson. I was eager to track down and examine the cache because it was associated with red ochre. Since it had been found in eastern Wyoming, there was a good possibility that the red ochre may have come from the Sunrise site in Platte County, the only known Clovis red ochre mine. Because Sunrise red ochre is physically and chemically very distinctive, and if red ochre still was present on the artifacts, I could compare it to samples from the Sunrise Mine and confirm or reject the source. I had already examined red ochre from the Anzick, Richey-Roberts, and Fenn Caches, and none of them conclusively matched the Sunrise Mine.

I called Pete Bostrom of the Lithic Casting Lab in Troy, Illinois, because Pete always has his finger on the pulse of Ice Age American discoveries. If anyone knew the whereabouts of the Crook County Cache, it would be Pete. My hunch paid off. Pete not only had seen the cache but also had photographed it. He told me that Forrest Fenn had just acquired the artifacts, so they were now just a phone call away. I immediately called Forrest and asked him for permission to examine the cache. He shipped it to me the next day.

The artifacts arrived within twenty-four hours. Lifting the individually wrapped specimens from the mass of foam peanuts, I was struck by their tremendous size and weight. I carefully removed the protective coverings, placed the artifacts on a bench covered with several layers of bubble plastic, then arranged the specimens by size, from the largest to the smallest, and began to examine them with a microscope under tungsten lighting.

The Crook County Cache consists of nine bifaces representing various stages in the manufacture and use of Clovis weaponry and tools, from rough preforms to the heavily resharpened. Five of the bifaces are well made and nearly identical to Clovis preforms in the Fenn Cache. The flaking patterns, edge treatment, and sheer size of these specimens are quite similar to preforms from the Simon and Anzick Caches. They also are reminiscent of some of the paleoliths described by Frederick Wright and so vehemently rejected by William Henry Holmes and Ales Hrdlicka a century earlier.

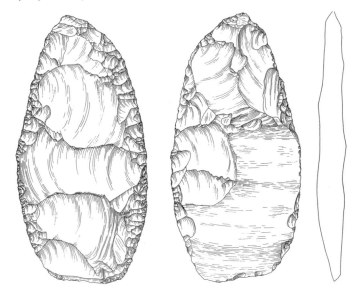

Crook County Cache, specimen 202, early stage Clovis biface.

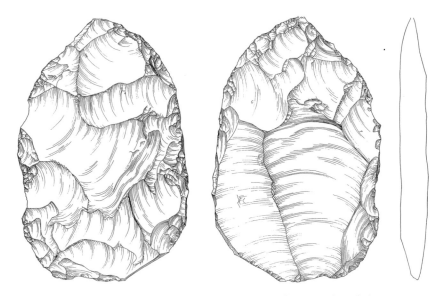

Crook County Cache, specimen 203, early stage Clovis biface.

The largest, most robust, and earliest-stage Clovis biface #203 measures 8.7 inches long, 5.3 inches wide, and 0.9 inches thick. It is irregular, with massive flake scars and a large flute-like, basal thinning flake on one side. A small portion of the edge has been prepared for additional flaking and some of the original cortex remains. Clovis biface #202 is slightly smaller, measuring 8.3 inches long, 3.9 inches wide, and 0.8 inches thick. It is boat-shaped with large, thinning flake scars, and a natural frost-fractured surface on one side. Clovis biface #205, which measures 7.9 inches long, 5.4 inches wide, and 0.7 inches thick, is teardrop-shaped and most of the edge has been well prepared for further flaking. Clovis biface #204, which measures 7.3 inches long, 4.7 inches wide, and 0.6 inches thick, is irregularly shaped with a huge overshot flake and edge preparation for additional flake removal. Clovis biface #206 is nearly identical in size, measuring 7.3 inches long, 4.3 inches wide, and 0.6 inches thick. It is oval-shaped with small flaking and grinding along the edge for the removal of more flakes and a small cavity on one face caused by the dissolution of impurities in the tool stone.

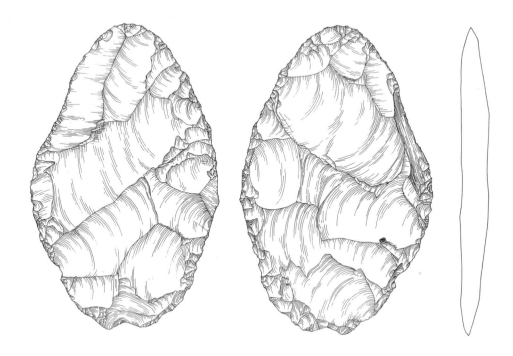

Crook County Cache, specimen 204, early stage Clovis biface.

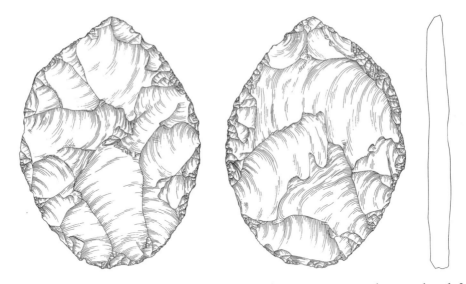

Crook County Cache, specimen 205, early stage Clovis biface.

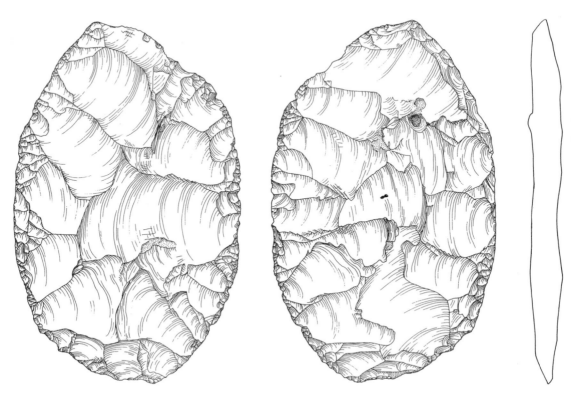

Crook County Cache, specimen 206, early stage Clovis biface.

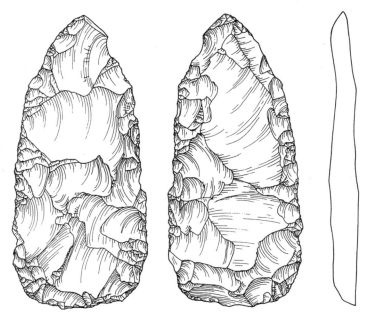

Crook County Cache, specimen 207, incomplete Clovis projectile point.

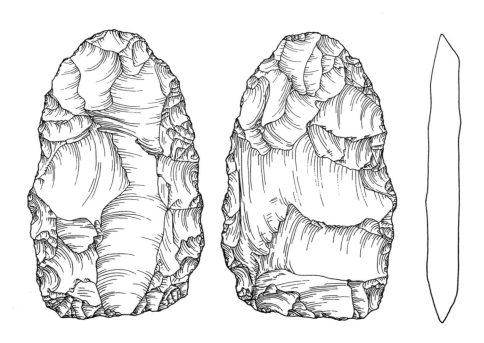

Crook County Cache, specimen 208, incomplete Clovis projectile point.

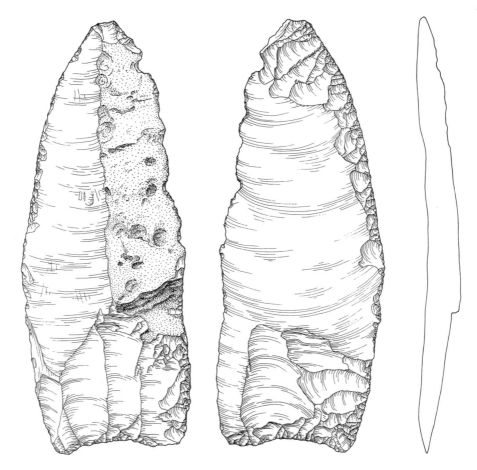

Crook County Cache, specimen 201, Clovis knife.

Two of the smaller specimens, which are incomplete Clovis points that closely resemble specimens in the Fenn Cache, exhibit secondary shaping flakes and reduced edge angles. The base of Clovis point #207, which has been prepared for fluting, measures 4.2 inches long, 1.9 inches wide, and 0.5 inches thick. Clovis point #208, which is fluted on one side and has pronounced platforms that have been set up for the removal of more flakes, measures 4.2 inches long, 2.5 inches wide, and 0.5 inches thick.

Specimen #201 is a large Clovis fluted knife that was made from a long expanding flake struck in the shape of a Clovis point. Aside from the concave base, fluting, and retouching along one edge, the knife retains most of the original surface, including the cortex on one side. In this regard, it is similar to one of the Clovis points from the Anzick site. The specimen is 8.5 inches long, 3.2 inches wide, and 0.7 inches thick, with a broken tip. It is larger than all but four of the Clovis fluted knives from the Richey-Roberts Cache.

The smallest specimen, #209, is a finished, slightly damaged and nearly exhausted Clovis point with irregular edges and lack of heavy grinding on the base, suggesting that it may have been reworked from a formerly larger point. Measuring 1.9 inches long, 0.9 inches wide, and 0.2 inches thick, it was manufactured from an even-colored yellow chert that compares favorably with Mississippian-age Madison Formation cherts exposed in the Hartville Uplift, Black Hills, and Wind River areas of Wyoming. This Clovis point differs from the other bifaces in its sand-blasted appearance.

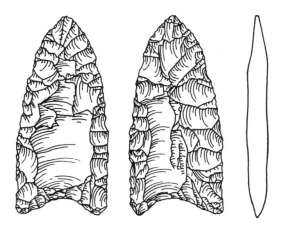

Crook County Cache, specimen 209, heavily resharpened Clovis projectile point.

The eight other Clovis bifaces were manufactured from large flakes of distinctive black-to-brown, silicified lake sediment commonly referred to as Tiger chert. Some of the stone is well banded while other examples are more irregularly patterned with mottling, impurities, and fossils. Interestingly, the fact that the banding can be matched between some of the artifacts suggests that they originated from the same nodules. The primary source of Tiger chert is more than three hundred miles from Crook County in the fifty-eight to thirty-seven million years old, Eocene-age rocks of the Green River Formation of southwestern Wyoming. This tool stone is the same material that was used to manufacture seventeen of the Fenn Cache artifacts.

At first it appeared that there might be two varieties of red ochre on the pieces in the cache, one that is deep red and another of pale rose, almost pink. Under the microscope, however, it became apparent that the lighter-colored material was actually part of the stone. A variety of Tiger chert in the Green River Formation has a natural rusty residue of iron oxide on the cortex or outer rind of the stone, which explains the pinkish powder on both the cortex of the Clovis fluted knife #201 and in the solution cavity of the Clovis biface #206.

True red ochre, which is present in varying degrees on all of the artifacts, deeply penetrates the microcrystalline texture of the stone. On two of the Clovis bifaces, #204 and #206, the red ochre appears as a well-defined diagonal pattern that can be enhanced under long-wavelength ultraviolet light. Under the microscope, linear outlines of red ochre and polish across flake ridges and flake-scar interiors suggest that the bifaces were wrapped with strips of a material such as sinew or rawhide. In that situation, red ochre would form a stain on the surface of the stone that was not covered by the wrappings. In the Fenn Cache, similar diagonal patterns of red ochre appear on several finished Clovis points manufactured from chalcedony.

In nature, red ochre occurs naturally as a crystalline substance. When it is exposed to a concentrated source of X rays or a beam, it bends or diffracts the energy in a pattern that reflects the geometric arrangement of the atoms in the crystal. Because every mineral has its own unique atomic structure, X-ray diffraction patterns provide mineralogical fingerprints for red ochre sources. Sunrise red ochre, for example, contains a distinctive combination of minerals, including hematite (Fe_2O_3), quartz (SiO_2), and a magnesium-rich calcite ($[CaMg]CO_3$).

On Clovis bifaces #204 and #206, there was enough red ochre to obtain samples for X-ray Diffraction Analysis (XRD). While XRD identified both hematite and quartz in the samples, there was no evidence of high-magnesium calcite, but there were suggestions of a clay mineral. With this finding, I decided to reexamine the Crook County Cache under the microscope at high magnification (400x). At the Sunrise Mine, SiO_2 occurs as massive, white, barren quartz, what the old miners and prospectors used to call bull quartz, so I thought that I might be able to see particles of bull quartz on the Clovis bifaces.

Along with the red ochre, I found rounded multicolored grains of silt and sand present in the flake scars of all of the artifacts. Although the silt and sand grains were not bull quartz, they were likely the source of the SiO_2 in the XRD. On the other hand, their presence did give some credence to the story Byrd told of Erickson's discovery. Although I could not confirm the presence of Sunrise red ochre on the artifacts, I began to think that maybe the location was not lost after all. With a little old-fashioned detective work, geology, and a bit of luck, I thought that I might be able to rediscover the Crook County Cache site.

My reasoning was that if the cache site could be relocated, we might be able to determine the source of the red ochre and possibly locate other Clovis sites in the area that were related to the cache. More importantly, we could compare the Crook County Cache site to other Ice Age American sites. By comparing artifacts from one site to the next, or the geology and landscape of one site to another, we might find patterns of similarity or diversity. Looking for such patterns in prehistory, which may be found in the artifacts, the sites, or both, is the primary goal of all archaeologists. Such information helps us understand how the Ice Age Americans successfully adapted to the rapid and profound environmental changes that occurred at the end of the last Ice Age, approximately ten thousand years ago.

Did the Ice Age Americans alter their livelihood as the climate warmed and the environment changed? Or did they try to hold on to their old way of life as long as possible and then change when they were faced with no other choices? These questions should be of more than a little interest to all people because we are living at a time of global climatic and environmental change. Lessons for our own survival may be buried in the past.

The TRAIL to CROOK COUNTY

CHAPTER 7

Arial photograph of the Crook County Clovis Cache site, Wyoming.

In November 1997 when Forrest Fenn brought the Crook County Cache to the fifty-fifth annual Plains Anthropological Conference in Boulder, Colorado, I met with Forrest and a group of distinguished Ice Age American archaeologists—including Stan Ahler, Dan Amick, Bruce Bradley, George Frison, Adrien Hannus, Jack Hofman, Pegi Jodry, Dennis Stanford, and Alice Tratebas—to look at the cache. After examining the artifacts firsthand, there was no question in anyone's mind: the artifacts were magnificent examples of Clovis technology and ingenuity.

Dan Amick, an anthropology professor at Loyola University in Chicago, picked up biface #202, ran the tips of his fingers across a rough area, and said, "This is a natural surface. This biface was made from a naturally spalled, frost-fractured flake." Others agreed. The colorful bull's-eye pattern on the flake may have been what caught the eye of the Clovis knapper.

Bruce Bradley and George Frison were amazed at how closely the large bifaces resembled those in the Fenn Cache. Bradley, a Cambridge-trained archaeologist known around the world for his expertise at flint-knapping, is also the foremost authority on Clovis flaked-stone technology. Frison, a member of the prestigious National Academy of Science, is the leading expert on the prehistoric hunters of the High Plains. He also has excavated some of the most important Ice Age American sites in the Western Hemisphere. Bradley and Frison, who have spent almost a decade studying the technology and stone used in the manufacture of the Fenn Cache, said that the flaking patterns and materials of the Crook County Cache were nearly identical to those in the Fenn Cache.

We reviewed the laboratory findings and the story of how Harold Erickson had discovered the cache. I explained that the artifacts were found in the summer of 1963 during an exploratory oil and gas survey in northern Crook County, Wyoming, but the exact location and geologic nature of the spot had never been documented. Although Erickson passed away without revealing the locality, there were twelve clues that might lead us to the cache site.

- The cache was discovered in the northern part of Crook County, Wyoming.

- The cache site was located in the checkerboard country.

- An oil and gas field underlaid the area.

- A reservoir had been constructed in the vicinity of the find spot during the summer of 1963.

- There was a well near the reservoir.

- The dam of the reservoir was situated on a small spring in the bottom of a broad coulee near its head.

- The cache site was located in a dirt road that was bulldozed the length of the coulee at the time of the dam's construction.

- The cache was discovered directly beneath a low sandstone bluff, six to eight feet high.

- The cache was found about five feet below the surface in a pocket of red earth.

- The exposure of red earth was about four feet wide, at most six inches thick, and thinned to nothing on either end.

- The red earth was compact.

- There was a survey stake near the find spot.

While no one clue provided enough information to be useful, combined there were just enough specific geographical and geological references that might lead us to the cache site. Frison added that a number of important Ice Age American sites had been excavated in the area since the late 1950s—Carter/Kerr-McGee to the west, Mill Iron to the north, Jim Pitts to the east, and Hell Gap and Agate Basin to the south.

Alice Tratebas, an archaeologist for the Bureau of Land Management (BLM) and fellow alumnus of Indiana University, pointed out that there are several different Mesozoic sandstones, 245 to 66 million years old, in Crook County—Cretaceous, 144 to 66 million years old, in the west; and Jurassic, 208 to 144 million years old, in the east. She suggested that if I could compare the sand grains on the artifacts with those from bedrock samples of known locations, I could narrow my search to a quarter of the county rather than a half.

Tratebas also added that if the cache had been discovered on land managed by the BLM, it would be worth investigating the state and federal records for the first half of 1963 in the northern half of Crook County. Permits would have been filed for the construction of the reservoir and the road, and for the oil and gas survey. While it would be unlikely that there was only one road constructed, one dam built, and one survey filed for northern Crook County during the summer of 1963, she said the permits would help limit the search to a number of specific locations. If they could be obtained, they would indeed provide vital information because of the sheer number of potential sites.

When Fenn added that he had a plane and could fly us over the area if we came up with some good prospects, I became considerably more optimistic about the search, even though Crook was an enormous county that took up most of northeastern Wyoming.

Over the next year, I collected a myriad of geographic and geologic data. With the help of my wife Jenny, a geographer, I examined state maps, county maps, road maps, BLM maps, topographic maps, relief maps, bedrock geology maps, structural maps, oil and gas maps, hydrogeology maps, soil maps, aerial photographs, and even satellite images. The enormous amount of information available on the area was not surprising since northeastern Wyoming includes the Black Hills and the Powder River Basin. Economically, the area is rich in coal, and the oil and gas deposits are legendary. It also has been extensively mapped and photographed because of its active geological past. Volcanic features are both so abundant and spectacular in the area that people come from all over the world to see the unique Devils Tower National Monument.

The more data I collected, the more daunting the task seemed. According to the BLM maps, almost the entire northern part of Crook County, Wyoming, could be classified as checkerboard country. Furthermore, there were thousands of broad coulees, and most of them had dammed reservoirs situated on small springs. To make matters worse, almost every reservoir appeared to be associated near a well. However, it was not hopeless.

The bedrock geology allowed me to eliminate significant portions of the county as potential site locations. Ruling out areas with green, gray, black shales, claystones, and intrusive igneous rocks—a considerable part of northern Crook County—I focused my search on areas with sandstone outcrops, coulees, and reservoirs.

Then, in the spring of 1999, Tratebas provided me with a crucial clue—all of the oil and gas survey permits and related construction for the first half of 1963 were filed for the western side of the county. Petroleum exploration was concentrated on the eastern end of the historic Powder River Basin oil and gas fields. This information restricted the investigation to a nine-by-four-mile rectangular area. Geologically, the bedrock of this area is composed of Cretaceous shale in the east and sandstone in the west. Since the cache had been found near a sandstone outcrop, we would only have to survey a seven-by-six-by-three-mile triangular tract of land located in the extreme northwestern portion of Crook County.

Tratebas's clue was vital because it allowed me to restrict the search to a single seven-and-a-half-minute USGS topographic map, which revealed there were only three places with dirt roads near sandstone exposures in the vicinity of wells. Of these, only one led downhill from a bench top to a small reservoir at the base of a broad coulee. Now I had enough data to conduct a surface survey of the area.

I invited C. Vance Haynes, Jack Holland, and Forrest Fenn to join me in the survey. During the past century, no archaeologist has done more to further our knowledge of Clovis than Vance Haynes. In fact, he has received numerous awards, including membership in the National Academy of Science and Geoarchaeologist of the Twentieth Century, for demanding nothing less than the highest standards in Ice Age American research. Vance is also known for his extraordinary ability to use geology to provide a better understanding of the archaeology of Clovis sites.

Holland, who established the Holland Lithics Laboratory at the Buffalo Museum of Science, which contains the largest comparative collection of tool stone and raw materials used by the Ice Age Americans, was anxious to obtain additional specimens for his laboratory. Although he had been in the field with me many times in Wyoming, this would be his first trip to the northeastern corner.

Fenn is no stranger to Clovis archaeology. Over the past forty years, he has worked with Emil Haury, Frank H. H. Roberts, Joe Ben Wheat, Cynthia Irwin Williams, and Marie Wormington, the pioneers of Ice Age American research. Fenn, a longtime supporter of scientific archaeology, is also an accomplished pilot, having served with the United States Air Force during the Korean and Vietnam Wars. He enthusiastically agreed to fly us into northeastern Wyoming.

We decided to conduct the survey at the end of June when the prairie would be green and dry and the days long and blue. Holland and I would fly into Albuquerque, New Mexico, and drive up to Santa Fe to meet Fenn. From there, the three of us would fly to Guernsey, Wyoming, to pick up Haynes, who would be finishing his fieldwork at the Hell Gap site.

On June 24, 1999, I boarded a 727 and flew to Albuquerque. Passing over the High Plains of southern Colorado and northern New Mexico, I looked out the window at the expansive landscape below. It was filled with coulees, reservoirs, dirt roads, and sandstone outcrops that all looked alike; any one of them would fit the description of the cache site. Were we going to find the same situation in Crook County? Feeling a bit panicky, I returned to my notes and maps, checking them over and over again, while asking myself, "Could I really find this place?"

Although I was quite confident of our abilities in the field, I also knew that northeastern Wyoming was as vast as the great prairie beneath my feet, a reality that induced an intimidating feeling. Then I started thinking about the words of the late Louis Leakey, who recalled them many times in his pursuit of early archaeological sites: "I know they are there. Now I just have to find them." And remarkably, with the help of his wife, Mary, he always succeeded. Well, almost always.

Descending over the Sandia Mountains reminded me that, for comparative purposes, Holland and I needed to collect geological samples of yellow ochre from Sandia Cave. Sometime before the end of the last Ice Age, people climbed the mountain and entered the cave to mine yellow ochre from its depths. Although yellow ochre has never been found on a Clovis site, it could easily have been transformed into red ochre in a campfire. With that thought, I landed at the Albuquerque airport with its adobe buildings that beautifully contrast with the ever-present turquoise-colored sky of New Mexico, a true "Land of Enchantment."

Holland was waiting for me inside, standing among displays of contemporary and traditional southwestern art and Lincoln Fox's bronze sculpture, *The Dream of Flight.* We wasted no time picking up a car, loading up our gear, and driving to Santa Fe.

We pulled into Santa Fe and the circular driveway of Forrest Fenn's house. Within minutes, we were sitting in the kitchen examining maps of Crook County, Wyoming, over a glass of iced well water and discussing our itinerary for the next day. Forrest had made arrangements to have Haynes meet us at the Guernsey airport in Wyoming the following morning, so Holland, Fenn, and I agreed to rendezvous at sunup.

We met Fenn the next day at the crack of dawn. We drove straight to the Santa Fe airport where Fenn's pressurized Piper Malibu Mirage was gassed and ready to go. As quickly as possible, Holland and I loaded up the field packs, while Fenn checked out the plane in preparation for departure. The tower cleared us for take off, and before I knew it, we were gently rising above Pecos and on our way over the Turkey Mountains.

Flying between the Spanish Peaks, Fenn asked me, "How does it feel to put your career on the line like this?" Somehow, Fenn knew exactly what I had been pondering the past couple of days. We were investing a great deal of time and money in a project based on my professional opinion. It was an ominous feeling.

I nervously replied, "What do you mean?"

Fenn smiled and said, "If you can't find this site, you are going to lose all credibility!" I knew he was teasing, but Fenn reminded me of the haunting words of an old Cherokee friend, "Ken, a man is only as good as his word." Fenn was essentially telling me the same thing.

We flew high above numerous Ice Age American sites in Colorado including Lamb Springs, Dent, Lindenmeier, and Drake. At seventeen thousand feet above Denver you can see all the way to Wyoming. It was a very clear day and I could see the tall smokestacks of Wheatland in the distance. Although I could not yet make it out, I knew that Guernsey was directly behind it.

North of Cheyenne, Wyoming, Fenn began a slow but steady descent towards Guernsey. I spent a lot of time looking out of my right-side window. After passing over Chugwater, I could see the sunny reflection of our plane racing across the prairie like an illuminated ghost passing through the sagebrush. Prairie dogs jumped into their holes as the mirage rushed toward them.

The Guernsey airport is not much more than a few well-maintained strips of asphalt. Our final approach took us over the North Platte River and the remains of the Oregon Trail—two deeply rutted grooves in the Arikaree sandstone created by the relentless procession of wagon wheels rolling west from Fort Laramie toward Fort Phil Kearney. Nearby, I could see Register Cliff, a rock face where thousands of pilgrims and pioneers carved their names in the sandstone. Fenn was landing the plane by the time I turned my head forward. We moved to the hangar and slowly came to a stop in front of the office. As Fenn turned off the engine, removed his communications gear, and opened the cabin door, I was shocked to hear him say, "Well, that's another one we walked away from!" Fenn is, in fact, a natural pilot, one of those few gifted people who were born to fly, and fly high.

Haynes pulled up in his blue four-wheel-drive truck and got out with a pack and camera in hand, ready to go. This time Jack climbed into the copilot's seat and I sat in the back with Vance. Forrest finished his preflight check, started the engine, and away we went. We quickly rose above the town of Guernsey and some of the most famous Ice Age American sites in the west—Hell Gap, the Sunrise Mine, the Spanish Diggings quarries, and Agate Basin. After a smooth flight over hundreds of teepee rings and thousands of prairie dog towns, we landed in Gillette on the same narrow piece of ground where the first airplane took off in Wyoming, eighty-eight years earlier.

Fenn made arrangements to have a four-wheel-drive truck waiting for us at the gate. We grabbed a quick lunch in the airport, transferred our gear to the truck, and hit the road north. Jack and Vance sat in the back, I navigated, and Forrest drove. It was two-lane blacktop until we reached the turnoff to Thunder Basin National Grassland. Although it is more than a forty-mile drive on a dusty winding road, the grassland is quite beautiful. Thunder Basin is the quintessential short-grass prairie of the High Plains, which, in late June, looks like a great endless sea of Little Bluestem waving in the wind. Western meadowlarks flying in front of our truck reminded me of dolphins swimming at the bow of a ship.

Haynes leaned forward and said, "Ken, do you have a copy of Byrd's article with you?" I pulled a manila folder out of my pack and handed Haynes a copy of the essay. After reading it, Haynes asked, "Can I take a look at your map?"

I felt uneasy as I passed back a folded copy of the USGS seven-and-a-half-minute topographic map. Would Haynes draw the same geographic conclusions that I had? He spent about twenty-five minutes carefully examining the map, then leaned forward and asked, "Ken, where do you think the cache was found?"

"I have three possible locations. The middle one, along the dirt road that runs past well #4104, is my best guess."

"That would be my best guess, too," Haynes said.

I felt a sudden surge of confidence, a sensation that soon faded as we drove onto the land covered by the map. Looking at a topographic map of the High Plains is one thing; matching it to the actual landscape is another, especially when the map is almost thirty years old! Towns that were thriving in the early '70s were now abandoned buildings and foundations. Cemeteries were all that remained. To make matters worse, most of the roads leading off our dusty thruway were nothing more than tire tracks fading onto the lonesome prairie.

"Forrest, stop the truck at the next bend in the road," I requested.

"Why?" he inquired.

"We're here," I replied.

"Here where?" I understood Fenn's response because it looked as if we were in the middle of nowhere, sitting on the edge of a flat featureless landscape.

"Let's go back a few miles. I want to begin counting the bends in the road. This stretch has twenty doglegs in it, one right after another. If we go back to the first bend, I can match them with the ones on the map, assuming, of course, that the road has not changed in the past thirty years."

Forrest complied with a big smile, turning the truck around after the last curve. The area that I wanted to explore was in the northwest corner of the county, half-way between the twelfth and thirteenth bends, counting south to north. We drove slowly as I tallied the bends and followed our location on the map with the tip of my index finger.

After the twelfth bend, I said, "Take the next road on the left." Although it was smaller, the road was well traveled.

After a mile or so the road ended in a cul-de-sac of barns, corrals, and a ranch house with a grassy front yard. The map made the location look like Grand Central Station with roads branching out in six different directions. A bit confused, Holland and I got out of the truck, walked up to the ranch house, and knocked on the door. Given the remote location, we expected to be greeted by a double-barreled shotgun and a vicious attack dog with teeth exposed to the gum line. Instead, we met a cheerful Wyoming ranch woman armed with a glass of fresh cool lemonade and a puppy vigorously wagging his tail. It is true what they say about Wyoming ranchers: they are simply the nicest people in the world.

I introduced everyone and explained that we came to Wyoming from New York, Ohio, New Mexico, and Arizona in search of an ancient archaeological site that had been discovered somewhere in the vicinity in 1963, but its location had long since been lost. I showed her the map of where I thought we were and said that we were looking for a dirt road that ran past a well near a pond. She confirmed our location and told us that there were two wells: one was a dry hole on the other side of the butte, and the other was a water well.

"You're welcome to look around all you want. Just go on up and over the hill about a mile or so. The dry hole is on the west side of the butte, and the water well and ponds are just a little bit farther to the north. You can't miss them. You'll see the pump house and the pond next to it. It's all part of our ranch, so no one will bother you. We have cattle in those fields, so just make sure that you close all of the gates behind you."

"Where exactly is the road?" Fenn asked.

"It's over there on the other side of the fence. You can't see it too well because it was made so long ago; the grass has just about covered it up."

After examining her collection of rocks and minerals from the ranch, we resumed our search. We drove around the barn and across two corrals. The prairie grass on the other side of the fence was as high as the tailgate, so it was difficult to tell the road from the cattle trails. We headed north, up and over the hill and along the eastern side of an isolated sandstone butte. The western countryside looked a lot like the Black Hills of South Dakota.

After we continued across a small coulee and up and over another rise, the pump house and pond appeared directly in front of us. A dirt track ascended from the pond to a high grassy bench. Fenn parked the truck nearby, and we all got out to explore the area.

The broad coulee of the Crook County Clovis Cache site.

Not surprisingly, Vance had already spotted a terrace cut and was on his way to look at the exposed sediments. Fenn followed closely behind and Holland began looking for stone. I started slowly walking up the old dirt track with my eyes closely focused on every inch of exposed earth. I have never forgotten the words that David Carradine once spoke in an episode of *Kung Fu*, "The wise man walks with his head bowed to the ground, humble like that of dust." That is pretty much the way it is on an archaeological surface survey. With your head bowed to the ground, good peripheral vision, and some luck, you can examine about six feet of surface at a glance, but you cannot afford to take your eyes off of the ground, not even for a second. I've lost count of the number of times that I've picked up a Clovis point near or under the foot of another archaeologist because he or she was looking elsewhere.

The low sandstone bluff above the bulldozed dirt road
at the Crook County Clovis Cache site.

About a quarter of a mile farther and 120 feet above the truck, I was standing beneath a low buff-colored sandstone bluff. The road that cut about five feet into the hillside exposed a seam of red ochre about six inches thick, a dense deposit that continued across the dirt track from the outcrop. An old survey stake appeared on the other side of the road, and on the ground in front of me was a fragment of fossilized bone. Harold Erickson had reported finding two broken, cylindrical bone artifacts that he described as "tent pegs as big as your finger and a foot long." The fragment looked like mammoth bone and it was the right size to fit Erickson's description—a half-inch wide and less than a half-inch thick.

As Fenn and Haynes approached, Fenn asked, "Find anything?"

As I showed him the piece of heavily mineralized bone, much to my surprise, he pulled a bone fragment out of his pocket that he had just found. Haynes looked at the bones and said, "They're bone all right. They could be mammoth, or they could be the remains of a large marine reptile or even a dinosaur. The rocks around here are full of them." He was right; the bone splinters were suggestive, not definitive.

Haynes squatted down in front of the red ochre, pinched it between his index

C. Vance Haynes next to a pocket of compact red earth exposed
in the dirt at the Crook County Clovis Cache site.

finger and thumb, put some in his mouth, and rubbed the rest between his fingers.

"Well, that's mighty fine red ochre. It's occurring here as a thin band of blood-red hematitic mudstone within this light, greenish-gray shale, probably a discontinuous bed within the Fox Hills formation. It extends to the surface with almost no soil development. The overlying sediment here has slumped from above."

"If that's the case, then the cache must have been intentionally buried in the red ochre," Fenn observed.

"It wouldn't be the first time. Clovis artifacts were found buried in the red ochre at the Sunrise Mine," Haynes replied.

This was a novel idea since conventional archaeological wisdom suggests that red ochre was transported and buried in cache pits along with flaked-stone and bone weapons and tools. That scenario is completely understandable because red ochre was a valuable raw material that could be used as an abrasive, a pigment, a preservative, and even as packing material. But why would the Ice Age Americans bury a tool kit in red ochre?

"Ken, I have a Brunton so I can line up the site with Devils Tower. Do you want me to take a compass reading?" Haynes asked.

"You bet!" I replied.

Devils Tower, Crook County, Wyoming.

As I turned to look at Devils Tower on the horizon, I was struck by the view. The cache site overlooks a spectacular southeastern vista that not only includes Devils Tower but also the Missouri Buttes, Inyan Kara, Sundance, and the Bear Lodge Mountains, volcanic bodies that have been sacred features to the hunters of the High Plains since time immemorial. Even today, they make up part of *Cangleska Wakan*, the Sacred Hoop in the Lakota constellations.

The geologic and geographic setting may have been what was culturally significant about the cache site. It may have been associated with a ritual or spiritual element of the Clovis culture, perhaps hunting magic. Traditionally, the Lakota return to the earth part of what they take from it. Did the Ice Age Americans have a similar practice? As archaeologists, we can never prove or disprove such ideas. Although some might debate the point, getting into the minds of the dead is a feat beyond the realm of science.

Although we could not prove why the cache had been buried in red ochre, we felt confident that this was the site. Everything fit—we were in the northern part of Crook County, Wyoming, in the checkerboard country, atop a petroleum field, overlooking a reservoir in the bottom of a broad coulee, standing on a pocket of red earth exposed in a dirt road that was bulldozed beneath a low sandstone bluff, and next to a survey stake. Now, if we could only prove that the road and tank dam were constructed in 1963.

For laboratory comparison, we collected samples of red ochre with the material adhering to the artifacts. Then Forrest, Vance, and I decided to survey up the hill and across the coulee, hoping to find a Clovis campsite while Jack continued his search for stone.

The dirt track led us to a high grassy bench, the original land-survey marker, and scattered groves of yellow pine where the shade was a welcome relief from the hot summer sun. We took a short water break in the pines and admired the panorama that looked like a scene out of the movie *Dances with Wolves*. With a little imagination, we could almost see Oglala, Hunkpapa, and Cheyenne warriors crossing in front of us on their way to their encampments along the Little Big Horn River. Little has changed in the past hundred years or so; the view before us would have looked the same then as it does today. Appropriately, Haynes reminded us that it was the anniversary of the Battle of Greasy Grass.

"On this very day, General George Armstrong Custer and the Seventh Cavalry were defeated in battle, just about 140 miles northwest in Montana. By this time 123 years ago, the bodies of Custer and more than two hundred cavalrymen lay dead in the sun. Looking out at the Plains from up here, it's easy to see why the Indians fought so hard to keep this land."

In addition to being the foremost authority on Clovis, Haynes is also an expert on the Indian Wars. Not only has he followed in the footsteps of General Custer and the Seventh Cavalry, but he has also excavated their battlefields and investigated their weaponry. Haynes is the only person I know who actually owns one of Custer's guns, a model 1866 trapdoor Springfield sporting rifle, and he is a published author on the subject.

Having rested, we decided to follow the ridge, descend the coulee, and meet Holland back at the truck. Just before we reached the edge of the ridge, the ranch owner and his family drove toward us in a pickup truck. They stopped to talk with us.

"Find what you were looking for?"

I recounted the story of how the cache was discovered in 1963, along a freshly bulldozed road that led to a recently constructed dam, but forgotten thereafter.

"Well, that dam down by the pump house is fairly new, but the one behind it was built by my father in the summer of sixty-three."

I was so focused on the reservoir next to the pump house that I didn't even notice the one behind it.

"How about the road, when was it built?" I asked.

" 'Bout the same time as the dam," he replied.

That was it! We had found the Crook County Cache site on the first try.

"Have you ever found any arrowheads or Indian relics around here?" Fenn asked.

"Well, not right here, but up the road a bit, next to the spring. I can take you there if you want. You can hop in the back and I'll drive you back to your truck."

We got in and they drove us across the coulee. Riding in the back of a pickup, off road, and down an eastern Wyoming hillside is an experience that is akin to riding a buffalo bareback. We picked up Jack and our packs and followed the rancher and his family to the spring situated at the head of a deeply cut ravine, about a half mile northeast of the cache site. The gulch, which exposed the interior of an old river terrace dating back to the last Ice Age, had plenty of soil profiles exposed along the walls. While Haynes and Fenn began cleaning some of the exposures, Holland and I looked for artifacts. After we split up to cover more ground and make the most of our time, I found an end scraper and Holland found a few flakes. Unfortunately, the artifacts were not diagnostic of any particular period of time or culture.

We compared our finds and walked back to see how Vance and Forrest were doing. Haynes had identified a number of *paleosols*, ancient buried surfaces that were full of wood charcoal, so he was taking notes and collecting samples for radiocarbon dating. The spring site was clearly stratified and might contain Ice Age American artifacts.

"You know, there could very well be a mammoth kill site here, or there may have been one, and all of the bones and artifacts have long since been washed downstream," Haynes said. "I won't know the age of the paleosols until I get the charcoal dated, but they sure look like the same sequence that we have back at Hell Gap."

Hell Gap, unquestionably one of the most important Ice Age American sites, is beautifully stratified, well dated, and artifact-rich. To discover another site the same age of Hell Gap would be icing on our cake.

The southeastern vista of the Crook County Clovis Cache site.

The spring site was situated on the highest terrace above the Little Missouri River, so we decided to drive cross-country to the end of the terrace and look for other geologic features that dated to the last Ice Age. The terrace ended in a broad flat scarp that we descended, then we looked back at a textbook example of a late Pleistocene terrace on the High Plains. We drove over the lower terrace and followed its edge to the head of the coulee. The rancher was right; there was a second spring-fed reservoir. Standing on the older tank dam, we could see the old bulldozed dirt track descending from the high grassy bench, down into the coulee, under the low sandstone bluff, and leading straight to the reservoir in front of us.

I turned to Holland and said, "You know, it just does not get any better than this!"

The sun was getting low on the horizon, so it was time to head back to Gillette.

THE SUNRISE MINE

CHAPTER 8

Early the next morning, Fenn gassed up the plane and prepared for departure, Holland took the copilot's seat again, and Haynes and I sat in the back. Before heading south to Guernsey, Jack wanted to see Devils Tower and the volcanic features around it, and I wanted to catch a glimpse of the cache site from the air. After a swift, smooth takeoff, we headed straight for the tower, a prominent feature protruding from the Crook County countryside. With the late June heat rising off the sage-covered prairie, the plane rose and fell as we flew over cliffs and canyons along the way.

We approached Devils Tower from the west and circled around the sparsely vegetated pinnacle, about thirteen hundred feet off the ground. As Forrest swung the plane round the neck of the ancient volcano, I could see the Crook County Cache site tucked away to the northwest, concealed in the pine-capped sandstone hills that surround the tower. It was no wonder that the cache remained a hidden treasure for some thirteen thousand years.

We dropped about three hundred feet and banked southward, passing in front of the distinctive, lichen-covered columnar walls of Devils Tower. While I have admired the tower from a distance, stood at its base, and scaled its cliffs, the view from the wing of a plane is by far the best I have ever seen. It must be as close as a human being can come to feeling like an eagle when it soars in the thermals around the monument.

After flying past the western wall of Devils Tower, Fenn asked, "Well, Jack, did you get a good look at the tower?"

Holland was speechless.

"We were so close, I could see the feldspar crystals in the rock," Haynes commented.

"Crystals!" I excitedly replied. "I could see ants on the crystals!"

136

Fenn looked back and smiled at both of us.

"Say, Forrest, would you mind passing over Hell Gap and the Sunrise Mine before we land in Guernsey? I would like to take some photos of the area," Haynes asked.

"No problem," Fenn said.

We headed south between the Bighorn Mountains and the Black Hills, crossing over the Belle Fourche and Cheyenne River basins. Vance loaded his camera as we flew over the headwaters of the Niobrara River, between the Rawhide Buttes and Pine Ridge. From the air, you can see that Hell Gap is a unique spot on the landscape, a mountain gap that leads to a box canyon on the edge of the prairie where the Crescent Basin meets the north end of the Haystack Range.

The countryside around Hell Gap has changed little since the days when Calamity Jane drove the Cheyenne-to-Deadwood stagecoach through the area. Along nearby Cottonwood Draw, you can still see where Lakota warriors sat down to make arrowheads from the broken bases of wine bottles discarded by passengers on her stage. Many of the old cottonwoods along the draw are the same ones that provided

The historic setting of the Sunrise Mine.

much-needed shade to the western travelers as they waited for Calamity Jane to water her team of horses. And the roads, well, they too have changed little since they were last used by the stage.

After making a couple of passes over Hell Gap, we flew over the Haystacks and directly above the Sunrise Mine, five miles north of the Guernsey airport. The mine looked like a Martian landscape: large gaping craters in the brittle, up-thrown metallic crust, surrounded by a red-stained, arid mountain landscape. We were anxious to reexamine the Sunrise Mine because it was the only other place besides the Crook County Cache site where Clovis artifacts had been deliberately buried in red ochre. This discovery was closely tied to the history of the mine itself.

In the late 1880s, shortly after the end of the Indian Wars, soldiers stationed at nearby Fort Laramie began exploring the Lakota treaty land for sources of gold, silver, and copper. They staked out claims on an extremely rich ore deposit a few miles east of the town of Hartville and soon began surface-mining for the precious metals. At the beginning of their excavation, the miners exposed an ancient red ochre mine where they found a narrow fissure descending headlong into a cave-like grotto, a ten-by-fourteen-by-seven-foot room dug into a soft deposit of iron ore and littered with ornaments and other artifacts. The mine was attributed to the Lakota because it was on their treaty land, and a similar location was described in one of their traditional myths:

> "A young man was once hunting and came to a steep hill. The east side of the hill suddenly dropped off to a very steep bank. He stood on this bank, and at the base he noticed a small opening. On going down to examine it more closely, he found it was large enough to admit a horse or buffalo. On either side of the door were figures of different animals engraved into the wall. He entered the opening and there, scattered about the floor, lay bracelets, pipes and many other things of ornament, as though they had been offerings to some great spirit. He passed through this first room and on entering the second, it was so dark that he could not see his hands before his face, so becoming scared, he hurriedly left the place, and returning home told what he had seen."

While Lakota myths are not meant to refer to specific events in time, most of them are based, in part, on real places. If the myth does refer to the ancient mine, then the story suggests that the mine was dug by a group of people other than the Lakota. The discovery of the old mine sparked many cowboy stories and western legends that have been told for more than a century about lost Indian gold and silver mines. Although the Sunrise Mine actually did produce some quantities of gold, silver, and copper, the deposits were shallow and soon depleted.

In 1898, open-pit mining focused on the deeper, more abundant, high-grade iron ore. By the 1930s, the Colorado Fuel and Iron Steel Corporation moved their mining operations underground. With the shift from open pits to subterranean shafts and tunnels, a new railroad system was needed to accommodate the massive movement of iron ore from the mine to the blast furnaces three hundred miles away in Pueblo, Colorado. Construction of the railroad cut right through another ancient red ochre mine.

The Sunrise Mine.

The Ice Age American red ochre mine was discovered by Wayne Powers, a coach at the local high school, while walking along the recently constructed railroad spur. He spotted a flaked-stone artifact exposed on the high iron-stained scarp of the Sunrise Mine, and immediately recognized it as an important discovery. Powers was an enthusiastic collector with a real knack for finding Ice Age American artifacts. He had worked with Frank H. H. Roberts of the Smithsonian Institution at the Lindenmeier site and discovered the now-famous Powers Folsom site in Colorado.

Over the next fifty years, Powers came back to the Sunrise Mine many times, amassing from the eroding margins of the site a diverse collection of artifacts, including finished flaked-stone weaponry, knives, preforms, tools, hammer and anvil stones, bone tools, and bone and shell ornaments. In 1980, he brought part of the collection to the Smithsonian Institution and showed it to George Frison, who was there conducting research on Ice Age American sites in Wyoming. When Frison returned to Wyoming the following year, he looked for the red ochre mine in the cut-banks along the railroad grade between the towns of Hartville and Sunrise. Unable to find any evidence of the mine, he suspected that the site had been completely destroyed.

By happenstance, when Powers was invited to attend a class reunion in southeastern Wyoming during the summer of 1986, he used the homecoming as an opportunity to search for remnants of the red ochre mine. Remarkably, he discovered that fourteen hundred square feet of the mine had survived but was about to be destroyed by a mine reclamation project. Right away, he got on the telephone to the Smithsonian Institution and alerted Dennis Stanford of the situation. Stanford immediately contacted Frison at the University of Wyoming, who, in turn, contacted Mark Miller, the Wyoming State Archaeologist. Frison and Miller drove straight from Laramie to the Sunrise Mine, arriving just in time to stop heavy earthmoving equipment from completely obliterating the remains of the site. In July, they were able to conduct a test excavation and verify that the site was, in fact, an Ice Age American red ochre mine. Powers's relentlessness and Frison's quick thinking resulted in the preservation and protection of the site.

From the Sunrise Mine, we descended into the North Platte River Valley and on into the Guernsey airport. Although it was still early in the morning, the puffy white cumulus clouds were growing gray and the wind was picking up, so we decided to tie the plane down for safekeeping. Afterwards, we transferred our packs to Vance's four-wheel-drive truck and headed north out of town through Hartville Canyon, passing through a complex sequence of terraces that date to the last Ice Age and beyond. The canyon terraces are the same age as sediments exposed at the Sunrise Mine and Hell Gap sites, and are probably the same age as the terraces around the Crook County Cache site.

We followed the canyon to Hartville, the oldest incorporated town in Wyoming. It still has the atmosphere of an early western mining town, and the "Oldest Bar," established in 1864, is, in fact, the oldest bar in Wyoming. The original, solid, cherry-wood back bar is so well preserved that you expect to see old Wild Bill himself walk in and ask for a drink. We stopped in town to ask the property owner for permission to visit the Sunrise Mine and collect samples of red ochre to compare with the Crook County Cache site. After getting the go-ahead, we drove out to the mine and the town of Sunrise.

Behind locked steel gates, the old mining town of Sunrise is undergoing a long careful process of historic restoration. While Haynes and I had been to the town and mine many times before, this was the first time for Holland and Fenn. As Haynes parked his four-wheel-drive truck in front of one of the oldest YMCA buildings in the United States, I could see from the expressions on their faces that they were underwhelmed with the location. Today, most of the inhabitants of Sunrise are brittle tumbleweeds, sagebrush, and rattlesnakes.

We found the mine completely fenced off. After the Colorado Fuel and Iron Corporation shut down its operations, the Wyoming Abandoned Mine Reclamation Program began to eliminate environmental and safety hazards around the mine with the installation of chain-link and barbed-wire fencing. We grabbed our packs and carefully made our way through the barbed wire.

"Ken, why don't you lead the way," Haynes suggested.

"Oh sure, I get to flush out all of the rattlesnakes," I jokingly replied.

"Don't worry, Ken, rattlesnakes usually bite the second person on the trail!" Fenn added, and Holland and Haynes nodded and smiled in agreement.

I have stepped on my share of rattlesnakes, and, thus far, have never been bitten. Still, the word "usually" did not sound very comforting, but we made our way safely through the brush without seeing a single snake.

Haynes examined the scarp face, Holland collected specimens of specular hematite, Fenn looked for artifacts, and I climbed to the top of the terrace to search for manifestations of the ancient mining operations. The contact between the mined surface and the natural sediments is poorly defined, but from the top of the terrace, if the conditions are right, you can see the outline and sunken dimensions of pit features created by Clovis miners. When I realized that I was standing at the same spot where Clovis people dug into a deposit of red ochre during the last Ice Age, the hair rose on the back of my neck.

"Alright, Ken, where's the mine?" Fenn shouted up from the base of the steep talus slope. I could see from the expression on Holland's face that he too was wondering the same thing.

"This entire slope is filled with stone and bone artifacts, but the actual mining features are up here, just below my feet." I pointed to a compact and complex deposit of ancient mine tailings; spoil dirt about six feet thick from the Ice Age American mining process. "It is difficult to see the outline of the pits because everything is dusted with red ochre."

At the Sunrise Mine, everything, absolutely everything, is covered with red ochre dust—the buildings, regardless of whether they are made of wood, brick, stone, or steel; the cars and trucks; the trees, bushes, and grass; even the animals have a pinkish hue to their fur. Archaeologists who spend too much time at the mine end up with permanently ochre-stained clothes and skin. The particulate red ochre dust deeply penetrates the epidermis and will not wash off; it must be shed! This discovery was first made when Frison and his crew conducted test excavations at the site during the summer of 1986. Since then, many of the Guernsey motel owners will ask before you check in, "You're not an archaeologist, are you?" If the answer is "Yes," they quickly give you a wry face and ask, "You're not going up to the Sunrise Mine, are you?"

Forrest Fenn points to a Clovis artifact in the Sunrise Mine red ochre.

Before I knew it, Fenn had not only scaled the slope but found a Clovis artifact manufactured from Hartville chert in the pit feature directly beneath my feet. Holland and Haynes came over to examine the specimen.

"The last time I was here, Stan Ahler found a Clovis point at that very spot," Haynes said.

I photographed the artifact still in place and studied the composition of the surrounding mining feature. There was no question about it, Ice Age Americans were collecting high-grade, earthy red ochre from the site, but the pit features were an archaeological mystery. Given the large quantity of readily available red ochre, Ice Age Americans did not have to mine this material. They could have easily collected more than enough red ochre from the surface.

Why did the Ice Age Americans invest a great deal of time and energy digging into the red earth? Did the process of digging red ochre from the deeper deposits have some symbolic, ceremonial, or ritualistic significance? Were the deeper deposits of red ochre more concentrated or more pure than those exposed on the surface? Or, were the Ice Age Americans interested in another form of iron?

The composition of what I found in the pit feature, as well as what was missing, provided clues to what the Ice Age Americans were mining. The pit feature was filled to the surface with earthy red ochre, and the presence of hammer and anvil stones at the site suggested that they were extracting something besides the red-colored dust.

From a strictly geological standpoint, red ochre is an impure variety of the mineral hematite, chemically known as ferric oxide (Fe_2O_3). The word hematite is derived from the Greek heimatites, which means "blood-like," an allusion to the vivid blood-red color produced when the mineral is powdered. It can occur in sedimentary rocks, concentrated and enriched by meteoric water, as is the case in the Crook County Cache site, or, like the Sunrise Mine, in metamorphic deposits from hot mineral-rich water originating from the earth's hot molten magma.

Hematite ranges in color from the specular steel blue and blood red of the Sunrise Mine to the brick red and dull earthy pink of the Crook County Cache site. Variation in the color results from chemical impurities. While almost all red ochres are composed of 69.9 percent iron and 29.9 percent oxygen, the remaining 0.2 percent may include trace amounts of such other elements as silicon, calcium, magnesium, and aluminum. At the Sunrise Mine, impurities of silicon occur in the form of bull quartz, and calcium and magnesium in the form of calcite.

The deep penetrating power of the earthy red ochre from the Sunrise Mine results from two microorganisms that feed on iron. One is a variety of fungus and the other is a very primitive rod-shaped bacterium that lives in irregular colonies on the surface of the hematite. As they feed, they reduce the solid, steely metallic iron ore into a more-weathered particulate state, a process known as microbial leeching. The resulting oxidized red-iron particle waste is almost atomic in size and much smaller than the average skin pore. The red ochre at the Crook County Cache site lacks these distinctive iron-eating microbes.

At the Sunrise Mine, high-quality specular hematite occurs beneath the surface, and it does indeed require mining. From the makeup of the discarded specular hematite fragments, it appears that bright, shiny metallic pieces free of inclusions, such as quartz and calcite, were the most desirable mining products. Nodules of specular hematite from the Sunrise Mine produce a high-quality, deep red pigment when powdered. Grinding this material on a hard stone in the presence of water produces the illusion that the rock is bleeding. The gleaming, steely, specular hematite transforms irrevocably to red ochre. It is quite possible that this phenomenon was an important quality to the Ice Age Americans. Perhaps it served as an allegory for the natural or spiritual transfigurations between birth, life, and death.

Kevin Tankersley standing in the excavations at the Hell Gap site, Wyoming.

Further evidence that Ice Age Americans were interested in both the earthy red and specular varieties of hematite comes from the Hell Gap site, located five miles north of the Sunrise Mine. Artifacts from the Hell Gap site are nearly identical to those found at Sunrise, suggesting a long-term relationship between the two sites. At Hell Gap, artifacts occur in layers, one stacked on top of the other in a pancake-like sequence. The deepest and oldest layer is about thirteen thousand years old and contains both artifacts of rounded nodules of specular hematite and red ochre powder.

Another archaeological enigma is that some of the bones and stone tools at Hell Gap appear to have been painted with the red pigment. Sites like Hell Gap, the Sunrise Mine, and the Crook County Cache are very important to archaeologists because they provide insights into the spiritual lives of Ice Age Americans that are beyond the more mundane aspects of everyday hunting and tool-kit manufacture.

Looking around at the arid mountainous setting of the Sunrise Mine and recalling the distant Black Hills environment of the Crook County Cache site made me realize that the Ice Age Americans were truly skilled prospectors. It also suggested to me that it was unlikely that the Crook County Cache site and the Sunrise Mine were the only two locations where they obtained red ochre. Then again, they were not just mining red ochre. Like the Crook County Cache site, Ice Age Americans cached entire tool kits in the natural deposits of red earth at the Sunrise Mine. While it is possible that some of the flaked-stone and animal bones, such as bison ribs, were actually used as mining tools, most of the weapons still have sharp cutting edges and pinpointed tips. Instead of digging implements, these artifacts—some of which were manufactured from exotic stones like Knife River flint from North Dakota—were intentionally buried in the red ochre.

Like the Crook County Cache site, we will never know for certain why artifacts were buried at the Sunrise Mine. Around the world and throughout time, red ochre has been used as an important source of red pigment. It has also played a significant symbolic role in the ceremonies and rituals of hunter-gatherers, usually associated with the power of reproduction and the proliferation of life, healing, and death. Consequently, the buried nature of artifacts at the Sunrise Mine and the Crook County Cache sites almost certainly had ritualistic significance.

Were the weapons buried in red ochre used successfully to kill or butcher a mammoth, camel, horse, bison, or tapir? Or, were they left behind as an offering to Mother Earth?

Today, when traditional Lakota obtain red ochre from the Sunrise Mine, they leave behind a *wowicakupi,* an offering on the spoil pile. Traditional Lakota use red ochre from the Sunrise Mine to paint things red, or *wasaya,* in their religious ceremonies of the seven sacred rites. To the Lakota, the color red symbolizes the red road, the good way, the straight way that runs north and south. North represents purity and south represents the source of life. The color red is also used as a symbol of the place where Morning Star lives, the place where the sun continues to shine, and gives men wisdom. According to the Oglala *wakan wicasa, Heha'ka Sapa,* or Black Elk, the color red is associated with the gift of the sacred pipe.

> *"It is the Earth, your Grandmother and Mother, and it is where you will live and increase. This Earth which He has given you is red, and the two-leggeds who live upon the Earth are red; and the Great Spirit has also given you a red day, and a red road."*

While it is not known if Clovis people had a similar symbolic system associated with the color red, the buried artifacts at the Sunrise Mine and the Crook County Cache site do suggest that there was some kind of ideological element to both the sites and the ochre itself. The iron-stained bones of two children at the Anzick site in Montana also suggest a ceremonial aspect of Clovis red ochre use.

Red ochre has been found on the floor of Ice Age American campsites, on the surface of grinding stones, on the bones of megamammals, and on the tools and weapons used to kill and process those animals, suggesting that it also had utilitarian and domestic purposes. Red ochre has been found in similar contexts on archaeological sites in Africa, Europe, and Asia, spanning five hundred thousand years of time. The closest similarities, however, come from Russian Upper Paleolithic sites dating to the last Ice Age. For some archaeologists, those similarities suggest a cultural and, perhaps, genetic relationship between the two areas.

Having collected sufficient samples of both the earthy and specular varieties of hematite from the mine, we carefully made our way back to the road. This time we stayed in the more open ground, passing by rusty tire-less vehicles of yesteryear, including the hollow shell of a 1930s Bugatti. The ground was littered with flaked-stone artifacts that have washed from the slope of the mine since the day it was first exposed by railroad construction activities.

By the time we got back to the car, thunderstorms were building up over the mountains, tumbleweeds were racing down the center of Main Street, and Haynes' four-wheel-drive truck had a fine pink film over the navy blue paint. We decided to head over to the Oldest Bar for homemade sandwiches and cool drinks, and try to figure out what it all meant.

While we were amazed at the fact that Clovis artifacts buried in the red ochre deposits at the Sunrise Mine and the Crook County Cache site were manufactured from stones that were transported more than three hundred miles, their exotic natures are not isolated incidents. Clovis artifacts manufactured from Knife River flint were discovered at the Bostrom site in St. Clair County, Illinois, and in adjacent St. Louis County, Missouri, more than nine hundred miles from the source area in North Dakota. Clovis points manufactured from Gunflint jasper were collected from the Kilmer site in Steuben County, New York, and the Trojan site in Bradford County, Pennsylvania, some nine hundred miles from the source area in western

Jack Holland sits next to a high-quality stone source in the
Rocky Mountains used by Ice Age Americans.

Ontario. Clovis points manufactured from Hixton silicified sandstone were found at the Sandy Springs site in Adams County, Ohio, and near the historic entrance of Mammoth Cave, Kentucky, more than five hundred miles from the source in southwestern Wisconsin.

Fenn pointed out that these distances are truly remarkable when we consider that Clovis people transported stone over great distances without the aid of horses or the technology of the wheel.

Holland suggested that the long-distance transport of stone tools and weapons might be related to the initial movement of Clovis people across the landscape. If we assume they entered the Americas from the north and west, then the long distance movement of stone may be related to a west-to-east and north-to-south migration.

I find it significant that the movement of stone by Clovis people is unlike that found in the Ice Age archaeological record of anywhere else in the world, and it is unlike that of any of the hunter-gatherers documented by anthropologists during the nineteenth and twentieth centuries. University of Wyoming archaeologist Robert Kelly has shown that historic hunter-gatherers were economically tied to specific geographic regions. Clovis people, on the other hand, were more likely tied to the behavior of the animals they hunted.

In order to survive and adapt to the rapidly changing environmental conditions of the last Ice Age, Clovis peoples moved seasonally within loosely defined territories, scheduling their movements according to the availability of food, water, and the rocks and minerals they needed to manufacture tools and weaponry. High-quality stone would have been an invaluable asset to the survival of Clovis hunters because it is easy to sharpen, reshape, and recycle. Sources of high-quality stone likely formed the center of Clovis territories, and the return to a stone source was likely planned and scheduled into their seasonal movements on the landscape. By plotting the distribution of Clovis artifacts manufactured from specific stone sources, we can reconstruct the size and shape of Clovis territories and, in some cases, even determine the season when they were used.

Much of what we know about the seasonality of Clovis hunting and gathering cycles is based on the identification of animal remains from archaeological sites. Mammoth and mastodon tusks in cross-section provide a direct link to the seasons of the Ice Age and can be read like rings in a tree. The outermost rings in a tusk provide the season of death. Mammoth and mastodon tusks from Clovis sites suggest that they were hunted, killed, and sometimes scavenged during the fall and winter, the colder months of the year. Fall and winter hunting is also indicated by the discovery of a frozen mammoth-meat cache at the Colby near the Bighorn Mountains in Wyoming.

The seasonality of Clovis stone collecting can be obtained by looking at the geographic location and geologic setting of the stone sources. Clovis knappers collected high-quality stone from high elevations in localities such as the Bighorn Mountains and from the high northern latitudes of places like North Dakota. Over the past century, the ground in these areas is frequently frozen and snow-covered between November and April, and during the last Ice Age these monthly extremes were even more exaggerated.

Because of the seasonal limitations of high elevations and latitudes, Clovis knappers collected stone from these areas between the late spring and autumn while gearing up for mammoth and mastodon hunting during the colder months of the year. This is not to say that they did not work on their stone tools and weapons during the colder winter months; knapping activities likely took place throughout the year. The great diversity of the stone used by Clovis knappers suggests that they were versatile hunter-gatherers capable of adapting to variations in the availability of food and raw-material resources.

THIEVES OF TIME

Amateur archaeologists, collectors, and everyday citizens, such as Wayne Powers, have discovered the vast majority of Clovis artifacts. Their collections are an invaluable source of information about Ice Age American cultures. Ever since it was recognized that fluted points are among the oldest, most distinctive artifacts in the Americas, archaeologists have labored to inventory and document them.

Today, most states have some form of an ongoing fluted-point survey, and many of these inventories are incorporated into larger registries for the United States, North America, and the Western Hemisphere. Once encoded, these records are used to examine relationships between patterns of artifact distributions, bedrock geology, river systems, and other environmental information to reveal clues about human adaptation, migration, and land use during the last Ice Age. But what if the artifacts included in the survey are fakes and their reported locations fraudulent?

While most archaeologists actually examine artifacts firsthand and conduct face-to-face interviews with curators of public and private collections, this is not always the case. Many of the inventories of fluted points have been made by telephone interviews or questionnaires. As with any survey, the results assume that everyone was honest in their responses. University of Arizona anthropologist William Rathje has shown that it is fairly common for people to lie during a survey. Rather than answering truthfully, Rathje found that people tend to respond the way they think they should reply, or what they perceive to be the social norm. Unfortunately, some people lie during a survey with the deliberate intention to deceive for profit.

Imagine that you are conducting a fluted-point survey and you ask the curator of a collection a series of questions: Who found the artifacts? Where were they found? When were they found? Now imagine that this information is combined with measurements of the artifacts, photographs, drawings, then used in a master's thesis or doctorate dissertation, or published in a scientific journal. Now imagine that all of the points are fakes and their locations are phony. Such a scenario would not only weaken our interpretations about the past, it would also damage an essential relationship between artifact collectors and professional archaeologists.

Forgeries and bogus sites exist because the vast majority of archaeology students and professionals lack the skills needed to distinguish the authentic from the fraudulent. They presume that all of the artifacts and site records curated in public and private collections, museums, universities, and colleges are genuine. Unfortunately, this is not a safe assumption.

In order to establish a pedigree for a point or an entire collection, it is important to have the artifacts included in a scientific study. Pristine fluted points with verifiable pedigrees are worth tens of thousands of dollars. The more surveys that an artifact is included in, the longer the lineage of documentation. In some cases, entire sites have been faked and falsely reported. The people that perpetrate these frauds are thieves of time because they rob us of the truth about the past.

In the summer of 1996, I met a cantankerous old anthropology professor. I found the short ashen-faced man eager to show me what he considered a "significant and substantial" collection of fluted points from one of the "most important" sites. The old professor went on to tell me that he was going to sell the entire collection to a museum of natural history for a mere "$40,000." As a research associate for that particular museum, I knew that they had a "no-buy" policy, but I really wanted to see the collection and, if possible, the site too.

Early on a hot and humid Saturday morning in August, the old professor picked me up at my home and drove me to what had once been a productive steel mill town. It was filled with abandoned, graffiti-covered factories, empty warehouses with broken and boarded-up windows, and entire neighborhoods in disrepair. We pulled into the cracked concrete driveway of an old yolk-yellow house sitting on top of a small hill beneath the shade of mature hardwood trees.

The friendly smiling face of a man, one who given the right costume would have made the perfect Santa Claus, greeted us. With his fluffy white beard, long wiry hair, red nose, and rosy cheeks, it was difficult to tell that he had recently suffered a stroke. According to the old professor, they had collaborated on numerous archaeological surveys and excavations. We sat down in lawn chairs in his backyard and exchanged pleasantries.

"Can I get you anything?" the bearded man politely asked.

"I would really like to see the artifacts and any field notes or maps that you have from the site."

"Do you have any whiskey?" the old professor asked.

The bearded man went into the house and returned with several rolls of field maps, a stack of line drawings, and a dusty unopened bottle of Canadian whiskey. As I looked at the detailed documents with amazement, the old professor began to drink whiskey, one glass after the other.

Much to my amazement, the artifact illustrations were superb and among the best I had ever seen. They were carefully drawn with black ink on white paper, skillfully shaded, and well labeled. They were cross-referenced on exquisitely drafted maps of the site, which had been squared off into a systematic grid. The exact location of every fluted point, scraper, and flake tool was precisely recorded. I was genuinely impressed. It was indeed one of the best-documented collections that I had seen in a long time.

"This is truly a remarkable site! Is there any possibility of conducting an excavation to obtain radiocarbon samples?" I asked.

"Most of the site has been destroyed, but you can see the layers of the glacial deposits along the stream. There are even places where you can see old logs protruding from the bank," the bearded man said.

Stratigraphy, materials suitable for radiocarbon dating, and a large collection of perfectly plotted artifacts, what more could I ask for?

My enthusiasm had become almost unbearable. I really wanted to see the collection. However, it was becoming clear that we were not going to see the artifacts anytime soon.

The old professor continued to pour glass after glass of whiskey and reminisce about his archaeological exploits from way back. The crusty conversations ranged from swapping silver artifacts for whiskey to making movies of a drunken field-school student who later became an anthropology celebrity. After an hour and a half of field yarn and two-thirds of a bottle of whiskey, the old professor and bearded man agreed to show me the artifact collection.

From a side door along the drive, we stepped down a steep stairway and entered a dank, dimly lit basement that smelled of mildew, musty books, and wet cardboard. There was a large room filled with tables covered with large sheets of rotting cardboard and beneath them was the collection. The artifacts seemed to be arranged in patterns that corresponded to the excavation grid plotted on the well-drawn maps. In the beginning, I was like a kid in a candy shop!

The first three artifacts I examined were typical of fluted points that you would expect to find in the area—variable in size and color, mostly broken or resharpened, and made of non-local cherts. The fourth specimen, however, was quite different; it was a biface manufactured from a poor-quality, local glacial chert with flaking patterns that were distinctive of later Archaic weaponry and tools. I took the wide-angle hand-lens that was hanging around my neck and began to examine the flutes. Much to my surprise, the poorly produced flutes had been flaked with a metal tool that was softer than the stone—the metallic marks were still present on the striking platforms.

The next artifact I examined was another Archaic biface, except that the flutes had been ground on with an electric sharpening stone. The flutes were not only in the shape of the sharpening stone, but they retained the parallel gray striations of a carbocorrundum compound. I began to realize that there was something seriously wrong—an economically depressed town, heavy drinking, talk of making $40,000, and now forgeries and most likely a spurious site.

While I could rationalize that two of the artifacts, an Upper Paleolithic-like Venus figurine and an engraved ground slate gorget with figures of bow-wielding hunters shooting arrows at a mammoth, were part of some kind of prank, the rest of the collection was plotted, mapped, and illustrated with pen and ink and presented as having been precisely excavated.

The bearded man saw the growing concern on my face and exchanged whispers with the old professor, who was leaning against a wall on the other side of the basement with the bottle of whiskey in one hand and a glass in the other.

I walked up and down the aisles between the tables, looking at the artifact collection from all angles. I did manage to find a handful or so of real fluted points and end scrapers on the tables, but most of the artifacts were much later in age, and someone had tried to alter them to look old. Although the black-ink illustrations depicted real artifacts, the actual specimens were not even good fakes. My nose caught the smell of alcohol, and I knew that the old professor and his friend were approaching from behind.

"Well, what do you think of the site?" the bearded man asked as I turned around to face them.

I picked up one of the most blatant fakes from the table, held it in front of them, and asked, "Where was this one found?"

"Along with the others," the bearded man said. "It's all plotted there on the maps."

"This flaking pattern is Archaic, and the flutes look like they were made with a metal tool," I replied with a wry face.

The atmosphere in the basement became tense. The bearded man had a grave look of disappointment, and the old professor was visibly agitated. He turned to the bearded man and said, "I think that $40,000 is a fair price for the entire collection, and the museum will be glad to have it for that."

"It is my understanding that the museum does not purchase artifacts," I commented.

The old professor's face had become pallid. He turned to me, bent his head down, and said in a low and stern voice, "Shut up before you blow this deal!"

I was shaken to the core. It was apparent that the old professor was trying to broker the sale of a collection of forgeries and falsified site records, and I had been brought along because of my affiliation with the museum. This experience made me acutely aware that there were, indeed, modern hoaxes in Ice Age American archaeology, and they were more common than I previously suspected.

I, like many others, was taught that the stone tools and weapons of the Ice Age were manufactured by a technique called "flint knapping" that had been, until recently, "a lost art." Then, in the middle of the twentieth century, professional and amateur archaeologists such as Francois Bordes in Europe, Louis Leakey in Africa, and Don Crabtree in the Americas rediscovered the technology through years of systematic experimentation. This urban myth led to an assumption made by me and most professional and amateur archaeologists that flaked-stone forgeries were not produced until the later part of the twentieth century when there were tens of thousands of modern flint knappers.

Actually, flint knapping was never a lost art. Even today, Kim-Yal, the native people of Irian Jaya in the mountainous region of western New Guinea, still make flaked-stone tools, just as they have for thousands of generations. The Kim-Yal quarry basalt from a riverbed located almost a mile and a half below their village. They use hammer-stones to rough out teardrop-shaped bifacial preforms, wrap them in leaves, and place them in woven bags. The preforms are then carried back up the mountainside where the final thinning and shaping flakes are removed at a workshop site in their village.

The production of flaked-stone forgeries actually began during the nineteenth century when Lower Paleolithic hand axes were discovered along the Thames River. The people of Victorian England quickly became infatuated with their Ice Age past and everyone wanted to have a piece of it. The market for fakes emerged when the demand for authentic Ice Age artifacts exceeded the supply. One of the earliest forgers was Edward Simpson, known to many as "Flint Jack." Like modern forgers, he used a rock tumbler and chemical stain to create a false patina on the fakes that he produced with nothing more than flint nodule and steel hammer. Even some of the most reputable museums and private collections in the world contain Flint Jack's forgeries.

Today, the people who make Clovis-point forgeries are premeditated in their actions, stalking their targets like drug dealers preying on the vulnerable. In the fall of 1998, I received a phone call from Forrest Fenn about the possible discovery of another Clovis cache near Greeley, Colorado. An artifact dealer told him that twelve Clovis points had been found, carefully wrapped in the pages of a 1946 *Life* magazine, in the attic of a recently deceased cowboy. In other words, the artifacts were older than the era of modern flint knapping. The dealer knew that Fenn had two Clovis caches in his collection and that he might be interested in acquiring a third.

Fenn told me that he did, indeed, want to acquire the cache for his collection, but he first wanted to make sure that the artifacts were authentic. Aside from having the largest collection of Ice Age American artifacts in the world, Fenn is internationally known in the art community and well aware of the deceitful ways of forgers and the knockoffs that they market. Fenn said that George C. Frison and Robson Bonnichsen, both well-known authorities on Clovis artifacts, examined the points and considered them to be wonderful examples of Clovis flaked-stone technology. Three of the points had also been inspected and papered by a professional artifact authenticator, Calvin Howard of Springfield, Illinois. Fenn told me that he wanted to be absolutely certain about their authenticity, and asked if I would be willing to use a scientific approach to test the authenticity of the artifacts. I told him that I would be more than happy to look at them.

Initially, Fenn mailed me a partially broken Clovis point preform manufactured from rock crystal quartz and a photograph of the other eleven specimens. When I unwrapped the layers of bubble-plastic, I could see that the artifact clearly displayed the flaking characteristics that Bruce Bradley called the hallmarks of Clovis. It was unquestionable; the flake scar patterns were distinctive and sophisticated, produced by an edge-to-edge soft-hammer, or billet, percussion technique. I knew that this flaking technology was a signature of Clovis artifacts, and the quartz specimen was exemplary.

I immediately called Fenn and told him "it is as good as gold!" Fenn explained to me that he was more concerned about the Teflon-like film on the artifact than the flaking pattern. Gregory Perino, one of the oldest authenticators in the business, told him that he was beginning to see more and more of this material on artifacts that were being sent to him for authentication. The coating made him suspicious that someone was manufacturing fakes of the highest quality.

After talking to Fenn, I began a detailed microscopic examination of the artifact. Not only did I see a thin oily skin covering the stone, I could see that the artifact was manufactured from a rutilated quartz crystal. Rutile is the mineral form of titanium oxide (TiO_2), a fairly common mineral inclusion in quartz crystals that appears like golden strands of angel hair. Given the presence of rutile and the enormous size of the artifact, I thought that it might be possible to determine the source of the quartz crystal.

Quartz is one of the most common and abundant minerals on the planet. In its rock crystalline state, it is almost chemically pure silicon dioxide (SiO_2) and almost impossible to source. Impurities such as titanium dioxide, however, increase the probability that the source of the stone can be pinpointed. If the artifact was actually discovered in Greeley, Colorado, then I should be able to trace the rutilated quartz to a location somewhere on the High Plains, Rocky Mountains, or Great Basin. From the microscope, I decided to turn to the geology library to research the occurrence of rutilated quartz crystal in the Americas.

I found that while rutilated quartz does occur in western North America, most of the crystals are much smaller than those used to manufacture the Clovis point preform that Fenn sent me. Much to my surprise, crystals of rutilated quartz of that size are most common from Itibiara and Bahia, Brazil. With this information, I reexamined the biface under the microscope and compared the rutile inclusions in the Clovis preform to those described for the Brazilian source. They matched! At this juncture, I decided to call Fenn and ask him for permission to examine the rest of the artifacts. Fenn's philosophy about artifacts has always been to seek the truth; the entire cache arrived the next day.

All of the Clovis points were well labeled with an alphanumeric catalog system. I placed the artifacts side by side, in order, on a lab table so I could compare the flake scars one against the other. The points were remarkably similar. On almost all of the specimens, I found alternating, circular flake scars near the tips that were almost identical in their dimensions and platform removal, suggesting that a single individual had made them all. It also indicated that a lever might have been used to produce the flutes. Unfortunately, this observation neither supported nor negated their authenticity. If it was a real Clovis cache, we might expect that the entire collection was manufactured by the same knapper, and levers were used prehistorically to flute bifaces. I needed the kind of evidence that would hold up in a criminal court of law—beyond a reasonable doubt.

I decided to examine the artifacts with a battery of tests including low- and high-magnification optical microscopy, ultraviolet spectrometry, dissolution of surface residues with solvents, and gas-chromatography mass spectrometry. Just as Fenn suspected, I found traces of a resinous material on all of the Clovis points. In all but one specimen, the chemical occurred as a coating over both faces of the Clovis points. On the latter specimen, the residue was present in the deepest flake scars. It varied from translucent to opaque, suggesting that it could be anything from a plant resin to animal protein, bitumen, petroleum, or a modern petroleum product.

Many natural and synthetic compounds have a characteristic fluorescence when they are exposed to ultraviolet radiation that can be qualitatively described in terms of color, or more precisely, with measurements in nanometers (nm). Fluorescence refers to the luminescence of a compound when it is exposed to ultraviolet radiation. Visible light is emitted from a substance as it absorbs long (< 380 to 290 nm) or short (< 290 nm) wavelength radiation. Because ultraviolet spectroscopy is nondestructive and inexpensive, it is an important tool for archaeologists and forensic scientists.

Materials may exhibit fluorescence in their solid state, in solution, or both. Most hardened plant resins generally exhibit some kind of fluorescence. Acidic environmental settings can create a patina on the surface of plant resins and mask their fluorescence. In these situations, the patina can be removed by dissolving the resin in a solvent such as toluene. If the organic is bitumen, petroleum, or a petroleum product, it will only show fluorescence when it is dissolved in a solvent. Animal proteins, terrestrial or aquatic, generally will not manifest fluorescence in solid form or in solution.

In order to examine the fluorescence of the hard resinous coating on the fluted points, I needed to dissolve the compound in a volatile solvent such as toluene. I teased a minute sample from one of the Clovis points with a sterile, stainless-steel dental pick and placed it in a small glass beaker by rinsing the tip of the instrument with toluene. The material dissolved!

I then dipped Q-tips in toluene and rubbed the wet ends against the resinous material on each of the fluted points. I dipped the dirty ends of the Q-tips into small glass beakers filled with toluene, stirred, and exposed the solutions to long-wavelength ultraviolet light. The solutions in all of the beakers produced a pale white-green fluorescence which indicated the presence of a heavy molecular-weight hydrocarbon such as a petroleum product. How did a modern organic compound get on the surface of the Clovis points?

I began to recall my younger days as a teenager, riding atop an old Farmall tractor. If I saw an arrowhead or axe in my path, I would pause the tractor, grab the artifact, put it in the dirty, black, oil-stained toolbox under the seat, and resume my work. All of the artifacts I collected while working on the tractor had some amount of motor oil or grease on their surface. I rationalized that my qualitative chemical test had reasonable doubt and decided to focus my efforts on the red ochre.

All of the Clovis artifacts in the Fenn and Crook County Caches are covered with a single variety of red ochre, the mineral hematite (Fe_2O_3). On the Fenn and Crook County Cache artifacts, time has reduced the red ochre to particulate matter, almost atomic in size, and the individual particles have been adsorbed and absorbed into the microcrystalline texture of the stone's surface.

This collection was different; there were at least two different types of red pigment, one very fine grained and the other quite coarse. A couple of the points had a thin coating of fine-grained red ochre over their surface, but they showed no evidence of weathering, which is a natural chemical breakdown and mechanical disintegration of the hematite by an iron-eating bacteria, hydration, or oxidation. The rest of the specimens were covered in a red-ochre-like material known as terra rossa, a soil common to the limestone-rich landscapes of the southern U.S. I even found coarse- to medium-grained sand in some of the larger fractures and flake scars. Even more surprising was that the resinous compound was adhering to the outside surface of the terra rossa, as if it had been used as mastic to hold the red-ochre-like soil to the stone.

If I could completely remove the resinous material from one of the flake scars on each of the points, then I should be able to see the true texture of the surface of the stones and glean some information about the antiquity of the specimens. I decided to use a mixture of Proctor & Gamble's Ivory Soap and a pinch of Arm & Hammer baking soda to act as a mild abrasive and cleaner. I applied the mixture to a flake scar on each artifact and scrubbed it with a soft-bristled toothbrush. In every case, the soapy mixture completely removed the resinous compound, suggesting that it had been recently applied to the stone. But why would someone coat the stone unless they were trying to hide a freshly fractured surface?

Like resins, many of the stones used to manufacture Clovis points display a characteristic fluorescence that changes through time. With the exception of the two-rutilated quartz specimens, all of the points were manufactured from high-quality cherts from a variety of locations, including alibates in Texas and Knife River flint in North Dakota. Both of these cherts exhibit a different fluorescence when they are freshly flaked in comparison to ancient surfaces with well-developed patinas.

In the sunlight, Clovis artifacts manufactured from Knife River flint range from amber to white in color. Under long-wavelength ultraviolet light, the ancient amber patinas produce a green to orange fluorescence, and ancient white patinas an orange fluorescence. In contrast, freshly flaked Knife River flint exhibits a yellow fluorescence when it is exposed to ultraviolet light. Alibates has just the opposite reaction. Freshly fractured alibates is colorful in sunlight and displays highly variable day-glow fluorescence under ultraviolet light, while alibates with an ancient patina is almost nonreactive.

I placed the Clovis points on a flat-black velvet cloth to absorb superfluous radiation and held an ultraviolet light over the samples in a completely darkened room. The ultraviolet lamp had a filtered mercury tube to transmit long-wavelength radiation at precisely 360 nm. None of the areas where the resinous material had been removed displayed a fluorescence that was indicative of surfaces with an ancient patina. The cleaned surface of the Clovis point manufactured from Knife River flint appeared yellow, and the cleaned surfaces of the alibates specimens displayed brilliant fluorescence. In other words, all of the specimens had modern flaked surfaces.

If the Clovis points were recently manufactured and deliberately covered with a chemical to mask their fresh flake scars, I began to wonder if there were discrepancies in the more minute details of manufacture, such as basal grinding. Marvin Kay, an expert on the microscopic analysis of flaked-stone weaponry, has shown that Clovis basal grinding is quite distinctive when it is examined under high magnification. I illuminated the edges of the Clovis point bases with tungsten fiber optics and scanned their surface with an optical microscope between 70 and 450 magnifications. Although the edges of the bases were all well ground, there were deep sharp microgrooves in the polish, suggesting that they were made with an abrasive moving at a high speed. A close examination of the flutes and adjacent flake scars revealed similar scratches on their surfaces. They too were likely made by a high-speed grinding stone. At the higher magnifications, I also found a number of thin, delicate, overhanging microflakes that should have been lost to thirteen thousand years of freezing and thawing.

At this juncture, there was no doubt in my mind—the artifacts were fakes. In order to help expose who perpetrated the fraud, it would be necessary to precisely determine the chemical composition of the compound that had been applied to the stone using gas-chromatography mass spectrometry. Before I made any further tests, however, I felt that it was time to call Fenn and tell him that the Clovis points were unquestionably fakes. It was one of the hardest things I have ever had to do.

Mastodon bones in a Missouri spring site.

Sunrise Mine

Aerial photograph of the Sunrise Mine, Wyoming.

The author, Kenneth B. Tankersley, holds a cane torch while Chico Dulac, a traditional Oglala Lakota, examines a recently mined selenite crystal during the filming of the National Geographic Explorer *Mysteries Underground* program.

A hand-axe similar to the one discovered by Jacques Boucher
de Perthes in the Ice Age gravels near Abbeville, France.

Clovis points from the Kimmswick site.

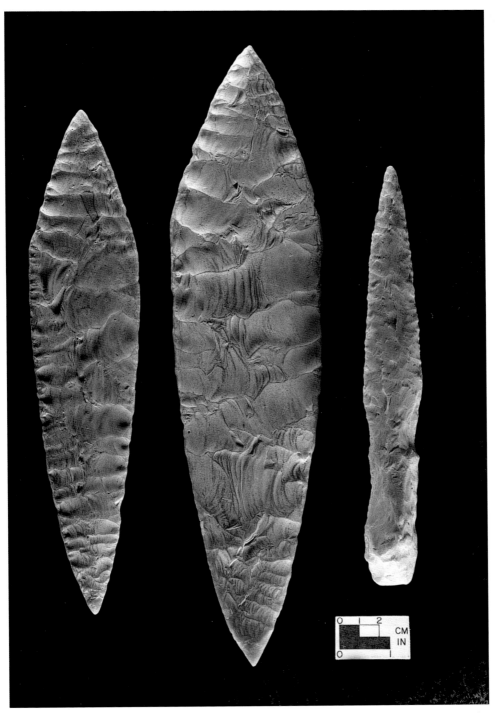

Upper Paleolithic, Solutrean artifacts from the Iberian Peninsula.

Clovis-like, Solutrean blade and core from the Iberian Peninsula.

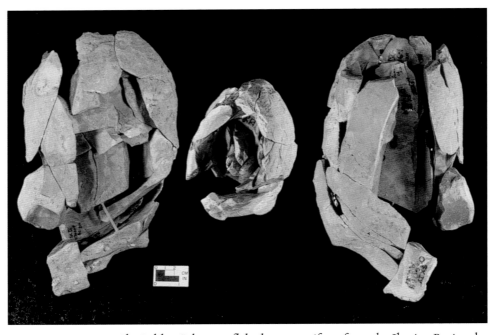

Clovis-like, Solutrean flaked-stone artifacts from the Iberian Peninsula.

A mastodon tusk exposed underwater.

Archaeologists investigate an Ice Age American site that is completely underwater.

Excavations at the Kimmswick site near St. Louis, Missouri.

A glacial outwash plain similar to that once traversed by the First Americans.

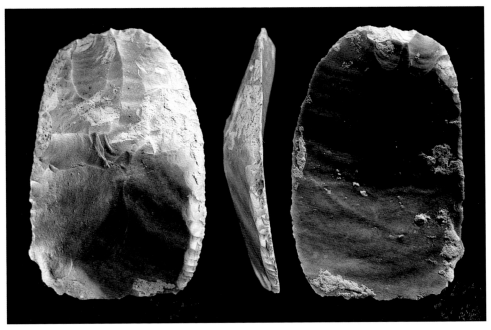

A flaked stone artifact from the Ice Age deposits of Sheriden Cave.

The entrance to Sheriden Cave, Wyandot County, Ohio.

Remains of the extinct flat-headed peccary from Sheriden Cave.

A bone spear point from the Ice Age deposits of Sheriden Cave.

A close-up of the highly engraved surface of a bone spear point from Sheriden Cave.

Excavations at the San Lazaro Pueblo near Santa Fe, New Mexico.

An Ice Age spear point manufactured from exotic stone, rock crystal quartz.

An Anasazi water tank and bedrock metate at the San Lazaro Pueblo site in New Mexico.

A Santa Fe Black-on-White potsherd in a pottery-filled stone cist at San Lazaro Pueblo.

A packrat nest containing large sherds of ancestral Pueblo pots.

An illustration reconstructing the Ice Age environment.

Rather than continuing with the more sophisticated quantitative gas-chromatography mass spectrometry, Fenn asked me to put the results of my tests in writing. I sent him a summary of my findings along with a videotape of the modern-made features viewed under high magnification with the optical microscope. Fenn told me that he had a strong suspicion that Woody Blackwell, a flint knapper from Georgia, had committed the fraud, and he was right. In fact, Blackwell had already swindled some of the most prominent collectors of Ice Age American artifacts in the United States for more than a hundred thousand dollars. Ironically, an article in the Society for American Archaeology's journal *American Antiquity* referred to Woody Blackwell as one of the more productive and reputable knappers of twentieth-century Stone Age.

Blackwell had acquired high-quality casts of Clovis points in the Fenn and Drake Caches from Pete Bostrom's Lithic Casting Lab in Troy, Illinois. With the exception of the rutilated quartz crystals, he traveled the western countryside to collect the same stone used in the manufacture of authentic Clovis points in the Fenn cache. Blackwell even went to the Smithsonian Institution to study the flaking patterns of the original Clovis points in the Drake cache found in northern Colorado. The Clovis points in Blackwell's fraudulent cache exhibited flaking techniques that were a combination of those found on specimens in both the Drake and Fenn caches.

As it turns out, Blackwell used a rock tumbler, just like Flint Jack had done in Victorian England more than a hundred years ago, to dull the fresh surfaces of the flake scars, not realizing that the process would leave a residue of modern heavy-molecular-weight hydrocarbons on the stone that could be detected in the laboratory. While he rubbed fresh red ochre on a few of the fakes, Blackwell smeared most of them with his own red Georgia soil. In order to antique the fakes, he coated them with a strong oxidizer, potassium permanganate ($KMnO_4$).

It is not surprising that Blackwell used potassium permanganate, because it is one of the oldest, most common, and aggressive inorganic oxidants available. At the microscopic level, it quickly oxidizes the iron, manganese, and sulfide mineral inclusions that are common in American cherts. Potassium permanganate also creates brown bloom-like stains of manganese dioxide on the surface of chert that mimics the natural decomposition of organic matter over thousands of years. Most collectors consider the presence of manganese dioxide blooms as a sure sign of an authentic artifact. Fortunately, the phony manganese stains can be easily removed using a solution of common chemicals found in most households—three parts hydrogen peroxide, four parts white vinegar, and three parts tap water.

Potassium permanganate is an odorless, dark purple crystal with a blue metallic sheen, and it is moderately soluble in water. Like any oxidizer, it is hazardous if not handled with care—rubber or neoprene gloves to protect the skin, goggles to protect the eyes, and a well-ventilated area to protect the lungs. Fakes coated with potassium permanganate can burn the skin and eyes, and when dust from the surface comes in contact with the respiratory system, the air passages swell, the trachea and bronchi become irritated, and breathing becomes difficult. In addition to producing fakes, Blackwell was also exposing innocent, unsuspecting collectors to a poison. Because it looks like a dark red wine in solution, potassium permanganate has been responsible for human deaths by accidental poisoning, suicide, and even murder.

Blackwell's exploits are by no means unusual among artifact swindlers. People who fake Clovis points go to many extremes to create false patinas, especially when a successful hoax can net them hundreds of thousands of dollars. Perpetrators will soak fake points in dirty motor oil, rotting leaves, and hydrofluoric acid, a dangerously corrosive substance that actually dissolves the stone. Some charlatans have even wrapped their fakes in meat and fed them to their dog so that the stomach acid of their pet creates a high-gloss polish on the stone similar to sand blasting and desert varnish. Fortunately, all of these psuedopatinas can be detected in the laboratory.

A professional authenticator recently told me that seven out of every ten artifacts he examines are fraudulent, regardless of whether they are in private or public collections. I suspect that his estimate is conservative and the number of forgeries is actually around eighty percent. How can so many fakes go undetected by the vast majority of professional archaeologists, museum curators, and collectors?

Unlike the art and art history communities, there is not a single laboratory devoted to full-time artifact authentication. While there are Clovis-point surveys, there is no registry or database containing a list of authentic artifacts. This situation is similar to the one that paleontologists and fossil collectors faced near the turn of the twentieth century.

After the publication of Charles Darwin's *The Origin of Species,* professional paleontologists and fossil collectors scoured the countryside in search of the bones of primitive humans. Fossils were eventually found in France, Germany, China, and Java, and the news of each discovery made headlines around the world.

In 1912, Charles Dawson announced that he had discovered ancient human fossils in the Piltdown quarry near Sussex, England. For almost half a century, the reading public called the fossils Piltdown man, paleontologists called them *Eoanthropus dawsoni*, and anthropologists called them the "missing link." In 1953, Dawson's fossils were subjected to a battery of scientific tests and shown, beyond a reasonable doubt, to be fraudulent and part of an elaborate hoax.

There are a lot of interesting parallels between Blackwell's fake Clovis points and Dawson's phony fossils. Both hoaxes had every physical feature that professionals and collectors expected them to have; they had an anonymous individual who could verify the story of their discovery; they were artificially ground, broken, and chemically treated to make them appear ancient.

Dawson's fakes were treated with chromic acid, iron sulphate, and the Van Dyke–brown pigment. Like Blackwell, Dawson's hoax was exposed in the laboratory. The bones were shown to be modern fraud using fluoride dating, a chemical technique that was developed in 1844. If the technology needed to expose the Piltdown fraud had been around for more than a hundred years, then why did it take more than forty years to expose it?

Again, there are parallels between the Blackwell and Dawson hoaxes. The professional community assumed that antiquity forgeries were either extremely rare or nonexistent; consequently, there were neither laboratories nor analytical techniques dedicated to authentication. In both cases, professionals and collectors were not trained to distinguish the authentic from the fraudulent, and the people involved in both forgeries had excellent credentials and were highly skilled at fabricating hoaxes.

Both Blackwell and Dawson knew exactly what the professionals and collectors wanted to find, and they constructed their forgeries to meet those expectations. Both forgers knew the physical properties and exact proportions of authentic specimens. They also knew that the vast majority of professionals would examine drawings, photographs, and casts rather than the original specimens. Actually, this is a fairly standard procedure for rare and precious specimens in both private and public collections. Both the Blackwell and Dawson hoaxes required the assistance of at least one co-conspirator, and they were both guilty of committing more than one ruse. Both frauds were premeditated and systematically developed over a long period of time.

Recognizing hoaxes as soon as possible is essential in any discipline. If undetected, they can take away from the importance of real discoveries, and, even worse, they can waste irreplaceable years of people's lives. Consider the amount of time that has been spent researching and writing professional journal articles, popular articles, and books about what later turned out to be a hoax, not to mention the amount of time spent by the readers of those articles and books. No matter what spin is placed on hoaxes, they are destructive and severely weaken the public's respect for scientists, as well as scientists' respect for collectors.

Though most people are honest, as with any profession or hobby, there are always going to be a few devious, manipulative, Machiavellian people who will commit deliberate frauds for profit and fame. They have no regard for the past, present, or future. They are thieves of time.

How Old is Clovis?

CHAPTER 10

"How old is it?" is the single most important question in American archaeology. If we do not know the answer to this simple question, then everything we say about the past is going to be based on pure speculation. For more than three hundred years, archaeologists have relied on the "Law of Superposition" to determine the relative age of stones, bones, and pots excavated from archaeological sites.

Seventeenth-century geologist Nicolaus Steno conceived "superposition" as the fundamental principle of dating the earth's sediments. He reasoned that each layer of earth was formed after the one before it and before the one above it. Since the days of Steno, superposition remains our most powerful and accurate dating tool.

In 1844, British chemist J. Middleton discovered that changes in the chemistry of fossil bone could be used as a relative measurement of time. Middleton found that the element fluorine occurs naturally in the ground. After burial, fluorine begins to accumulate in the bone. As time passes, the amount of fluorine in bone increases at a rate that is directly proportional to its age—the older the bone, the greater the concentration of fluorine.

If human skeletal remains are found among the bones of extinct Ice Age animals, then fluorine dating can be used to determine if they are the same age. Fluorine dating was made famous when it was used during the twentieth century to expose the infamous Piltdown hoax.

While fluorine dating and superposition can tell us, beyond a reasonable doubt, if one artifact-bearing layer is older or younger than another, it cannot tell us the age of the layers or the artifacts they contain in terms of years. At the time of his death in 1875, Charles Darwin was working on the problem of dating archaeological sites. He reasoned that if he could determine how much earth an earthworm moved per year, then the depth of naturally buried artifacts could be used as a measurement of time. The technique was never developed.

The greatest breakthrough in dating the past came during the twentieth century when amateur archaeologist and physical chemist Willard Frank Libby envisaged the radiocarbon dating technique. It was Libby's dream to one day combine his love for archaeology and chemistry. As a young college student, Libby built the first Geiger counter in America, improving on Hans Geiger and Walther Müller's original 1928 German design. As part of his doctorate research project completed in 1933 at the University of California at Berkeley, he found new ways to amplify the Geiger-Müller counters so they could detect and measure the radioactivity of ordinary elements such as carbon.

As the United States entered World War II, Libby volunteered his service to the Manhattan Project at Columbia University. While he was working on the development of thermal-nuclear weaponry for the United States war effort, Libby used his spare time to calculate the half-life of radiocarbon. Although his WWII-era calculations were off by tens of thousands of years, Libby correctly determined that radiocarbon had a long half-life, a property that made it ideally suitable for dating.

The first radiocarbon laboratory,
created by Willard F. Libby.

Immediately following the war, Libby accepted an academic position in the department of chemistry at the University of Chicago. After his move to the Midwest, Libby kept his radiocarbon dating research a closely guarded secret because he was certain that his colleagues would think he was crazy. Libby knew that if he publicly announced that he was trying to use radiocarbon to date the ancient past, he would be lampooned and labeled a crackpot, and his work would never be funded.

During the summer of 1946, Libby assembled all of the facts needed to develop radiocarbon as the first precise dating technique. Libby assumed that radiocarbon formed naturally in the earth's atmosphere as cosmic rays bombard the air. Cosmic rays are an extremely energetic source of radiation that is generated well beyond our solar system. This small-scale nuclear reaction results in the production of radiocarbon (^{14}C), which then combines with oxygen (O_2) to form radioactive carbon dioxide ($^{14}CO_2$). Radioactive carbon dioxide quickly becomes part of all living things as plants use it in the process of photosynthesis. Herbivores then eat the plants containing radiocarbon, and carnivores eat the herbivores. As long as the plants and animals remain alive, they contain the same amount of radiocarbon in the atmosphere at any given point in time. After death, the amount of radiocarbon begins to decrease, or decay, at a steady rate known as a half-life.

By the summer of 1946, Libby learned that the half-life of radiocarbon had been calculated to about five thousand years, and with this figure he knew that he would be able to determine the age of an archaeological site by measuring the amount of radiocarbon in artifacts.

Over the Christmas holidays of 1946, Libby's student assistant, James Arnold, disclosed to his father, another well-informed amateur archaeologist, Libby's secret plans to use radiocarbon to date the archaeological past. Overwhelmed with excitement, Arnold's father leaked Libby's secret to Ambrose Lansing, the director of the New York Metropolitan Museum.

In January 1947, Lansing sent Libby samples of cypress wood to be dated by his revolutionary new technique, radiocarbon. The wood was from the Sakkara tomb, which contained the remains of the ancient Egyptian king Djoser. Unbeknownst to Lansing, there was no such thing as a radiocarbon-dating technique. While Libby assumed that radiocarbon occurred naturally in nature, he had not yet confirmed it. Even if his assumption was correct, he had not developed an easy and inexpensive way to measure it. With his secret exposed, Libby hastened his research.

Libby moved his experiments to Baltimore, Maryland, where he was able to use radioactive sewage gas to confirm that radiocarbon was, indeed, a naturally occurring substance in the earth's atmosphere. On May 30, 1947, the *New York Times* released the news of Libby's discovery, which told the public that radiocarbon may "provide a new yardstick" to measure the past forty thousand years of prehistory. Libby's finding eventually attracted the attention of Paul Fejos, director of the Viking Fund for Anthropological Research, and with his support, Libby and his former student, Arnold, began their search for radiocarbon samples of known ages.

In January 1948, the Viking Fund invited about thirty archaeologists and geologists to a supper lecture in New York City with Libby as the guest speaker. Libby told the audience that he called his revolutionary new dating method "radiocarbon" because it used the amount of natural-occurring radioactive carbon in ancient wood, burned or unburned, to measure time within a reasonable margin of error.

Journalists later reported that you could have heard a pin drop at the end of Libby's presentation. The archaeologists were stunned! Aside from sheer disbelief, most of them were uncomfortable because their published speculations about antiquity were about to be put to the test.

While some of the archaeologists were more than a little interested in the possibility of determining how old their archaeological sites were, they had not saved a single scrap of carbon from their digs. Why should they? After all, both conventional wisdom and their professors had taught them that wood and charcoal were worthless materials that should be tossed out. Now, Libby was telling the archaeological community that carbon, a messy black residue from old campfires, was their most significant find!

The silence was broken when Ice Age geologist Richard Foster Flint stood and said, "Well, if you people are not interested in this, I am!"

Flint's unbridled enthusiasm led to a key position as a representative of the Geological Society of America on the first Committee on Radioactive Carbon. The committee was formed to carefully select samples of known ages from private and public collections from important archaeological and geological sites that could be used to test the technique.

The first sample selected for radiocarbon dating was the cypress wood from the tomb of King Djoser that Lansing had sent Libby more than a year earlier. Libby's first radiocarbon age determination correctly placed the wood in ancient Egypt's third dynasty, confirming that the dating technique did, in fact, work. However, it was too early to celebrate.

John Wilson, an Egyptologist at the University of Chicago, selected the second sample of known age. Wilson provided Libby with a piece of wood that he said was Hellenistic in age. Much to Libby's surprise, the artifact had the same radiocarbon content found in modern wood. Something was seriously wrong; it should have been exactly half the age of the wood from Djoser's tomb.

Libby had too much confidence in his dating technique to question his age determination. Instead, he questioned the authenticity of the artifact. Wilson had not taken Libby seriously. He did not realize that the first samples submitted for radiocarbon dating had to be of an unquestionably known age because they were being used to test the technique. Wilson had given Libby a modern fake that had been purchased from an unscrupulous antiquities dealer in Egypt. Although this was not the last time Libby was given a fraudulent artifact to date, fortunately they were few in number.

In May 1949, during the fourteenth annual meeting of the Society for American Archaeology held at Indiana University, and hosted by amateur archaeologists Glenn A. Black and Eli Lilly, Arnold reported the results of Libby's first seven radiocarbon dates obtained on authenticated samples. The first radiocarbon dates were published later that year in the December 23, 1949, issue of *Science*. Now Libby was ready to move into the great unknown ages of prehistory.

In 1953, Libby used radiocarbon to date an important American Ice Age deposit known as the Two Creeks Forest Bed, an ancient layer of spruce trees thought to have formed just before the end of the last Ice Age, about the same time Clovis hunters killed mammoth and bison at Blackwater Draw, New Mexico. Libby dated five samples of wood from a Two Creeks Forest Bed in Wisconsin, producing an average age of 11,404 ± three hundred fifty years old. Ernst Antevs, a Swedish-born geologist, adamantly refused to accept the radiocarbon dates and began a long dispute with Libby and his dating technique.

Antevs was the first person to attempt to date Clovis artifacts. In 1934, he visited the Clovis type-site with Edgar B. Howard to examine the geologic nature of the

Ice Age pond sediments that contained Clovis artifacts and an abundance of mammoth and extinct bison bones. Antevs used water-evaporation rates and runoff calculations to determine that the artifacts were deposited in the pond sometime between thirteen thousand and twelve thousand years ago.

In the spring of 1954, Elias H. Sellards collected numerous samples from Blackwater Draw for radiocarbon dating. Although they were submitted directly to Libby's lab, they were never dated. It was not until the mid-1960s that archaeologists had enough radiocarbon samples to show that all of the Clovis sites dated to the end of the last Ice Age. C. Vance Haynes, using the University of Arizona Radiocarbon

Radiocarbon Time (years ago)	Calendar Time (years ago)
550	520
1,000	930
1,500	1,350
2,000	1,940
2,500	2,610
3,000	3,190
3,500	3,770
4,000	4,440
4,500	5,150
5,000	5,730
5,500	6,300
6,000	6,840
6,500	7,380
7,000	7,790
7,500	8,270
8,000	8,860
8,500	9,500
9,000	9,980
9,500	10,510
10,000	11,160
10,500	12,420
11,000	12,920
11,500	13,420
12,000	13,990
12,500	14,850
13,000	15,350
14,000	16,800
15,000	17,950
16,000	19,100

Lab, was the first person to obtain acceptable radiocarbon dates for the Clovis type-site; they ranged from 11,040 ± five hundred to 11,630 ± four hundred years old, comparable to those obtained by Libby for the Two Creeks Forest Bed.

Antevs's calculations for the age of Clovis were correct. As it turns out, radiocarbon years do not equal calendar years because the production of radiocarbon in the atmosphere through time has not been constant; it varies as much as 15 percent from Libby's original calculations, making radiocarbon time older or younger than calendar time. Fortunately, other dating techniques have been used to calibrate radiocarbon dates to calendar years.

In the case of Clovis, a radiocarbon age range of 11,000 to 11,600 years is actually about 13,000 to 13,500 years old; the radiocarbon dates are about 2,000 years short. Nevertheless, Libby's radiocarbon dating technique remains the greatest archaeological discovery of the twentieth century.

On November 3, 1960, Libby received the Nobel Prize in Chemistry for his use of radiocarbon to determine age in archaeological and geological time. Despite the fact that Libby had become an internationally recognized physical chemist, he always referred to himself as an amateur archaeologist, not only because of his lifelong passion to date the past but also for the people whom he most enjoyed working with, the ultimate source of his most important radiocarbon samples.

Since the days of Libby, radiocarbon samples have become the single most important discovery that can be made on an Ice Age American site. Not only can they be used to answer the most fundamental of questions—how old is it?—but radiocarbon samples can also ultimately determine whether the site will be respected or rejected. However, assigning an age to a site has become more than just sending a handful of charcoal to your local radiocarbon lab.

Today, a technique known as accelerator mass spectrometry (AMS) is routinely used in laboratories around the world to precisely measure the radiocarbon age of minute samples by literally counting atoms. Instead of measuring the radioactive decay in 1.0 gram of carbon, AMS detects and counts the number of radiocarbon atoms in less than 0.0001 of a gram of carbon. AMS can date samples as small as a mouse tooth or strawberry seed.

Working at this minute scale, archaeologists have heightened their awareness of the many outside factors that can influence the interpretation of a radiocarbon date.

Materials that are older or younger than a radiocarbon sample can forever alter its chemistry and result in an incorrect date. The presence of peat, lignite, bituminous coal, anthracite, petroleum, bitumen, or black shale can make radiocarbon samples date older than their true age. Organic acids naturally occurring in soils can make a sample date too recent if the acid is not completely removed. And, even if the radiocarbon sample is chemically perfect, human bias can distort our interpretation of the date.

Since the last Ice Age, insects, roots, burrowing animals of all sizes, freezing and thawing, and erosion and redeposition have moved many radiocarbon samples from their original position. Through time, older and newer radiocarbon samples are moved into layers containing Ice Age American artifacts. If these natural processes go unrecognized by the excavators, then the age of a site will be misinterpreted.

Past disturbances of radiocarbon samples can be identified at the microscopic scale. A close inspection of the sediments will not only reveal disturbances that moved radiocarbon samples and artifacts after their burial but also helps us understand how the site formed and how it compares with the formation of other sites of the same age. This information can also be compared to the geology of the region in order to look for temporal consistencies that can be used to strengthen the interpretation of the site's age.

Human bias is unquestionably the most severe of all of the factors that can lead to the misinterpretation of radiocarbon dates. Preconceived notions and conventional wisdom about the age of an artifact or a site before a sample is dated determines whether or not an archaeologist accepts or rejects a radiocarbon date. This statement from Harvard professor John Otis "Jo" Brew is representative of the attitude of many archaeologists about radiocarbon dating:

> *If a radiocarbon date supports our theories, we put it in the main text.*
> *If it does not entirely contradict them, we put it in a footnote. And if it*
> *is completely out of date, we just drop it.*

Brew's statement is particularly true when it comes to Ice Age American sites. An accurate interpretation of what exactly is meant by "out of date" depends upon the geology of the site and the purity of the radiocarbon sample. If the geology and chemistry were not investigated, then the radiocarbon date will always remain in question.

Every radiocarbon date has some margin of error. Therefore, one of the best ways to precisely date a site is to obtain numerous radiocarbon samples, not only from the layer containing artifacts but also from the deposits above and below them. By showing inconsistencies in the age sequences, a large battery of radiocarbon dates can reveal if the geology of the site has been misinterpreted or if the samples have been chemically contaminated.

Prior to radiocarbon dating, the presence of Folsom points among the remains of extinct bison was enough evidence to prove beyond a reasonable doubt that people had been in America before the end of the last Ice Age. Clovis was later shown to be unquestionably older than Folsom when Clovis points were found in a layer beneath Folsom points. Now archaeologists are feverishly searching for sites that contain artifacts beneath a Clovis layer. Although many sites have been offered as pre-Clovis possibilities during the last half of the twentieth century, none have stood up to the scrutiny of rigorous radiocarbon dating.

Thanks to AMS, a pre-Clovis site does not need to have an overlying Clovis layer. In fact, the most credible pre-Clovis site would be one that contains human remains that are older than the oldest Clovis radiocarbon dates. In the absence of human remains, undeniably human-made artifacts discovered in a layer that pre-dates Clovis would also be convincing evidence of a pre-Clovis site. However, determining whether or not the specimens were made by people or by nature is not always an easy task. Mother Nature can modify bone and stone in ways that mimic human behavior.

At the Calico Hills site in southern California, nature has created the same flaking patterns on stones that were also produced by ancient humans in the manufacture of stone tools and weapons. Calico Hills contains a deeply buried deposit of gravel, pebbles, cobbles, and boulders that are at least 200,000 years old. Many of these stones are extremely high-quality forms of quartz that, when struck, produce a sharper-than-razor edge. When a sizable earthquake occurs, the stone-rich deposit of Calico shakes to the point that it behaves like a liquid. Brittle pebbles and cobbles of chalcedony, agate, and flint are struck repeatedly between larger, denser stones such as granite, removing multiple flakes from their edges that mimic the human-worked edge of a tool or weapon. Liquefaction also produces debris that resembles human stone-tool making, flakes that have striking platforms and bulbs of percussion.

The Calico Hills site in southern California.

Similar patterns can be created on bone. The powerful jaws and teeth of carnivores such as lions, bears, wolves, coyotes, and raccoons can split open and fracture bone in a way that resembles the work of ancient humans. Splinters of bone that pass through the gastrointestinal tract of carnivores become so highly polished that they can be mistaken for a skillfully human-made bone awl or needle. Large herd animals can trample bone in such a way that it mimics the fractures, flakes, and cut marks produced by human bone-tool manufacture and butchering. African elephants have been known to inadvertently flake long bones by picking them up with their trunks and striking them against the ground. Freezing and thawing can move a bone against the sharp edge of a stone, creating cut marks that resemble those produced in butchering. If an archaeologist fails to recognize that the bone was naturally split, flaked, or cut, then even the most precise pre-Clovis age radiocarbon dates become meaningless.

The best way to limit human bias is to invite numerous archaeologists and geologists to visit the excavation of an Ice Age American site so they can see firsthand the relationship between the radiocarbon samples, the geology, and the artifacts. The more people that examine the radiocarbon samples and their find spots, the less chance there will be for misinterpretation.

A pseudo-artifact produced by earthquake-generated liquefaction at the Calico Hills site.

It is important to remember that no one radiocarbon date will forever change our view of the past, and no one site will ever contain all of the answers. It is only by looking at all of the radiocarbon dates from all of the sites and working together with open minds that we can adequately interpret the archaeological record of Ice Age America.

Were Clovis the First Americans?

CHAPTER 11

Among the most fascinating questions in American archaeology are the most basic: Who were the first Americans? Where did they come from, and when did they arrive? Our modern explanations about the origins of Ice Age Americans are almost half a millennium old.

The Spanish Jesuit priest Fray José de Acosta suggested in his 1590 *Historia Natural y Moral de las Indias* (book 1, chapter 20) that people from Asia initially settled the Americas and that overland or coastal migration was their likely route of entry.

> *I coniecture then, by the discourse I have made, that the new world, which we call Indies, is not altogether severed and disioyned from the other world; and to speake my opinion, I have long beleeved that the one and the other world are ioyned and continued with another in some part, or at the least are very neere. . . . For that wee must beleeve they could not so conveniently come thither by Sea as travelling by Land, which might be done without consideration in changing by little and little their lands and habitations. Some peopling the lands they found, and others seeking for the newe, in time they came to inhabite and people the Indies with so many nations, people, and tongues as we see—*

The English scholar Edward Brerewood speculated in his 1622 book *Enquiries Touching the Diversity of Languages, and Religions, Though the Chief Parts of the World* that the Tartars, today known as Mongolians, were probably the first people to enter the Americas. Twenty-six years later, the philosopher and traveler Thomas Gage argued that Mongolians likely entered the Americas through the narrow channel of water known as the Bering Strait. Other writers during the sixteenth and seventeenth centuries suggested that the first Americans might have arrived in boats from Europe or from China or other areas in the Pacific. Amazingly, these explanations sound like the story lines of recent articles in the *New York Times, Newsweek*, and *Time* magazines. Indeed, all possible routes of human migration into the Americas during the Ice Age were proposed before the birth of either Thomas Jefferson or Benjamin Franklin.

Despite centuries of debate, there still is no consensus on the initial peopling of the Americas, only controversies and contradictions. While some of the arguments have been logically consistent through the centuries, others have confused possibilities with probabilities and certainties. In the face of new discoveries, technologies, and methods converging on the issues of human migration, the questions raised hundreds of years ago still linger.

Archaeologists today disagree on many—perhaps most—of the important issues concerning the peopling of the Americas, and that is as it should be in the pursuit of knowledge. Perhaps the biggest obstacle is the fact we do not have a tight chronological framework for discussing and analyzing the cultural and biological origins of Ice Age Americans. It is safe to assume that people were present in Beringia—the temporary, dry-land passage between Siberia and Alaska—sometime after fifteen thousand years ago, and that they moved southward, hunting wild animals and gathering wild plants. But were these the first people to inhabit America?

Disagreement swirls around who the first Americans were, the timing of their

Beringia, a bridge into the Western Hemisphere.

arrival, the number and nature of migrations, how quickly and by what strategies they moved across the landscape, and how they are related to contemporary American Indians. The answers to many of these questions hinge upon the exact timing of the arrival of the first people in America.

Essentially, there are two diametrically opposed temporal models for the initial peopling of the Western Hemisphere: an early entry, sometime before the peak of the last Ice Age, more than twenty thousand years ago; and a late entry, sometime just before the appearance of the oldest, unquestionable archaeological record in the Americas, less than fifteen thousand years ago.

If people first entered the Western Hemisphere by way of Beringia, then the answers we seek about the origins of Ice Age Americans should be found in Siberia. After all, Russian archaeologists have been searching for Ice Age sites in Siberia for more than a century.

Perhaps the oldest archaeological site in Siberia is Diring Yuryakh, deeply buried

An archaeological excavation in the homeland of Clovis, eastern Siberia.

on a terrace of the Lena River in central Yakutia. It was discovered in 1982 by a group of Russian scientists during an international geology field trip, and subsequently excavated by Yuri Mochanov and Svetlana Fedoseeva. The deepest deposits of Diring Yuryakh contain simple chopping tools and flakes manufactured from local cobbles of quartzite. Buried beneath almost fifty feet of windblown sand and silt, the artifacts appear to be Lower Paleolithic, pebble tools similar to those first described by Louis and Mary Leakey from Olduvai Gorge in Tanzania.

In 1993, Mochanov announced to the world that Russia could very well be the cradle of humanity. He believed that the Diring Yuryakh site was between three and two million years old, based on the primitive nature of the artifacts and the age of the landscape. Other Russian scientists such as Yaroslav Vladimir Kuzmin disagreed, however, arguing that the geology of the artifact-bearing deposits were much younger.

Michael Waters, an American archaeological geologist, examined the site in 1995 and collected sediment samples for optical-stimulated luminescent dating. The resulting age was more than 250,000 years old! While this date is not as ancient as Mochanov first proclaimed, it is consistent with the early Stone Age artifacts excavated from the site, and it means that people were present in Siberia hundreds of millennia earlier than previously suspected. But what happened to them? Were they forced to retreat southward when the climate became colder, or is it possible that they migrated on to the Western Hemisphere?

In western Siberia, a group of Ice Age sites known as Afontova contain artifacts that are similar to those found on Clovis sites in North America, including flake tools, blades, large bifaces, and composite bone and ivory tools and weapons. Two Afontova sites are particularly intriguing—Makarovo 4, located in the headwaters of the Upper Lena River basin, and Ust-Kova, situated in the Angara River basin. Although the flaked-stone tools and weapons from Makarovo 4 and Ust-Kova are more than twenty thousand years old, they are within the range of variation found in the Crook County and Fenn Clovis caches.

Of the two sites, Ust-Kova contains flaked-stone weapons that are not only Clovis-like in their form but also in their method of manufacture. Four complete weapon tips excavated from the site show the same large, percussion-produced, flake scar patterns found on Clovis points from the High Plains of North America. They were produced by the same manufacturing techniques that Bruce Bradley and George Frison call the hallmarks of Clovis. Two of the weapons from Ust-Kova even have flute-like basal thinning flakes, and one of the specimens is similar to Clovis points from the Hoyt and Dietz sites of Oregon.

In eastern Siberia, Ice Age sites called Dyuktai, named after a cave in the Aldan

The Ust-Kova site on the Upper Angara River of eastern Siberia.

River valley, are between sixteen thousand and fourteen thousand years old. Dyuktai sites differ from Afontova in age, the presence of microblades, and long, narrow, flaked-stone weaponry. Interestingly, the stone weaponry of Dyuktai closely resembles El Jobo and Lerma points from Ice Age sites in the Western Hemisphere, including Monte Verde in Chile, Taima-Taima in Venezuela, and Santa Isabel Iztapan in Mexico.

Although questions remain about the dating of Santa Isabel Iztapan and Taima-Taima, Monte Verde is among the oldest sites in the Americas. Monte Verde is a wet bog site located in southern Chile and excavated by Thomas D. Dillehay of the University of Kentucky. The site was brought to the attention of Dillehay in 1976, when a student at the Southern University of Chile brought in a small collection of large bones and a tooth from an extinct elephant-like species. Dillehay, who was teaching and conducting research at the university, recognized the potential of the discovery. With a team of more than eighty professionals, the site was excavated over a period of eleven years. Unambiguous artifacts and a plethora of faunal and floral remains were recovered from stratified contexts that have been radiocarbon-dated to about 14,850 years ago.

In western Beringia, the closest archaeological site comparable in age to Monte Verde is Ushki I, located on the Kamchatka Peninsula; it is about sixteen thousand years old. Flaked-stone weaponry found at the site is delicately flaked and tanged—more reminiscent of dart tips found on Ice Age sites in the Rocky Mountains of western North America than the El Jobo or Lerma points of Mexico and South America.

The Ushki I site on the Kamchatka Peninsula of eastern Siberia.

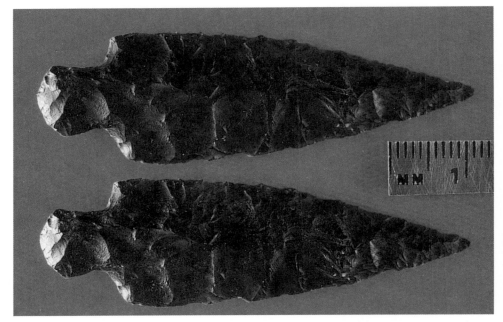

A spear point from the Ushki I site in eastern Siberia.

In eastern Beringia, there are at least two different groups of Ice Age archaeological sites that resulted from direct human migration from Siberia—Nenana and Paleoarctic. Flaked-stone artifacts from Nenana sites are nearly identical to those of Afontova, indicating that their cultural roots are deep in western Siberia and that they may represent the Beringian ancestors of Clovis. Artifacts from Paleoarctic sites are almost indistinguishable from the Dyuktai sites of eastern Siberia, including the proliferation of microblades. It is clear that the Ice Age technology of both Dyuktai and Afontova was well established and widespread in Beringia twelve thousand years ago.

While many continue to search for the oldest sites in Siberia and Beringia, a growing number of archaeologists have turned to other avenues of anthropological research. In 1987, Joseph H. Greenberg of Stanford University published a provocative book called *Languages in the Americas*. Using linguistic data, Greenberg believes that the Americas were settled by multiple waves of people from various parts of the world. He bases his proposition on three American Indian linguistic families, the relatively recent Eskimo-Aleut and Na-Dene, and a residual category he calls

Amerind that includes the rest of the languages. Greenberg considers Amerind a descendant of an ancestral or proto-Amerind family—the language of Ice Age Americans. While most anthropologists agree with the Eskimo-Aleut and Na-Dene classifications, Greenberg's Amerind category and his inferences about the peopling of the Americas remain controversial.

Greenberg's linguistic model is backed, in part, by molecular genetics. This is not a surprising source of support if we assume that the people in the Americas' past who spoke the same language were, in fact, related. Like molecular geneticists, linguists establish language groupings based on patterns in historically shared words. Although some anthropologists argue that this comparative methodology cannot be used to establish relationships that date to the Ice Age, there are striking similarities between phylogenetic trees based on Greenberg's linguistic data and genetic distances calculated from the DNA of American Indian populations. Congruences between the linguistic and genetic trees are of more than a little interest to archaeologists because they illustrate patterns of human migrations and population dispersal.

Direct evidence of human lineages is obtained at the molecular level from mitochondrial DNA, passed on from mother to daughter, and the Y chromosome, passed on from father to son. Because mitochondrial DNA and the Y chromosome are inherited from only one parent, they provide the ancestries of both the female and male lineage. Given that mutations in both mitochondrial DNA and the Y chromosome are permanent and indicative of the geographic region where they first occurred, and come about in a linear and predictable rate, it is possible to determine the timing and source areas of human migrations.

Theodore Schurr found variation in the mitochondrial DNA of modern Native Americans that not only suggests there were multiple migrations during the Ice Age from a number of different homelands, it implies that the first wave of people arrived in the Americas more than thirty thousand years ago. Schurr discovered that the mitochondrial DNA in modern Native American populations separate into four haplogroups, or lineages, which he designates A, B, C, and D on the basis of a specific set of genetic markers. On the basis of mutation rates, haplogroups A, C, and D originated about thirty-five thousand to twenty-five thousand years ago in both Siberia and America. Although haplogroup B appears to be more recent in America, it was present in East Asia sometime between thirty thousand and twenty-four thousand years ago.

Perhaps the most exciting and controversial of Schurr's findings is the discovery of a rare, fifth haplogroup, designated X, genetically linked to European, Middle Eastern, and West Asian populations, but completely absent in both East Asia and Siberia. While the idea of European-like physical features among Ice Age Americans sounds preposterous, early-nineteenth-century explorers from the Lewis and Clark expedition, and later artist George Catlin, wrote about the occurrence of light-colored skin, hair, and eyes among the Mandan of the Great Plains. Because the Mandan moved into the land of the Lakota from somewhere to the east, some ethno-historians argue that their physical features represent traces of early contact with the Norse settlements of about A.D. 1,000 near L'Anse aux Meadows, Newfoundland. However, Schurr's genetic data indicates that the haplogroup X is far more ancient, having arrived in the Americas sometime between thirty-six thousand and thirteen thousand years ago.

Schurr's genetic evidence shows that during the Ice Age different groups of people migrated to the Americas over long periods of time from different areas of the world. These findings are exciting, if not revolutionary. While the archaeological record supports the late entry model for the peopling of the Americas, the molecular genetic data suggest that the early entry model is a more precise view of America's past. Actually, we should not be surprised by Schurr's findings given that Charles Darwin cautioned, more than a century ago, that the archaeological record is imperfect. The importance of molecular genetics is further emphasized when we consider that our knowledge of the past is, and forever will be, incomplete—all evidence of entire cultures have vanished without a trace.

Are the answers we seek about the peopling of the Americas going to be found in population genetics rather than traditional archaeology? Genome variation analysis is rapidly becoming a powerful and productive tool that is leading toward a quantum leap in our knowledge of human migrations and origins. Case studies of gene flow and genetic variation in the Yanomama and other native South American groups suggest that genetic inferences can be made about ancient populations. Data obtained from mitochondrial DNA, Y chromosomes, and human population genetics are also producing intriguing new questions. It is becoming increasingly evident that genetics in the twenty-first century will have as profound an effect on American archaeology as radiocarbon dating did during the twentieth century.

These advancements in technology, methods, and theory do not suggest that we abandon the search for early sites; rather, they point to exciting new directions to look for answers about the initial peopling of the Americas. Rather than seeking clues by measuring bones and stones, more precise answers to questions about the ancestry of Ice Age Americans may instead be found in molecular genetics and historical linguistics.

It is also evident that the search for Ice Age Americans is no longer a single-minded archaeological endeavor; rather, it demands interdisciplinary field and laboratory research teams that include geologists, geographers, physicists, chemists, and biologists. No one individual can do it all or know it all. It is equally apparent that archaeologists in the twenty-first century are not searching for the oldest site to be duly confirmed or rejected by a blue-ribbon panel of their peers. Instead, contemporary archaeologists are working toward more heady goals such as searching for the mechanisms of human adaptation to periods of rapid and profound climatic change, or adaptation to different ecosystems with different resources. Not only are these more rewarding avenues of research, the answers to these questions may help us understand the economic consequences of future environmental change associated with global warming. Nevertheless, arguments over the exact timing, origins, and processes of human migration will likely continue to fuel many heated debates.

Our questions about the origins of Ice Age Americans are epistemological—they are about the very nature of human knowledge, its limits, and validity. Most scientists argue that truth is the ultimate goal of their research. As a science, modern archaeology seeks truth through the rigors of the scientific method.

- An ancient archaeological site is serendipitously discovered.

- A number of hypotheses, or educated explanations, are offered about its age and human behavior.

- Data needed to test the hypotheses are collected (artifacts, ecofacts, features, stratigraphy, and chronometric dates).

- The hypotheses are evaluated.

In this endeavor, archaeologists do everything they can to reject the explanations. If one of them cannot be negated, then that explanation comes as close to the truth as the scientific method allows. It should always be remembered, however, that new data might come to light at any time, which forces the archaeologist to reevaluate their explanation.

As scientists, archaeologists do not prove their interpretations of the past; rather, they disprove what is not true. Verification is a vital part of the scientific process. But, unlike researchers in other disciplines, archaeologists destroy their data as they collect it. Archaeological sites are nonrenewable and, once excavated, they are gone forever. Thus, it is the responsibility of every archaeologist to document the precise location of every exposed artifact, ecofact, feature, and layer. With this data, another archaeologist should be able to verify the temporal and spatial relationships at the site. If the data cannot be independently validated, then the interpretations of the site fall into question. If the data is verified, then the discovery may lead to the formulation of a new paradigm.

To paraphrase the late Thomas S. Kuhn: science progresses by the replacement of paradigms. A paradigm is a conceptual framework with an overall research strategy, a unique set of goals, methods, and theory. According to Kuhn, science goes through a period of tranquility with an approved paradigm. A crisis occurs when a new paradigm is introduced. Conflict between the old and the new usually leads to a revolution and the emergence of a new paradigm.

By the end of the twentieth century, archaeology was in a state of crisis. There was a conflict between the early- and late-entry models. For most of the twentieth century, Clovis has been recognized as the oldest unambiguous prehistoric culture in the Western Hemisphere. This situation created what many archaeologists have referred to as the Clovis-first paradigm; that is, Clovis were the first people to inhabit the Americas. During the last two decades, archaeological evidence presented from Ice Age sites in South America suggests that people were in the Western Hemisphere long before the advent of Clovis. If this evidence could be substantiated beyond a reasonable doubt, then a new paradigm would emerge—and so it seemed.

A philosopher of science, Thomas Kuhn might have argued that only blind stubbornness can account for the continued resistance of some archaeologists to recognize the early entry model as valid and accept the new pre-Clovis paradigm. On the other hand, disagreement on important issues is proper conduct in scientific inquiry. To paraphrase another philosopher of science, Abraham Kaplan: premature closure on important conceptual and analytical matters ill serves the field. As long as there are alternative rational interpretations of the data, the questions that have been raised about the initial peopling of the Americas should remain open and not be arbitrarily finalized. At the same time, we must remember that potentiality is not the same as truth.

Unfortunately, "paradigm bias"—an over-commitment to a favored model—has created a breakdown in communication among some archaeologists. Paradigm bias creates unrealistic expectations of the archaeological record by closing an investigator's mind to alternative explanations and possibilities.

Some would argue that history is repeating itself, a time similar to the nineteenth century when proponents of an early entry presented paleoliths as evidence of ancient human occupation of the Americas. They looked nothing like the more sophisticated artifacts found at the Folsom site, which finally proved beyond a reasonable doubt that people were in the Americas during the Ice Age.

Actually, the Folsom artifacts—as it turns out—were exactly what we should have expected to find in the Ice Age deposits of North America. The finely flaked Folsom artifacts are typical of the flaked-stone weaponry and tools of the Upper Paleolithic, the final phase of the Old Stone Age, which had been recognized fifty years earlier in Europe. Even the points of the Folsom site were not unique. In 1923, a concave-base weapon resembling the Folsom point was recovered from the Upper Paleolithic, Laugerue-Haute site in Dordogne, France.

Several interpretations, some of them contradictory, will fit the current evidence on the initial peopling of the Americas. Consequently, our questions—and our minds—should remain open as we seek more data; a choice between the early- and late-entry models should not be made arbitrarily. But we must also remember that possibility does not equal certainty. Despite intriguing possibilities of an early human presence in the Western Hemisphere, the evidence so far is only suggestive, not conclusive. While we remain hopeful, we must also remember that there may never be complete resolution about when and from where the first Americans arrived. Still the search goes on. Fortunately, as George Frison has reminded me many times, "Ken, we still don't have all of the answers."

ROUTES OF ENTRY

During the Ice Age, American summers were much cooler than the present, allowing winter snowfall to remain year-round in the western mountains and northern latitudes. In time, the accumulating snow turned into ice and, under growing pressure, glaciers began to flow outward. Eventually, the expanding mountain glaciers of the west collided and welded with the expanding continental glacier of northern Canada, creating an impenetrable barrier between Alaska and the contiguous United States.

In the oceans, polar sea ice extended southward into the Atlantic, merging with the expanding continental glacier of eastern North America, Greenland, and Iceland—ice also covered all but the southernmost areas of Europe. As a significant amount of the earth's water remained on land in the form of snow and ice, the level of the oceans began to drop, exposing the continental shelves. In the north Pacific, the floors of the Chukchi and Bering Seas were exposed, creating a passage of solid ground between Chukotka and Alaska known as the Bering Land Bridge.

Thus, a number of possible migration routes into the Americas were created by the climatic conditions of the Ice Age—across the Bering Land Bridge from Siberia, along the circum-Pacific coastal rim from Asia, and along the ice margins of the Atlantic Ocean from Europe. For almost half a millennium, philosophers, historians, and archaeologists have suggested that the first people walked into America from eastern Siberia, and they migrated southward into Canada, the United States, Mexico, and beyond. Since 1933, this explanation has been based on the assumption that a long, narrow, ice-free corridor was open between Alaska and northern Montana about the same time the Bering Land Bridge was exposed.

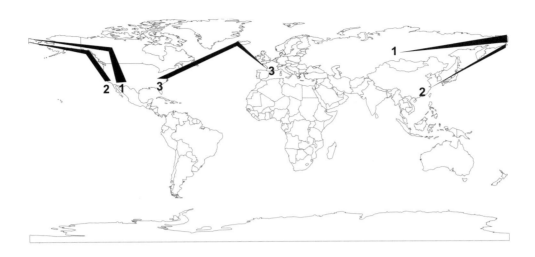

Map of the world showing the possible routes of entry during the Ice Age: (1) overland, from eastern Siberia, through Alaska and Canada, and into the Great Plains; (2) along the Pacific Rim, from Asia and the Far East, and onto California; and (3) across the Atlantic Ocean, from the Iberian Peninsula to the southeastern United States.

A group of paleontologists have found a conspicuous absence of fossils in the sediments of the corridor that date between twenty-three thousand and thirteen thousand years old. They feel that this is evidence that the ice-free corridor was closed until thirteen thousand years ago, a time when people were already hunting mammoths and bison on the High Plains of North America. C. Vance Haynes counter-argues that the absence of animal remains does not make the ice-free corridor a dead issue. In fact, the opinions of glacial geologists vary greatly. The only real consensus among geologists is that the corridor was closed at some time; the duration of the closure remains in question.

Canadian geologists Arthur Dyke and Victor Prest have shown that a narrow corridor about sixteen miles wide opened up fifteen thousand years ago. At this time, the corridor was probably a saturated muddle of quaking muskeg and barren glacial-melt water streams with a severe windchill. By fourteen thousand years ago, the land would have dried substantially, with prairie grasslands replacing many of the bogs and swamps.

A mounting body of genetic and linguistic data, as well as Ice Age sites such as Monte Verde, imply that people were in the Americas before fourteen thousand years ago. If the pathway into the Americas was, in fact, blocked by a mass of ice, then the circum-Pacific coast, navigated in part or completely by watercraft, would have been the most likely route of entry. Arctic archaeologist James Dixon believes that a coastal route, extending from Alaska to Washington State, began to open about seventeen thousand years ago and was well established fifteen thousand years ago. Unlike in the ice-free corridor, the bones of land and sea animals dating to fifteen thousand years ago are well preserved in the caves, high terraces, and beach ridges of the Northwest Coast. Not only was the coast a viable route of entry into the Americas during the Ice Age, it contained an abundance and diversity of food resources. We have not found a single Ice Age American site along the Northwest Coast, but this area is largely unexplored by archaeologists.

If people made it below the limits of the continental glaciers by fifteen thousand years ago, they would have found no significant barriers in their route southward, just a landscape filled with a mosaic of wetlands, open prairies, rivers, lakes, and springs. In this water-rich environment, megamammals such as mammoths, mastodons, horses, camels, tapirs, and bison would have flourished, as well as a plethora of smaller game and aquatic resources.

If people could navigate the circum-Pacific during the Ice Age, is it also possible that they could have circumvented the North Atlantic? Archaeologists Dennis Stanford and Bruce Bradley believe that a small group of Ice Age European seafarers followed the ice margin from the Iberian Peninsula to northeastern North America between twenty-two thousand and seventeen thousand years ago. They argue that an Ice Age migration of Europeans across the Atlantic Ocean is the best way to account for Schurr's haplogroup X. Stanford and Bradley emphasize that such a voyage would not have been the first Ice Age boating adventure. Indeed, people migrated to Australia from Southeast Asia some forty thousand years ago during a period of extreme cold, crossing the Wallace Line, and more than sixty-five miles of open water, and across the Sahul Strait, one of the deepest bodies of water in the world.

Stanford and Bradley believe that the origins of Clovis can be traced directly to the Upper Paleolithic Solutrean of Europe. Since the discovery of Blackwater Draw, archaeologists have pointed to the fact that Clovis and Solutrean flaked-stone and bone artifacts were manufactured with nearly identical technologies. Stanford and

Bradley suggest that the artifacts from Solutrean sites in Spain, France, and Portugal have more in common with Clovis than any other Stone Age technology in the world. Like Clovis, there are even Solutrean tool-kit caches that resemble the Fenn and Crook County Clovis caches—they both contain extra-large bifaces manufactured by the same technology.

Additional support for Stanford and Bradley's Ice Age voyage from Europe comes from a growing number of radiocarbon-dated sites in eastern North America that are older than those in the west. Also, the densest concentrations of fluted points occur in the Ohio, Tennessee, and Cumberland River Valleys. As Ronald Mason and Dave Anderson, specialists in the archaeology of eastern North America, have pointed out, there are more Clovis artifacts in three of the southeastern states than in all the western sites combined.

Art Jelinek and Lawrence Straus, archaeologists who have both spent a lifetime studying the Solutrean, argue that there are a number of significant counterpoints to consider. First, there is almost a five-thousand-year time gap between the age of the Clovis and Solutrean sites. Second, there is no evidence for a maritime-based economy at the Solutrean sites that contain Clovis-like artifacts. Third, the differences between Clovis and Solutrean artifacts are greater than the similarities—Clovis sites lack shouldered points and bipointed knives. Fourth, the technological resemblances between Clovis and Solutrean may simply represent similar technologies adapted to similar environmental stresses. In other words, the Clovis and Solutrean technologies are convergent rather than derived—they represent independent inventions; one is not related to the other. In terms of the philosophical tool Occam's Razor, convergence is a less-complex explanation. And finally, the great quantity of fluted points in southeastern North America may be the result of collector bias, a longer residence, or a longer persistence of the technology in this region.

Stanford and Bradley counter that a Solutrean origin for both Clovis technology and Schurr's haplogroup X is a more parsimonious explanation of the evidence than an Asian or Siberian ancestry. Given that direct evidence of human lineages can be obtained at the molecular level from ancient tissue by extracting, cloning, and amplifying small lengths of DNA contained within bone collagen, the ultimate test will be to compare the genome variation between the skeletal remains of Ice Age Americans to those of Ice Age Europeans. Until then, the Solutrean-Clovis cultural and biological link will have to remain an alternative hypothesis.

We still cannot reject the centuries-old explanation that people entered the Americas during the Ice Age from Siberia and Asia. What remains in question, however, is whether or not people migrated by land across the now-inundated Bering Land Bridge and southward into the continent, around the circum-Pacific coast, or both. The peopling of the Western Hemisphere was undoubtedly a complex process that occurred over a long period of time and probably involved many groups of people from many different places. Consequently, we must keep our minds open to the many ideas that are offered to explain the peopling of the Americas. Dixon emphasizes that the timing and processes of human migration into the Americas are important because the adaptations of the first inhabitants would have formed the foundation for all subsequent cultural development in the Americas.

Human geographers have observed that when people migrate away from their homeland, they settle upon the same kind of landscape, with the same geological formations and the same food and water resources as they had back home. If people grew up on the open plains, hunting mammoths along willow-lined streams, then it is likely they would migrate to areas where they could hunt mammoths just like they did back home. If people grew up along a volcanic-rock-lined coast, fishing, harvesting shore birds, and collecting shellfish, then they would likely migrate to areas where they could fish, harvest, and collect aquatic resources. Along the circum-Pacific coastline, migrating people would have found consistency in both the volcanic-shaped landscape and its bountiful marine resources. Likewise, migrating mammoth hunters would have found a megamammal-rich habitat from the central Russian Plains to the Great Plains of Canada, the United States, and Mexico.

There is, however, an even more important question to consider than whether or not the first Americans arrived in boats or on foot; why did the ancestors of Clovis migrate to America in the first place? Was it simply a matter of wanting to see what was on the other side of the mountain, or were there natural and cultural forces that pulled them to America? Unfortunately, there are no simple answers to these questions.

Most theories of Ice Age human migration suggest the pressures of a changing environment, an advanced technology, or population pressure as a catalyst. The environment alone, however, is an unsatisfactory explanation to account for the initial peopling of the Americas. While we know that people reached America during a major climatic downturn, a period of rapid and profound environmental change, it was by no means the first; there have been many Ice Ages in the past two million years and none of them resulted in the peopling of the Americas.

In terms of technology, the first people to migrate to America faced the challenges of the Ice Age with the most complex and sophisticated tools and weapons of the past two million years. They were armed with lethal weaponry, which was capable of killing, on a one-on-one basis, the largest and most powerful creatures on the land. They were unstoppable.

Population pressure combined with an ever-changing environment and a superior technology seems to be the most powerful explanation for the peopling of the Americas. People migrated at a time when the size and density of human population was an entirely new situation. For the first time in earth's history, people were everywhere, occupying all habitable areas on the planet except Antarctica. Never before had the earth been filled with people. It is estimated that the human population had reached a record fifteen million. The combination of an Ice Age, overpopulation, and people equipped with deadly weaponry were an unprecedented set of circumstances in the earth's history.

Some economic anthropologists such as Barry Isaac have shown that population pressure alone could have been enough to trigger human migration during the Ice Age. Living at a time when the human population is measured by the billions, a mere fifteen million sounds more like a deserted planet than an overcrowded landscape. However, to people who survived by hunting wild animals and gathering wild plants at a time of rapid environmental change and mass extinctions, finding another person within five hundred square miles may have been a threat to their very survival.

Consider for a moment the relationship between environment, technology, and population of the Tutchone, a group of Athapaskan hunter-gatherers of the Yukon Territory. At one person per hundred square miles, the Tutchone had one of the lowest population densities in all of native North America. Given their technology to fish at lake narrows during the winter and hunt whatever was possible when they moved from one camp to the next, their population density of one person per hundred square miles often resulted in periods of starvation. In order to completely eliminate hardship, deprivation, and death from famine, the Tutchone population could not exceed one person per five hundred square miles.

Isaac emphasizes that a people's attitude about overcrowding is another important demographic issue that helps explain why humans migrated to America. Consider for a moment the conversation between cultural anthropologist Doug Wilkinson (a resident of Manhattan, New York) and Idlouk (a Baffin Eskimo living on the remote arctic island of Aulatseevik).

Idlouk asked the anthropologist, "How do your people live?"

"Nearly two million people live on Manhattan Island in innumerable houses, apartments, tenements, and housing projects set row on row," Wilkinson replied.

Idlouk shook his head slowly and said, "I cannot understand how people live under such conditions."

Idlouk was appalled. Manhattan Island is no bigger than his home, Aulatseevik Island, which has only thirty-one residents. To Idlouk, Aulatseevik Island was disturbingly overcrowded! The very possibility that a place such as Manhattan could actually exist was enough of a culture shock to give Idlouk nightmares. He later told Wilkinson,

"Since you told me of all those people living on one small island I have not slept well at night. I awaken thinking about the men and women and children all crammed into such a small space, pushing and shoving, fighting for air to breathe. I see people stacked up one atop the other and I become one of them striving to climb upward to reach open air. I awake in a sweat, light a cigarette, and for a long time I cannot sleep. I lie there thinking of what life must be like for all those poor people in New York. . . . When I am in my house, I am happy for a while for it is warm and there is always food. But, after a few days, I grow tired of the house; I grow tired of many people so close to me. I want to get away, off on a hunt, out into the open spaces of the ice-covered sea where I can look out and see no other soul. Then I breathe deeply; I am happy; I feel like a man again. . . . How people in your land can live day after day, month after month, year after year in the same house and not go off to hunt I do not know, I could not do it."

Idlouk's conversation with Wilkinson sounds very similar to a discussion Daniel

Boone had with his fellow pioneers. Daniel Boone was a mobile hunter-gatherer of America's early western frontier. During the eighteenth century, Boone explored most of the land from Pennsylvania to Florida with his three essentials of life: "a good gun, a good horse, and a good wife." By the nineteenth century, the population of America had doubled and people began to pour into Kentucky and Tennessee on the Wilderness Road that Boone had created with his own two hands. Once people began to settle in Boone's revered hunting ground, the Cumberland Gap, he told his friends and family that it was time to move west "to get a little more elbowroom."

Although Idlouk's and Boone's conversations are concerned more about mobility than migration, Isaac believes that Ice Age hunter-gatherers would have had similar feelings looking out of their camps and onto the open landscape before them. As long as there were uninhabitable lands that lay ahead, Ice Age hunter-gatherers could break off into smaller groups and explore new territories when the population of their camp became uncomfortably large.

Some anthropologists might argue that the stories of Daniel Boone and Idlouk are androcentric—they only give us clues to the male perspective of mobility. What about Ice Age women and children? What were their concerns as members of a migrating group of hunter-gatherers? Using ethnographic case studies of twentieth-century native peoples of Australia, South Africa, and the Arctic, there are certain broad-sweeping inferences that we can make about Ice Age American women and their children.

Women likely traveled at least twelve miles per day. Because infants and young children had to be carried, women would have spaced their children at least four years apart to avoid having to carry more than one child at a time. This burden would have been a strong enough incentive to enforce some kind of fertility control such as infanticide, abortion, or ritualized sexual abstinence. Children likely did little, if any, productive work before they married. Just try to imagine sneaking up on a herd of mammoths with a screaming child!

Whether the ancestors of Clovis walked onto the continent or arrived in boats, their hunting and gathering culture was well established and widespread across America by thirteen thousand years ago. At the time Clovis hunters were most active, continental glaciers were retreating back to the northern latitudes and higher mountain elevations, streams were dramatically reduced in size, and water tables were dropping dramatically, falling to their lowest levels in the past thirty thousand years. Many springs, streams, and lakes dried up as water tables fell below the ground surface during a climatic period Haynes has termed the "Clovis Drought." By the end of the drought and the Ice Age, all of the Americas had been settled, some thirty species of megamammals had become extinct, and the Clovis culture was gone forever.

ICE AGE CAVE EXPLORERS

As the first Americans explored the Western Hemisphere for the first time, they would have come across the entrances of great caves, some of which were filled with mineral resources, that extended many miles underground.

Around the world, caves have always played an important role in archaeology. People ventured into caves in search of protection from the elements, to mine minerals, to dispose of their dead, to conduct ceremonies, and to simply explore the unknown. Ever since the 1868 discovery of Altamira, Spain, caves have added a new dimension to the archaeological record of the Ice Age. While the entrances of caves have long been known as important archaeological sites, Altamira proved for the first time that people living during the Ice Age had the technology and desire to explore the absolute darkness of caves, to illuminate spaces never before seen.

There is abundant evidence for Ice Age cave exploration in most of the largest caverns of Europe. In the Perigord region of western France, the Pyrenees, and Cantabrian Spain, more than two hundred caves containing Ice Age artifacts and features have been documented in the past century. Between thirty-five thousand and ten thousand years ago, people entered, explored, and used caves for ceremonial activities, as indicated by the footprints, pictographs, petroglyphs, mud glyphs, stone tools, and sculptures they left behind.

Similar artifacts and features have been found in the Nullarbor Plain of southern Australia. Like Europe, people entered caves during the Ice Age to explore the underground and conduct ceremonies. Perhaps the most impressive site in this region is Koonalda Cave, where the remains of torches, hearths, petroglyphs, and flint quarries have been dated as being between twenty-four thousand and fifteen thousand years old.

Older indications of Ice Age cave exploration and use have been found in Petralona Cave, located in the Katsika Mountain region of Greece near Thessaloniki, where the remains of an early human skeleton were found in a side-passage along with an ancient stone tool kit, encased in stone beneath a stalactite and deliberately placed in the darkness of the cave sometime between four hundred thousand and two hundred fifty thousand years ago.

If people were in the Western Hemisphere at the same time that the caves of Europe and Australia were being explored, then we should find comparable evidence underground. In America, the bedrock is thick, the valleys are deep, and many of the caves are millions of years old. The seeming absence of comparable evidence of Ice Age cave exploration and use in the Americas has been one of the great archaeological mysteries, especially given the fact that America contains Mammoth, Big Bone, and Jaguar Caves, some of the largest and oldest caves in the world.

Mammoth Cave, located in western Kentucky, is the longest cave in the world, with almost four hundred miles of passages large enough to permit human entry. It is more than two million years old, with six distinct levels and seven natural entrances. Archaeologists have been searching the corridors of Mammoth Cave for evidence of Ice Age Americans for more than a century. While a Clovis point was found near the main entrance, and the skeletal remains of the Ice Age short-faced bear, flat-headed peccary, tapir, and mammoth were found deep inside the cave, the oldest artifacts inside the cave are only about four thousand years old.

Big Bone Cave, located in south-central Tennessee, contains more than nine miles of passages large enough to permit human entry. Big Bone Cave is more than a million years old, with two entrances, and there are over two hundred vertical feet of passages; it is one of the driest caves in North America. Archaeologists have searched for evidence of Ice Age Americans in Big Bone Cave for almost two centuries. Although the remains of an Ice Age ground sloth, including portions of skin and hair, were found among ancient cane-reed torches, there was no archaeological association and the artifacts are only three thousand years old.

Jaguar Cave, situated in north-central Tennessee, contains more than four miles of passages large enough to permit human entry. Jaguar Cave is more than a million years old, with two entrances, five levels of passages, and a rich Ice Age fossil record. The remains of eight extinct animals have been recovered from the upper levels of the cave, including mastodon, long-nosed peccary, dire wolf, horse, tapir, and camel. Two Ice Age jaguar skeletons, along with paw and claw prints, vomit, and feces were found in more than a mile of cave passage. While more than 270 human footprints and artifacts were found in the same area of the cave, they are less than five thousand years old.

The absence of Ice Age archaeology in the largest caves in the Americas is, indeed, a great mystery. It would seem that wherever people found a dry cave with a reasonably accessible opening, they entered and explored it systematically. Patty Jo Watson, professor of anthropology at Washington University and a member of the National Academy of Science, believes that the prehistoric use of caves was related to a practical attitude toward the underground world. Caves that contain important resources such as salt, and workable stone such as chert and flint, were eventually explored and used later in prehistory. Prospecting, collecting, quarrying, and mining occurred in the remote corners of caves when mineral resources were unavailable on the surface or they were reduced in quantity or quality.

Perhaps there was a natural bounty of the raw materials needed to support human livelihood on the surface during the Ice Age—there was simply no need to venture underground. On the other hand, humans have an innate curiosity that drives them to explore the unknown, to cross an ocean, or to see what is over the next mountain. The darkened space of a cavern is nothing more than another unexplored territory.

If people were in America's cave country during the Ice Age, then the entrances may have gone unnoticed because people were too few in number or they were unfamiliar with the landscape. Or is it possible that evidence of Ice Age cave exploration actually does exist but is deeply buried beneath many tens of feet of rock, sand, and clay? A discovery made in 1990 by an amateur archaeologist in Ohio suggests that this is, indeed, the case.

Today, north-central Ohio is a flat, almost featureless landscape, covered with fields of corn, soybeans, wheat, and alfalfa as far as the eye can see. It is the last place you would expect to find a cave, especially one that contains the remains of animals, plants, and artifacts from the Ice Age. At Sheriden Cave, more than thirty feet below the surface, these vestiges of the past paint a very different picture of the landscape twelve thousand to thirteen thousand years ago.

If we had a time machine that could take us back to the end of the last Ice Age, the view from the sinkhole entrance would be unlike anywhere found in the world today. We would experience warmer winters and cooler summers, but they would be extremely erratic from one year to the next. We would see a mosaic of plant and animal communities, parklands of spruce and pine, open patches of grassland interrupted by an occasional cedar, and shallow streams and wetlands bounded by willows and poplars.

The waters would be filled with a variety of fish, turtles, and frogs. We would see beavers and muskrats swimming toward their lodges as raccoons washed their paws and pine martins, fishers, mink, and ermines hunted. We might see a red fox following a flurry of rabbits, lemmings, voles, or mice in the grassland near the edge of the woods as woodchucks stand watch. We may also see deer browsing under the watchful eye of a gray wolf while shrews burrow beneath the sod. We would see toads hopping, chipmunks scampering, and snakes sliding on the forest floor as flying squirrels leap from one tree to the next.

The air would be filled with the musty smell of bears while lizards warmed themselves on sun-baked glacial boulders. Salamanders crawling on damp rotting wood would go unnoticed as bats fly in and out of the cave entrance. Periodically, we would see caribou, herds of pig-like animals known as peccaries, short-faced bear, giant beavers, and stag-moose.

The stag-moose was a giant deer about the size of a modern moose. It had long legs and horizontal antlers. The short-faced bear was almost a foot taller than the modern grizzly, about twice its weight, and more carnivorous. It had long legs, a short sleek body, and a powerful short broad muzzle. It was the single most powerful predator of the American Ice Age. The giant beaver was a rodent the size of a black bear. It had enormous front teeth, short legs, small front feet, large and possibly webbed hind feet, and a long narrow muskrat-like tail. There were two kinds of peccaries that visited Sheriden Cave, the flat-headed and the long-nosed. Flat-headed peccaries were the size of European wild boars, with razor sharp canines and a gregarious nature. The long-nosed peccaries were about the size of a white-tailed deer, with long legs and long slender snouts.

In this game-rich environment, we would see a small band of hunters enter the cave. It provided them with natural housing and was a place where large and small game animals could be ambushed or scavenged. Turtles, fish, frogs, and plant foods could be gathered in the sinkhole and approaching game could be monitored from the slight rise in ground around the entrance.

An Ice Age American butchering a turtle in Sheriden Cave, Ohio.

To this sparse population of nomadic people, the cave would have been one of many stops during their seasonal rounds. But the landscape was deceptively idyllic because the climate at the end of the Ice Age was unstable, and as it changed, so did the distribution of plants and animals. The extent and abundance of trees and grasses changed continuously because every species has its own individual tolerance to climatic change. Animal communities were reorganized, their ranges shifted, and some thirty types of large game, known as megamammals, became extinct. The question of why they became extinct remains unanswered. Were these animals unable to respond to the rapidly changing environment, were they hunted into extinction, or was it a combination of both pressures? Sheriden Cave provides important clues about the demise of these animals.

Prior to 1990, Sheriden Cave was not visible at all; the only trace of it was a shallow basin-like depression, or "sink," situated immediately south of the commercial entrance to Indian Trail Caverns. However, Dick Hendricks, an amateur archaeologist from Vanlue, Ohio, suspected that clues to America's Ice Age past lay deep beneath the surface. Acting on his hunch, Hendricks purchased the land and used a clam bucket to remove more than fifteen thousand cubic yards of sandy soil from the depression. In the process, he exposed a funnel-shaped sinkhole more than sixty-five feet across and fifty feet deep. Near the bottom of the pit, he found a cave nearly filled with organic rich Ice Age deposits. Some of these sediments contained wood charcoal, the bones of extinct animals, and a large flaked-stone tool manufactured from Wyandotte chert, a type of stone that outcrops more than two hundred miles southwest of the cave in southern Indiana.

The discovery was eventually reported to H. Gregory McDonald, then-curator of vertebrate paleontology at the Cincinnati Museum of Natural History. After examining the cave, McDonald concluded that the artifact was an accidental inclusion among the fossil bones. Although the stone tool resembled prehistoric hide-scraping implements produced by North America's Ice Age inhabitants, there was no precedence in the region for such a find. In Ohio, Ice Age artifacts turn up in disturbed soils near the surface or are collected from cultivated fields along with more recent stone tools.

From 1990 to 1995, McDonald directed paleontological excavations in the cave under the auspices of the Cincinnati Museum of Natural History. During the summer of 1995, a second archaeological discovery confirmed once and for all that the cave was much more than a fossil site. While excavating the remains of an extinct flat-headed peccary, Kenneth Ford, a graduate student in paleontology at Michigan State University, uncovered a bone projectile point. Like the large scraping tool, the bone point or spear tip closely matched artifacts that had been found on western Clovis sites and in northern Florida. Unlike the scraper, however, the resting place of the bone point had been accurately pinpointed within the cave sediments.

In 1996, my wife Jenny and I visited the site and examined the artifacts. Further indications of a human presence within the cave were brought to light when Jenny discovered two small chert flakes in water-screened sediment. At that point, the decision was made to conduct an archaeological salvage excavation of the remaining deposits within Sheriden Cave.

We began our excavations with a crew of dedicated students, volunteers, and amateur archaeologists. Our research focused on the recovery of bone and charcoal samples that could accurately date the artifact-bearing layers in the cave, as well as provide more precise information about the nature of environmental change at the end of the Ice Age. The timing and circumstances of such change are of more than a little archaeological interest because they undoubtedly influenced the livelihood of Ice Age Americans and ultimately the survival of their culture.

In order to determine whether or not the artifacts were discarded in the cave or had fallen in from the surface, we opened excavation squares in various locations around the sinkhole. Dr. Donald Stierman, a geophysicist at the University of Toledo, was enlisted to conduct a geophysical survey of the surface to locate potential excavation sites. While his electrical resistivity survey very accurately identified a deep accumulation of sediment on the east side of the pit, our excavations failed to uncover an Ice Age site. Instead, we exposed another filled sinkhole beneath a nineteenth-century garbage dump. As it turned out, the deep layers of the filled sinkhole contained periglacial soil features created by the extremely cold temperatures of a near-ice-margin environment. All of the other excavations near the pit were sterile and produced no archaeological materials, suggesting that the artifacts in the cave did not wash in from a site on the surface.

Inside the cave, our excavations exposed at least four major episodes of deposition associated with the formation of the surrounding landscape. The deepest layer, more than thirty feet below the surface, was a dense accumulation of grayish-brown lake clays that predate the last Ice Age, more than seventy thousand years ago. The clays were deposited by surges of muddy water entering the cave through a system of pipe-like drains. Over the next fifty thousand years, the cave dried out with little deposition other than roof-fall occurring in the horizontal passage.

Geological studies of the region have shown that the last glacial advance over the cave occurred around seventeen thousand years ago. After the last remnants of glacial ice melted from the surface between sixteen thousand and fifteen thousand years ago, the domed ceiling of the cave collapsed to form the pit entrance. Following this event, a massive quantity of glacial till flowed into the newly exposed cave. This layer is barren of plant and animal remains, which reflects the desolate nature of a periglacial environment.

Approximately fifteen thousand years ago, the moist pit and cave became an environmental "magnet" for vegetation, animals, and eventually for the people who hunted and gathered them. Over the next three thousand years, through both natural and cultural processes, the bodies of numerous species of animals accumulated at the bottom of the sink and were transported downslope into the cave. One of the most obvious natural ways for animals to end up in the sinkhole pit was through accidental falls. In this way, the sinkhole acted as a natural trap, a function that was unlikely to have escaped the notice of Ice Age American passersby. Animal remains may have also accumulated as "leftovers" from the meals of predators such as bears or wolves that entered the cave.

During this time, the region experienced dramatic fluctuations in the water table. The water table plummeted to its lowest level ever, leaving the western basin of Lake Erie a shallow marsh. Analysis of the stratigraphy by Patrick J. Munson, a geoarchaeologist at Indiana University, and Robert Brackenridge, a geoarchaeologist at Dartmouth College, suggests that waterlogged sediments from the pit entrance moved downslope to the back of the cave by a process known as solifuction. Runoff into the cave from snowmelt and rainfall likely amplified the process.

Immediately following the end of the Ice Age, about twelve thousand years ago, the effects of glacial melting, climatic change, and a regional uplift of the land caused the water table to rise dramatically and inundate the cave. A continual in-wash of sediments from the surface, combined with a rain of decomposing rock from the ceiling and walls, eventually sealed the horizontal cave mouth with dark brown silt and sand. This culturally sterile layer contained only scattered bits of charcoal and the bones of modern species of "micromammals" such as mice and shrews.

The Ice Age deposits of Sheriden Cave contain a unique assemblage of animal remains that accumulated in a variety of ways. The micromammals most likely entered the cave on their own or in carnivore feces and undigested owl pellets. In order to recover the tiny remains of such animals, which happen to be good indicators of environmental change, fine water screens and flotation machines were used to process all of the excavated sediments. Since 1990, these procedures have resulted in the recovery of more than sixty species of animals of all sizes. With the exception of the masked shrew, all of the bones recovered from the uppermost layer are from amphibians, reptiles, and small mammals that are still living in the area today.

The bulk of the Ice Age animal remains were excavated from the artifact-bearing layers. They include formerly resident or "extralimital" species such as caribou, porcupine, yellow-cheeked vole, and heather vole. The extinct species are the giant beaver and flat-headed peccary. Approximately forty peccaries of varying age have been recovered. The discovery of several nearly complete but disarticulated skeletons of peccary suggests that they entered the cave alive—through accidental falls—or as fresh carcasses brought in by predators.

A cutaway view of Sheriden Cave, Ohio, during the Ice Age shows a hunter confronting two flat-headed peccaries.

Below the artifacts, we excavated the remains of extinct stag-moose, short-faced bear, long-nosed peccary, and the extralimital pygmy shrew, northern bog lemming, ermine, pine martin, and fisher. Most of the extralimital mammals at Sheriden Cave were living considerably south of their present-day ranges in arctic and subarctic environments. Interestingly, they co-occur with the bones of mammals that are living today in more temperate regions of the world. According to Holmes Semken, paleontologist at the University of Iowa, the geologic association of such environmentally diverse species is a defining characteristic of Ice Age animal communities.

An analysis by J. Alan Holman, paleontologist at Michigan State University, of reptile and amphibian remains recovered during the earlier paleontological excavations in Sheriden Cave indicates that the environment in the immediate vicinity was a mosaic of shallow marsh, grassland, and open woodland. Microscopic examination of wood charcoal by Frances B. King, ethnobotanist at the Cleveland Museum of Natural History, revealed the remains of willow or poplar, both of which tend to grow in wet environments. The presence of fish, frogs, water snakes, and aquatic turtles in the deposit further suggests that the bottom of the sink itself may have periodically held water.

The early discoveries of the flaked-stone scraper and bone point provided the first important evidence that humans used the cave; however, the event of greatest archaeological importance was the discovery of a fluted-stone spear point on July 19, 1998. Paul J. Barans, an avocational crewmember who uncovered the point, vividly remembers the momentous event:

> *It had a slight gleam to its surface. . . . I figured that it was a peccary tusk or something similar because that's usually what has a gleaming surface down there. It wasn't until I started working around the edge. . . . that I knew it wasn't a peccary tusk. Then I uncovered an ear. . . . at that point I was pretty sure that I had a fluted point.*

Found less than a yard from where the bone point was recovered, the fluted point is complete but heavily reworked. Stylistically, it is similar to small, thin, pressure-flaked points excavated from sites in the Great Lakes region, which suggests that such points date sometime between thirteen thousand and twelve thousand years ago. The issue of typology is complicated by the fact that the Sheriden Cave stone point was manufactured from the tip of a larger, broken fluted point.

On July 30, 2000, another remarkable discovery was made. Phil Cossentino, a devoted volunteer, exposed the tip of a second bone point within a yard of the fluted-point find spot. With the help of fellow avocational crewmember Rick Willaman, they exposed the point from an ash-like matrix that contained masses of wood charcoal, burned peccary bone, and the bones of smaller mammals. Like Paul Barans, Phil and Rick are dedicated volunteers. They are well trained in the excavation of ancient archaeological sites and have decades of experience. Every Sunday, they drive almost three hundred miles roundtrip so they can put in more than twelve hours of tedious backbreaking work in the cave.

Stylistically, the bone points are nearly identical. They are unmistakably similar to artifacts recovered from Ice Age American sites in Alaska, Saskatchewan, Washington, Oregon, Montana, Wyoming, New Mexico, and Florida. They are also surprisingly similar to some Eurasian Upper Paleolithic bone and antler artifacts that date between twenty-three thousand and eleven thousand years old. The bases of the artifacts are long and straight, with angular bevels that are covered with crosshatched patterns of incised lines. The incising of the beveled ends most likely represents an attempt to roughen the contact surface prior to their attachment to a wooden shaft. The opposite ends are tapered to points, and one of the specimens displays impact damage typical of what we would expect to find if it had punctured bone. Rick Willaman found a perforated fragment of a left pelvis of a large animal, perhaps a peccary, near the second bone point. The puncture wound approximates the size and shape of the bone points. However, further investigation is needed to demonstrate or negate their relationship.

Scanning electron microscopy shows that the surface of the first bone point is covered with marks from carving, grinding, scoring, incising, and polishing. Such distinctive manufacturing marks demonstrate that the point was worked while the bone was still fresh and resilient. Radiography of the point revealed that it was produced from a thick splinter of dense mammal cortical bone. If we assume that the tibia was the longest and thickest portion of cortical bone in most megamammals living during the Ice Age, then the point could have been manufactured from an animal at least the size of a modern bison. If the point was made from a rib, then it could only have been manufactured from a mammoth or mastodon.

The discovery of bone and stone projectile points in the cave suggests that Ice Age Americans were there to acquire animal resources. A neck vertebra of a snapping turtle bearing distinctive chopping marks is direct evidence of such activity. Remarkably, this butchered bone was recovered from the same one-yard square that produced both the bone and flaked-stone projectile points. Other artifacts such as burned and calcined bone, flaked-stone scrapers and gravers, and flake fragments produced from tool-edge damage and resharpening suggests that animal resources were also being processed at the site.

Dating is one of the most important aspects of any archaeological investigation. In order to accurately interpret prehistoric livelihoods, it is crucial to document evidence of human behavior within a temporal framework. The most precise and trustworthy chronologies are those developed from more than one dating method, using samples of known composition from well-documented geological and environmental contexts.

Thirty radiocarbon samples were dated from the artifact-bearing layers and the overlying and underlying deposits. The samples consisted of wood charcoal and animal collagen, a gelatinous organic substance obtained from bone and teeth. These samples were divided among four independent laboratories, using both conventional decay and the direct atom-counting method of Accelerator Mass Spectrometry (AMS). The radiocarbon dates for the artifact-bearing layers were between thirteen thousand and twelve thousand years old. Dates from the overlying deposit are between twelve thousand and eleven thousand years old, and the underlying sediments accumulated are between fifteen thousand and thirteen thousand years old.

While radiocarbon is the single best method to directly date the end of the Ice Age, its precision can be independently verified by comparing the results to other dating and environmental-detection techniques. For almost two hundred years, paleontologists have used fluoride dating to provide a relative geological age of vertebrate fossils. The fluoride content of more than one hundred samples of bone and teeth was measured at the atomic level. The results were remarkably consistent with the radiocarbon dates—bones from the deeper layers had the most fluoride and the amount of fluoride in the samples decreased in the higher levels.

As yet another independent measurement of time, we examined the magnetism of the deposits. Geologist Brooks Elwood of Louisiana State University has found that as surface soils accumulate in a cave, magnetic fields are created. A cooler and dryer climate produces a lower magnetic signal, and a higher signal results from warmer, wetter times. The artifact-bearing deposit has a low magnetic signal that is likely associated with the cooler and drier climate that occurred during the last gasp of the last Ice Age.

We compared magnetic variations in the Sheriden Cave sediments to the detailed climate record known from Greenland ice cores, which have annual layers like tree rings. In the ice cores, cold climates are reflected by low stable-oxygen-isotope values and warm climates with high values. Like the Greenland ice core data, the magnetic variations indicate periods of rapid and profound climatic change between fifteen thousand and twelve thousand years ago, oscillating back and forth from cold to warm and warm to cold.

The timing of climatic change is also reflected in the stable carbon isotope content of the radiocarbon-dated samples from the cave. Stable carbon is an indicator of the photosynthetic cycles of plants. Different plants produce different stable-carbon signatures. Plants in dry environments produce high stable-carbon values and more humid environments produce lower values. Plant consumption by herbivores, and the carnivores that eat the herbivores, makes the animals' collagen suitable for testing also. We found fluctuations in the stable-carbon values of animal bones and plant remains from the Ice Age layers. Like the magnetic and Greenland ice-core data, both sources of stable carbon from the artifact-bearing deposits point to climate instability and a major downturn at the time when people first entered the cave, just before the end of the Ice Age.

The artifacts at Sheriden Cave, as well as most of the animal and plant remains, were deposited during a period marked by extremely fast environmental change and the extinction of many species. What caused the extinctions at the end of the Ice Age remains an unsolved mystery, but the explanations offered most often are overkill by human hunting, rapid climatic change, or both.

At Sheriden Cave, the disappearance of the megamammals occurred over a period of about two thousand years, between fifteen thousand and twelve thousand years ago. Megamammals do not disappear from the deposits all at once. To some extent, the times of their disappearance and their sizes correspond—larger ones disappeared first, smaller ones more recently. For example, stag-moose remains from Sheriden Cave date to approximately fifteen thousand years ago, the short-faced bear to fourteen thousand years ago, the flat-headed peccary to thirteen thousand years ago, and the giant beaver to twelve thousand years ago. Similar patterns have been described from Ice Age deposits on the Great Plains of North America and eastern Siberia.

If the remains in the cave accurately reflect the animal community living near it, then the staggered disappearance of megamammals—which began before human use of the site—is likely the result of climatic change, not overhunting. In such a scenario, extinction would have been highly variable and related to the diversity of the surviving plant and animal resources and their individual response to climatic change. On the other hand, the disappearance of peccary and giant beaver coincides with the artifact-bearing deposits at Sheriden Cave dated between thirteen thousand and twelve thousand years ago. This period coincides with the dated extinctions of at least thirty species of megamammals in North America; thus, Sheriden Cave not only contains evidence of what the climate was like near the end of the Ice Age, it also holds important clues about the demise of megamammals.

Our investigations have revealed much about the amazing landscape that existed in the heart of North America at the end of the last glacial period. It was into this environment that the first Americans came, peopling the continent and witnessing the extinction of the megamammals. Sheriden Cave is one of a few dozen sites that contain evidence of people and the remains of extinct species in deeply stratified, well-dated geologic contexts. In order to resolve the complex issues of human inter-action with megamammals, extinction, and climate change at the end of the Ice Age, archaeologists will have to focus on identifying, excavating, and dating more sites like Sheriden Cave, and finding more people who are in a relentless pursuit of America's Ice Age past.

CLOVIS & BEYOND

Not long after the Blackwell hoax had been exposed, I found myself in a four-wheel-drive with Forrest Fenn heading south from Santa Fe, New Mexico, on the Turquoise Trail. We were on our way to meet Mark Mullins and Marisa Lile at the San Lazaro Pueblo, the largest ruins in the Galisteo Basin, continuously occupied from the ancient days of the Anasazi to the Pueblo revolt of A.D. 1680. The bright mountainous countryside was a wonderful backdrop to discuss our plans for the upcoming Clovis and Beyond Conference, a brainchild of Fenn to bring together in one room the nation's top experts on Ice Age Americans along with professional and amateur archaeologists, collectors, and the interested public. As we turned off onto a dirt road, Fenn expressed his concerns about the current state of archaeology and why he thought the conference was so vital to shaping the future of the field.

"You know, Ken, one of the problems with archaeologists today is that they fail to educate the public. Their reports are full of scientific jargon, an almost oppressive language that our good friend Charmay likes to call archaeospeak. I have always believed that if a fourteen-year-old cannot understand it, then something is wrong with it. If archaeology is going to survive in the twenty-first century, it is going to have to include the public."

The dirt road turned into the shallow sandy Galisteo Creek, and we crossed in a spray of water. Once we were up and over the bank on the other side, Fenn resumed.

"Ken, when I was younger, I spent a lot of time at places like Lindenmeier and Snaketown, having long conversations with the likes of Marie Wormington, Cynthia Irwin-Williams, Frank Roberts, Joe Ben Wheat, Emil Haury, and Waldo Wadel. They always made time for me. They did not care that I was an amateur or a collector, it was enough for them to know that I was genuinely interested in what they were finding and that I wanted to learn more about their work and the prehistoric past."

Just as I was about to reply, I saw another four-wheel-drive coming at us head-on with a large billowing cloud of dust behind it. At this juncture, our dirt road had become a set of two-wheel tracks stretching across the desert. We pulled to the right, the oncoming four-wheel pulled to the left, and we both came to a stop. As the dust cleared, Fenn unrolled his window, as did the driver in the vehicle next to us. Given that we had been traveling across private property for some time now, I was ready for the fireworks to begin.

"Hi, Forrest," an enthusiastically smiling face greeted us.

"Hey, Doug. How's it going?" Fenn replied. Then he turned to me and said, "Ken, I want you to meet Doug Preston. Doug, this is Ken Tankersley. He is the one that exposed the Blackwell fraud."

I smiled and nodded as Fenn continued. "Say, we're headed up to the pueblo. Why don't you join us? Ken can ride with you and he can tell you all about his lab work."

"I'll turn around, and we'll follow you," Preston replied.

I got in Preston's four-wheel-drive and we followed Fenn over a trail that had ruts big enough to consume a truck. We stayed far enough behind so we didn't have to eat his dust.

"So, Ken, tell me about how you determined that the Blackwell Clovis points were fake."

In addition to explaining to Preston about the inconsistencies that I found under the microscope and with the ultraviolet light, I told him about the parallels that I saw between Woody Blackwell, Charles Dawson, and the Piltdown hoax.

"Piltdown was a classic fraud. It gave the British nobility exactly what they wanted, proof positive that all of modern humanity originated from an English ancestor," Preston said with a smile.

We slowed to a stop. Fenn was out of sight and the tracks ahead forked. One side led to a high bluff overlooking Galisteo Creek, and the other went on to San Lazaro Pueblo.

"Well, Ken, which way?" Preston asked.

"There are a lot of forks in the desert between the Turquoise Trail and the pueblo, and they all look the same to me. Let's try the left."

I was wrong! When we rounded the bend, we could hear Fenn's horn beeping loudly behind a wall of Russian olive trees. He was warning us that we were headed for the edge of the bluff. Preston quickly swung the four-wheel around and we followed Fenn onto the site, where we found Mullins and Lile waiting for us. Preston parked next to Mullins, and Fenn introduced us as we stepped out.

We were standing in the middle of a large Anasazi pueblo that sits on the western side of the Arroyo del Chorro, which forms a natural boundary between the prehistoric and historic components of the site. The Anasazi ruins in front of us looked just like a natural group of earthen mounds hidden among patches of piñon and juniper.

"I think San Lazaro will be a perfect site for the Clovis and Beyond Conference fieldtrip," Mullins remarked as we looked out at the unspoiled ruins.

"Not much has changed around here since the days when Nels Nelson explored the site during his honeymoon in 1912," Fenn said.

Nels Christian Nelson was not only an archaeological pioneer, he also lived the American dream. Nelson was born on April 9, 1875, into a hard-working Danish farming family with little time or opportunity for school. At the age of seventeen, he immigrated to the United States to live with his aunt and uncle in Minnesota and to get a formal education. By the age of twenty-six, Nelson spoke English, attained a high school diploma, and moved to California as an unskilled laborer. After earning enough money for tuition, books, and board, he applied to Stanford University, then fell in love with archaeology after working on an excavation near San Francisco. Nelson went on to major in anthropology for his baccalaureate and master's degrees.

While he has worked on archaeological sites around the world, Nelson is best known for his work in New Mexico, where he broke new ground with his stratigraphic excavation techniques. At San Lazaro Pueblo and many other sites in the Tano District, Nelson determined the temporal relationship of five different types of pottery, each style succeeding and developing into the next one. His systematic stratigraphic excavation technique was later applied to Ice Age American sites on the Plains to determine the temporal relationship of distinctive spear-point styles; today it remains the most powerful excavation tool in field archaeology.

"I would like to go over the route of our field trip, step-by-step," Fenn said, as he led us southward to a place called Medicine Rock.

The ground between the four-wheels and Medicine Rock is absolutely covered with artifacts—flakes, potsherds, and hammer-stones are everywhere, and heavily worn *manos* and *metates* rest peacefully like fallen tombstones among the cat's claws and prairie grass. We followed Fenn to a tall pillar of sandstone that rises high above the ruins.

From the top of Medicine Rock, there is a panoramic view of the Ortiz peaks and the Sangre de Cristo and Jemez ranges of the southern Rocky Mountains. There is also a clear line of sight to the northwest that passes directly through the San Marcos Pueblo, between the peaks of Los Cerrillos, and onto the summit of Turquoise Hill— the largest source of turquoise in prehistory. The entrances to the Anasazi mines are located near the summit of Turquoise Hill, a ridge of volcanic rock known as rhyolite that sits high above the desert plains. For more than one thousand years, miners extracted turquoise from rhyolite with nothing more than simple rock hammers. Today, the ground around the ancient mines is littered with broken and worn hammer-stones.

For the Anasazi, turquoise was an important ritual item, used for the manufacture of elaborate art and jewelry, and traded to distant places such as the Toltec capital of Tula in central Mexico and the Mayan city of Chichén Itzá in the Yucatán. The use of turquoise by the modern Pueblo is thought to be a continuation of ancient Anasazi ritual practices. To the Pueblo, turquoise has religious significance as a symbol of life and good fortune; it is thought to prevent accidental injuries and to have healing properties for blindness, stomach disorders, internal bleeding, poisonous snakebites, and scorpion stings. Anasazi shamans used turquoise to tell fortunes, predict the weather, and influence dreams, and it was also worn as a good luck talisman.

The Anasazi likely moved to the sandstone ridge above the Arroyo del Chorro around A.D. 1180, near the end of a severe fifty-year drought. They had completely abandoned places like Chaco Canyon and Mesa Verde and moved to San Lazaro where there were reliable sources of water. Turquoise, however, continued to be mined, as it remained an important ritual part of Anasazi culture. Fenn showed us a large plaza in front of Medicine Rock where the Anasazi inhabitants of the pueblo likely assembled for religious ceremonies, festivals, and trade fairs, bringing with them their surplus dried corn, beans, and squash, which they exchanged for raw turquoise and craft goods.

We followed Fenn around to the western side of Medicine Rock, to an ominous-looking hand-chiseled rectangular shaft that plummeted into the bedrock, with a cowboy-era wooden ladder wedged into one corner. We carefully peered into the pit only to find a disturbing emptiness, a pitch-black hole. Even the ladder seemed to disappear into nothingness. It was easy to see why the Navajo called the ancient inhabitants of the pueblo the Anasazi, a Diné word meaning "old ancestors of the witchery way."

"I have a flashlight in my truck," Mullins said.

He ran back to his four-wheel and quickly returned with a Maglite. I laid flat on my stomach and shined the tungsten beam toward the bottom of the pit. Just below the surface, the walls of the shaft seemed to absorb all of the light. After a while, my eyes began to adjust to the darkness, and I began to make out tumbleweeds, packrat nests, and recently shed rattlesnake skins.

"Well, what do you think it is, Ken?" Preston asked.

"Given that water was extremely scarce and it was crucial to the Anasazi's survival in the desert, the shaft was probably dug as a well or a reservoir." I reached down and picked up a small lump of jet. "But, if this pile of shale next to the pit is ancient tailings, then they may have been mining jet, a fine-grain coal used for at least a thousand years in combination with turquoise and shell to make mosaic jewelry. Ancient jet mosaics have been found at Chaco Canyon, Snaketown, and Hawikuh. Then again, they may have been doing all three."

"This pueblo was built by the ancestors of the Southern Tawa, an extinct Tano-speaking people whose descendants are thought to be the Tewa. A while back, Charmay Allred and I brought eight Tewa-speaking elders up here and, with a young elder interpreting for us, we asked them that very same question. They told us that the pit was used during a rite of passage. Boys would descend this pit and enter a tunnel at the bottom, which led them upward through the rock and to the other side where they emerged as men," Fenn said.

Fenn then led us to the other side of Medicine Rock, where a large pile of rock and sand tailings hid the entrance to a narrow tunnel that reached diagonally down sixty-nine feet to join the twenty-nine-foot-deep vertical shaft on the other side of Medicine Rock. A trail of packrat scats, amberat, and bits of snakeskins led the way down to the bottom where the two shafts join. A pair of healthy looking bats flew past as I involuntarily ducked my head. Based on the makings on the wall, it too had been completely hand-chiseled from the sandstone bedrock.

"You know, Forrest, I have never seen anything like this."

"There are a lot of unsolved mysteries around here," Fenn replied.

From the rock shelter, Fenn led us through a maze of piñons and sandstone to a large outcrop near the south end of the pueblo. It was covered in a gray-and-black blanket of Anasazi potsherds, most of which were portions of thin bowls with decorated interiors facing the sky. The designs ranged from coal-black hatches to triangular pendant panels over a thin, lightly smoothed white slip. I picked up one of the sherds and examined it with my hand-lens. The exterior was unfinished and the paste was tempered with coarse sand, tiny bits of sherds, and volcanic tuff.

"These sherds remind me a lot of the Chaco and Mesa Verde Black-on-White types," I commented.

"In the Upper Rio Grande area, we call this type of pottery Late Pueblo III, Santa Fe Black-on-White. It dates from the time the Anasazi arrived to about A.D. 1325, and it is thought to be derived from earlier types, such as Gallina and Kwahe's Black-on-White. This stuff has a better slip and it is more carefully smoothed than the Chaco and Mesa Verde Black-on-White. The designs on the interiors are very similar to the corbelled line decorations of the Jeddito type, which date to about the same time," Fenn said.

Then he made a quizzical look at the rock. "Something's missing!"

"Did someone steal some of the pottery?" Lile asked.

"Not someone. Something!" Fenn replied.

We followed Fenn as he climbed over the edge of the outcrop and down into a small debris-filled gully. There, beneath a couple of sandstone boulders and wedged among the piñon twigs, cones, and needles, were the missing bowl halves, along with portions of an orange-colored Kayenta bowl with a black-and-red paint decoration.

"Packrats just love to decorate their nests with pottery. They have turned this nest into a regular art gallery," Fenn said with a smile.

"This will make a great stop on the Clovis and Beyond field trip. It is an excellent example of the power of nature to move artifacts from their original location," I commented.

From the packrat nest, Fenn led us to a block of rooms sitting on the sandstone bluff overlooking Arroyo del Chorro, the ruins of the historic San Lazaro Pueblo, and a Spanish mission, built in 1613.

"I want you all to take a look at something," Fenn said.

We followed him into an exceptionally well-preserved Anasazi room. The doorsill of the keyhole-shaped entrance was fitted with a rectangular piece of granite. Fenn reached down and gently moved his fingertips back and forth over the top of the stone. It was highly polished from the many years of dusty bare and sandal-covered feet stepping through the threshold.

"Ken, have you ever seen anything like this before?" Fenn asked.

"Just one other place," I replied. "In order to descend into Mummy Valley, deep inside Salts Cave, Kentucky, you have to step onto a small ledge high above the breakdown-covered cave floor. That ledge has that same kind of polish from more than a thousand years of feet stepping on the exact same spot, over and over again. Foot polish on stone is very distinctive."

Once we were all inside the room, Fenn showed us a slate *comal,* a flat stone griddle, still in place over a square stone hearth after nearly a millennium. A well-worn *mano* and *metate* were sitting next to it, and fragments of a gray corrugated utility vessel were scattered across the floor. The room was so well preserved that I could almost see the image of a raven-haired Anasazi woman grinding a bowlful of dried corn into meal while a fresh batch of tortillas sizzled on the grill.

My daydream was disrupted as Mullins asked, "How many rooms are there?"

"There are about two thousand ground-floor rooms on either side of the arroyo that we know about. There may be many more deeply buried beneath the sand, and some of the buildings are two and even three stories high. We think there are between forty-five hundred and five thousand rooms total," Fenn replied.

Fenn led us out of the block of rooms and onto the lip of a sandstone cliff. He stepped down onto a ledge, turned toward us, and said, "I am going to take you down a prehistoric trail that leads past a cave and on to an ancient water tank."

We followed him over the edge and down along the base of the rock face to a cave that Nels Nelson described and mapped almost a century ago. Inside, we found veins of selenite crystals protruding from the soot-covered walls and ceiling, and two monstrous packrat nests in the back of the cave. The stone around the crystals was battered, just like the prehistoric selenite mines in Salts Cave, Kentucky. I wondered if Nelson saw the similarities between the two sites; to my knowledge, he was the only other archaeologist besides me who had been in both caves.

"What is so special about selenite?" Preston asked.

"Selenite is the crystalline form of the mineral gypsum—hydrous calcium sulfate. Around the world, selenite is thought to have mystical, magical, and symbolic properties. On the Great Plains, Lakota mythology holds that one of the Great Spirits was conceived when his mother swallowed a selenite crystal. Traditional Lakota make a glittering powder from the crystals that is used as a sacred pigment in the Sun Dance ceremony. In the Southwest, both the Hopi and Zuni use selenite as sun symbols, which they place on altars during certain ceremonies. Zuni shamans swallow selenite, which they claim gives them supernatural sight to divine witches and diagnose the causes of illnesses. In the Rio Grande basin, selenite weapons have been excavated from Pueblo ruins along with other ceremonial items. In most cultures, the word for selenite usually translates into something that refers to the sun's rays. In Lakota, for example, selenite is *anpe'tu wi wahi'nkpe*, a sun arrow. For many traditionalists, the sun goes into Mother Earth at the end of the day and it rises from her in the morning. Now imagine going underground and capturing the sun's rays by mining selenite crystals from the earth. The power of the sun in the form of selenite could be removed from Mother Earth and held in a medicine or fetish bag," I replied.

Fenn added, "I had planned to cook the eight Tewa-speaking elders buffalo burgers on a grill using charcoal from the burned vigas of one of their ancestral houses in the Pueblo, and I was starting back to camp to build a fire. The oldest of the elders was tired and he walked back with me. Suddenly, he started speaking to me in English. I was startled, and asked him if he had spent much time away from Hano, where he lived at Hopi. He replied, 'No, except for the four years I was in the Air Force in Utah working as a helicopter mechanic.' You can imagine my surprise. As we walked past this cave I asked him what he thought about it. We stood around a long time looking at each other in silence. Then I asked the question again, and this time the elder responded, 'What cave?' I did not know what to think because he was

standing in front of the entrance! Was he blind? He must have seen the disenchant-
ment in my face because the elder further explained, 'I do not see any cave; all I see
is a clay mine used by the women of the bear clan.' He then pointed to a small,
horizontal, zig-zag petroglyph, barely visible on the sandstone face above the cave
entrance. It was a matrilineal clan mark of ownership. I had never noticed it before."

"What's remarkable to me is that Nelson, later archaeologists, and geologists
mapped this mine as a natural feature. Scientists often assume that if it looks like an
arrowhead, it must be an arrowhead. If it looks like a cave, it must be a cave. It
is always the assumptions that we make about the past that get us into trouble,"
I added.

"Where's the clay?" Preston asked.

Fenn broke an angular piece of gray rock from the cave wall and handed it to
Preston.

"This does not look like the clay that I use to make pots," Preston said, with a
questioning look on his face.

"Here in the desert, clay is almost anhydrous, every drop of water has evapo-
rated away, making it as hard as stone. If you take that gray rock down to the spring
and hold it underwater, it will almost magically transform into a really high-grade
clay, perfect for making pots," I said.

Pointing to a vein of selenite above our heads, I continued in my professorial
mode. "Selenite is an evaporate mineral that grows from the clay as it seasonally loses
water. Because it is a deleterious material in ceramic production, the selenite had to
be removed from the clay, here in the mine. It could then be carved into a fetish or
talisman, put into a medicine bag, or heated in a fire to make plaster for a kiva wall
or kachina mask."

The packrats began to rustle around ancient corncobs sticking out from their
nest; we knew it was time to move on. Fenn led the way down the prehistoric trail,
across a boulder-strewn slope, and away from the cliff face. Out of the corner of his eye,
Mullins caught the slow movement of something between the rocks and the two of
us stopped momentarily to peer into a small dark opening behind a patch of chaparral—it was a small rattlesnake, with the tail and hind legs of a lizard sticking out of
its mouth. Not wanting to interrupt the snake's lunch, we headed on down the trail.

By the time we caught up with Fenn, Preston, and Lile, they were standing next to a basin-shaped feature carved out of a sandstone outcrop. Every declivity and crack was modified and enlarged to capture and channel each drop of rain into the bathtub-sized basin. There was even a drain carved into the rock at the end of the basin to direct the overflow water to a ledge below, just big enough to hold a pot.

After the Anasazi moved to Arroyo del Chorro, they experienced another drought between A.D. 1216 and 1239. This time, they had developed an ingenious method of channeling and storing water. The Anasazi also constructed numerous dams across narrow sections of the arroyo, next to a broad terrace of arable land just outside the walls of the pueblo. The waterworks provided them with lots of water that could easily be carried to the intensively farmed fields.

"We have found a lot of long, hollow, highly polished bird bones in the ruins. Archaeologists tend to classify the bones as beads, but many of them are six to eight inches long. I think they were used as sucking tubes, bone straws to transfer the water from the bedrock basin to a water-storage pot," Fenn said.

"I didn't think that Anasazi earthenware could hold water," Preston questioned.

"You're right, Anasazi earthenware is porous, and over a period of time all of the water will percolate right through the pores. In the process, however, it cools, which is exactly what you want it to do on a hot summer's day. You can plug the pores with piñon resin or even by repeatedly filling the pot with muddy water," I replied.

"This is a good place to cross the spring," Fenn said.

From the prehistoric water tank, we followed Fenn into a grove of junipers along the floodplain. He stopped for a moment next to a low pile of stones arranged in a circle, about six to eight feet across.

"This is one of the many shrines that we have found among the ruins. Some are like this one, next to a spring along the bank of the arroyo, and others are along the ancient trails that lead up into Pictograph Canyon or to one of the summits of the surrounding hills. The shrines range from a simple pile of rocks to large cairns, stone boxes, and cists," Fenn said.

"The Diné word for shrine is *tsenadjihih*, it literally translates to 'picking up and putting on stones.' If we assume that the Anasazi used the shrines like contemporary Pueblo peoples, they would say a prayer and place an offering for good luck as they passed by a shrine. The offerings ranged from the feather of a beautifully colored bird to fresh pine boughs or even a twig from a juniper. The Anasazi would have prayed at the shrine when they were on the trail going toward their destination, but would never do so on their return because that would have brought them bad luck," I explained.

We continued on the trail, past a permanent spring in the arroyo, through a thicket of Russian Olive and juniper trees on the other side, emerging next to the remains of a large rectangular complex of Pueblo structures on a flat area of open ground that, from a distance, looked like it was covered with pea-gravel. In reality, it was a mound of trash from one of the largest ancestral Pueblo ruins in the American Southwest. Instead of gravel, the ground was completely covered with bits of obsidian, bone, pottery, shell, and turquoise. From the edge of the mound we could see the outlines of a seventeenth-century Spanish Franciscan mission rising above the cacti.

"Why did the Pueblo move to this side of the arroyo?" Mullins asked.

"Some archaeologists believe that the ancestral pueblos were abandoned in New Mexico because of the spread of smallpox from northern Mexico, just before the Spanish arrived, but it makes more sense to me that the epidemics of infectious European diseases happened after direct contact with the survivors of a Spanish shipwreck in 1527, or thirteen years later when Francisco Vásquez de Coronado and his army of three hundred Spaniards and mercenaries came through the area," I commented.

"When did the Spanish move into San Lazaro?" Mullins asked.

"The first Spanish colony in New Mexico was established in 1598, but no one really knows anything about the Spanish occupation of the pueblo until the mission was built, almost seventy-five years after Coronado's visit," Fenn explained.

We walked across the trash mound and toward the mission, side by side, with our eyes glued to the surface, stopping occasionally to pick up and examine pieces of burned bone, broken arrowheads, and crazed stoneware. About two-thirds of the way across the mound, Fenn stopped next to a massive complex of anthills and said, "I found shards of the church bell here and pieces of a candelabrum; they had been smashed with stone mauls at this very spot during the Pueblo Revolt of 1680."

When life under Spanish rule became intolerable for the Pueblo, who suffered devastating epidemics, Apache raids, and drought, they began to abandon Catholicism and return to their traditional religious practices. To make matters worse, the Spanish misinterpreted the traditional Pueblo religious ceremonies as something akin to witchcraft and magic.

Catholicism was crucial to the Spanish domination over the Pueblo, and in 1675, Governor Juan Francisco Treviño ordered the confiscation of all Pueblo religious items, the kivas burned, and the public hanging and beating of the religious leaders in the plaza of Santa Fe. One Franciscan priest later bragged about how he personally burned more than sixteen hundred kachina masks.

The Pueblo had been forced into labor, sold into slavery, and starved, but depriving them of their religious freedom was the last straw. Over the next five years, Po'pay, a Tewa from the San Juan Pueblo, worked with other religious leaders, such as Luis Tupatu, Antonio Malacate, and El Saca to unite the Pueblos and plan the eradication of the Spanish from their land. In the spring of 1680, Po'pay planned the revolt for the time when the corn ripened, during the new August moon. Copies of his plans were outlined as pictographs on deerskins and given to runners to take to more than seventy Pueblos, some of which were more than three hundred miles away. When the time was right, all of the Pueblos were to get their weapons, kill the Spanish, destroy the missions, and smash the church bells.

As the corn matured, Po'pay distributed knotted yucca rope to the runners, one for each Pueblo. At the end of each day, a knot would be untied, and when the rope was clear, the revolt would begin. Po'pay's plans were kept secret under penalty of death, even for members of his own family. Yet even after killing his own son-in-law for disloyalty, there were still leaks to the Spanish.

Po'pay changed the date of the revolt and sent runners once again to all of the Pueblos. Fearing that the revolution would be unsuccessful, representatives from five of the Pueblos alerted the new governor in Santa Fe, Antonio de Otermín, of the date change. This betrayal led to the capture and hanging of two young runners carrying knotted ropes. When word of the boys' executions reached their families, the revolt began.

Before fleeing for his life, the Spaniard in charge of San Lazaro likely took a wooden chest full of his personal belongings, including a diary, ledgers, and a change of clothes, then secreted it under some debris in a collapsing room, hoping to retrieve it at a later date. The Spaniard never returned—the mission was destroyed, 380 Spanish citizens and twenty-one priests were killed, and the church bells and candelabra were smashed into shards. On August 10, 1680, San Lazaro Pueblo was forever abandoned.

Fenn broke the solemnity of the moment. "When was the last time you got down on your hands and knees and watched a bunch of ants? I'm serious, it's very therapeutic!"

What the heck, no one was looking. We joined Fenn and dropped to our knees, each of us staring into the tiny tunnels of the anthills. From a distance, we must have looked ridiculous—crouched down on all fours, shoulder to shoulder, huddled together in a circle with our heads bowed to the ground like Shoulin monks in prayer. I don't know about the rest of the group, but I felt like a twelve-year-old kid on a warm, carefree summer afternoon.

We watched the ants emerge from their tunnels, one by one, carrying coarse grains of sand over their heads. Remarkably, each ant seemed to have its own unique personality and, after a while, I hearkened back to the days of ancient Anasazi miners bringing up and dropping off their tailings on the side of a spoil pile. It was such a mesmerizing process that I soon lost all track of time. Then it happened. One of the minute miners came out of a tunnel bearing the weight of a large sky-blue stone ring. I could not believe my eyes; it was a perfectly preserved turquoise bead about the size of Lincoln's nose on a copper penny. After the ant discarded the artifact, I pulled out the tweezers on the side of my Swiss army knife, picked up the bead, and placed it in my hand. I stood up and used my hand-lens to examine the tiny, delicate turquoise artifact resting on the dermal ridges of my palm.

"I'll bet this bead came from Turquoise Hill," I said.

"How can you tell a turquoise bead from the Cerillos Mine in New Mexico from the Silver Bell Mountain Mine in Arizona, or from a northern Mexican mine for that matter?" Fenn asked.

"That's a really good question. Every turquoise mine has its own unique chemical fingerprint. When compared to sources in Arizona, Nevada, and Mexico, the turquoise from Cerillos has a very low amount of aluminum, only about twenty percent."

From the trash mound, we headed up the hill and into the southwestern entrance of the historic San Lazaro Pueblo. As we entered the plaza, Fenn stopped and bent over to pick up a small piece of obsidian.

"Say, have any of you ever seen a Spanish arrowhead?"

We shook our heads as Fenn held out a small obsidian point. Early historic Pueblo arrowheads are finely flaked, well-thinned, and symmetrical, but this point was thick and crudely flaked.

"When the Spanish ran out of black powder and shot, they turned to making bows and arrows to hunt game," Fenn said.

"You would think that the Pueblo would have shown the Spanish how to properly flake stone," I commented.

"After more than four hundred years, people are still fighting back and forth about the degree of cooperation between the Pueblo and Spanish prior to the revolt, but in reality, no one really knows what it was like because most of the written records were destroyed. Some anthropologists believe that the Spanish were brutal, forcing the Pueblo to work for the powers that be as well as the missionaries, while others suggest that their relationship was much more complex, waxing and waning with the availability of food, water, and protection from the Apache. The truth is buried here, inside the walls of San Lazaro," Fenn said, as he walked over to a circular stone cist in the plaza.

The cist was filled with butchered animal bones such as sheep, goat, antelope, deer, elk, and bison, and minerals such as malachite, chrysocolla, and gypsum. The selenite crystals were undoubtedly obtained locally, and the malachite and chrysocolla were copper minerals that were probably mined from the rhyolite in Turquoise Hill.

The cist also contained an enormous pile of beautifully decorated Pueblo IV and V potsherds. I bent over and picked up one of the larger sherds. It was part of a bowl with red bands outlined in black over a yellow slip. I examined the broken ends of the sherd with my hand-lens; the paste was tempered with crushed rock and bits of sherd.

"That's an interesting piece of San Lazaro Polychrome, a type called Espinoso. It predates the Spanish occupation, sometime between A.D. 1425 and 1490. It was developed in the middle Rio Grande River basin, derived from the Heshotauthla

Polychrome pottery type, and introduced into this area by Zuni traders," Fenn said, as he picked up three different kinds of polychrome-glaze sherds and placed them side by side on a flat piece of sandstone. "The Espinoso Glaze Polychrome precedes the Largo Glaze Polychrome, which, in turn, precedes the San Lazaro Glaze Polychrome. All three of these types have been found in the ruins."

"Are there any prehistoric rooms on this side of the arroyo?" Mullins asked.

Fenn led us across the plaza, through the northwestern entryway, and around the side to a well-preserved wall where a historic Pueblo V room could be clearly seen resting directly on top of a prehistoric Pueblo IV room. Glazed polychrome sherds protruding from the room-fills formed a textbook sequence of the Rio Grande ceramics. It was easy to see why the San Lazaro Pueblo was an important site during the Nelson expedition of 1912.

"Would anyone like a cool drink of water?" Fenn asked as he exposed a cache of Arrowhead water bottles hidden near the pueblo wall.

The sun was high in the cloudless sky and waves of heat were visibly rising from the desert sand. Everyone was beginning to look a bit dehydrated and anxiously grabbed a bottle of springwater. After a refreshing drink, we headed down the hill and into a broad sandy wash festooned with a menagerie of animal tracks—roadrunners, tarantulas, lizards, and snakes. The drama of the night was written in the sand. A bull snake followed a lizard, which was stalking a tarantula, which, based on the sudden end of its tracks, became the prey of a roadrunner.

Fenn saw me looking at the animal trails in the sand and commented, "On occasion, I find the paw marks of black bear and mountain lions."

We followed the wash to a ravine of gray shale that was full of plant fossils and gypsum crystals. The gulch led us up to the crest of a hill and to the remains of a large square shrine protruding from the junipers. The center of the shrine overlooks a cowboy-era ranch and the Anasazi Pueblo on the other side of the arroyo. Fenn squatted down in front of the petrified trunk of a sixty-five-million-year-old tree standing in the middle of the shrine.

"When we brought the Tewa elders up to this shrine, they told us that it should have some petrified wood in it. We looked around the hill and, sure enough, we found this stone stump lying on its side. We moved it to the center of the shrine and set it upright," Fenn explained. Then he reached over and handed me a rock and said, "We found quite a few of these stones in the shrine. Do you know what they are?"

"It looks like a slickenside, a grooved and polished rock surface that was created on a fault during a strong earthquake. The canyons surrounding the shrine are full of tilted, folded, and faulted sandstone cliffs. The Pueblo probably collected slickensides as offerings because they look so much like the bark of a fossil tree," I responded.

Fenn nodded with a smile and then got up and led us away from the shrine, back down the ravine, over the wash, and across the floodplain. We stopped momentarily to look at a block of Anasazi rooms and hearths exposed in the western bank of Arroyo del Chorro.

Fenn placed his hand on an adobe wall and said, "Nelson exposed these rooms in one of his trenches. Since 1912, flash floods and erosion have removed most of the eastern walls."

Inside the rooms were bits of bone, potsherds, and charred maize cobs about the size of my little finger. What surprised me was that Nelson's crew ended their excavation before they reached the bottom. Perhaps they ran out of time or maybe they had gathered all of the information they needed to complete the San Lazaro ceramic sequence. Regardless of their reasons, the hair on the back of my neck rose as I stood there looking at the same profile that Nelson examined almost a century ago.

We climbed up the silty bank of the arroyo and walked over to a sandstone bench covered with an extensive Anasazi trash dump filled with Black-on-White potsherds, broken black-basalt hammer-stones, and flakes of beautifully colored translucent chalcedony. The sun was getting low on the horizon and casting long shadows across the ground, producing a series of faint circular patterns in front of us.

"Are those pithouses?" Mullins asked.

"They may be some of the pithouses that Nelson found," Fenn said.

By A.D. 500, increasing population pressures and the introduction of storable seeds from the valley of Mexico forced the ancestral Pueblo to give up their nomadic hunting and gathering for a more sedentary livelihood of maize and squash farming. Archaeologists refer to these people as Basketmakers because of their exquisitely woven baskets. They were living along the banks of Arroyo del Chorro in round pithouses that bear a striking resemblance to the kivas found in the Pueblos.

Aboveground, the pithouses were similar to Navajo hogans built over knee-deep pits, sometimes with a smaller foyer-like room facing the south. The pithouses were probably clustered in a small farmstead or village with a dozen or more structures and small garden plots next to the spring.

By A.D. 750, increasing population pressure and the introduction of beans, the bow and arrow, and irrigation farming strained the natural resources of the local environment, and the ancestral Pueblo moved away to places like Mesa Verde and Chaco Canyon where they made pottery and built aboveground, apartment-like, pole-and-adobe housing in long curved rows with a round pithouse, which probably served shamans as a place to conduct religious and ceremonial activities. Today, the traditional Pueblo refer to these ancient people as *Hisatsinom*, which translates to "our ancestors."

We circled back through the cacti to the trucks and headed onto Santa Fe. Behind us, flashes of lightning illuminated the heart of a large peach-colored thunderhead expanding in the navy blue sky over the pueblo. Slowly, a large luminous moon—a Comanche Moon—rose from the top of the thunderhead's great anvil.

On October 28, 1999, Fenn's dream was realized. The Clovis and Beyond Conference captured the true spirit of Howard and Chapman's 1941 Santa Fe meeting and was a turning point in American archaeology, bridging the gaps between amateur and professional archaeologists, between private collectors and public museums, and between the average American citizen and the active political community. America's interest in its earliest beginnings had clearly increased; instead of sixty people, seen in attendance in 1941, more than fourteen hundred people journeyed to the Land of Enchantment to attend what was the archaeological conference of the twentieth century.

People came to Santa Fe from many walks of life—Nobel and Pulitzer Prize winners; molecular biologists; geologists; chemists; physicists; forensic scientists; lawyers; representatives from the National Park Service, the United States Department of Justice, and the Bureau of Indian Affairs; and members of professional and amateur archaeology organizations. As we worked together in an open, informal hands-on forum, a clearer understanding of the earliest Americans was established.

On Sunday, October 31, we led a caravan of Clovis and Beyond participants from the front of the Santa Fe Hilton Hotel, down the Turquoise Trail, and across the desert to the San Lazaro Pueblo, just as we had practiced. For the first time in more than three hundred years, the Pueblo was alive again with a multitude of people. As we walked through the ruins and down the ancient Anasazi trail toward the arroyo, a nighthawk called above the cacti.

After stopping briefly in front of the clay mine, one of the visitors asked me, "In the past few days we sure have learned a lot about the First Americans. But, in your opinion, who were they?"

Her question and the space-like landscape reminded me of the ending of Ray Bradbury's *The Martian Chronicles,* and I responded accordingly, "Follow me."

I led the group down the rock-strewn slope to a pool of cool spring water in the arroyo below the mine. I knelt down in front of the flat, still water and pointed straight down.

"There they are—there are the First Americans."

The young woman who asked the question, as well as everyone else in our group, peered into the pool. The First Americans were there—in the spring, reflected in the water. The First Americans stared back up at us for a long silent time. They encompassed every race and country origins from all over the world, and regardless of how they identified their family, they were all Americans. Their fathers and mothers came to America from distant lands, just as the people of Earth came to Mars in *The Martian Chronicles.*

"They came because they were afraid or unafraid, happy or unhappy. There was a reason for each man. They were coming to find something or get something, or to dig up something or bury something. They were coming with small dreams or big dreams or none at all. The first men were few, but the numbers grew steadily. There was comfort in numbers. But the first Lonely Ones had to stand alone . . ."

—Ray Bradbury

247

INDEX

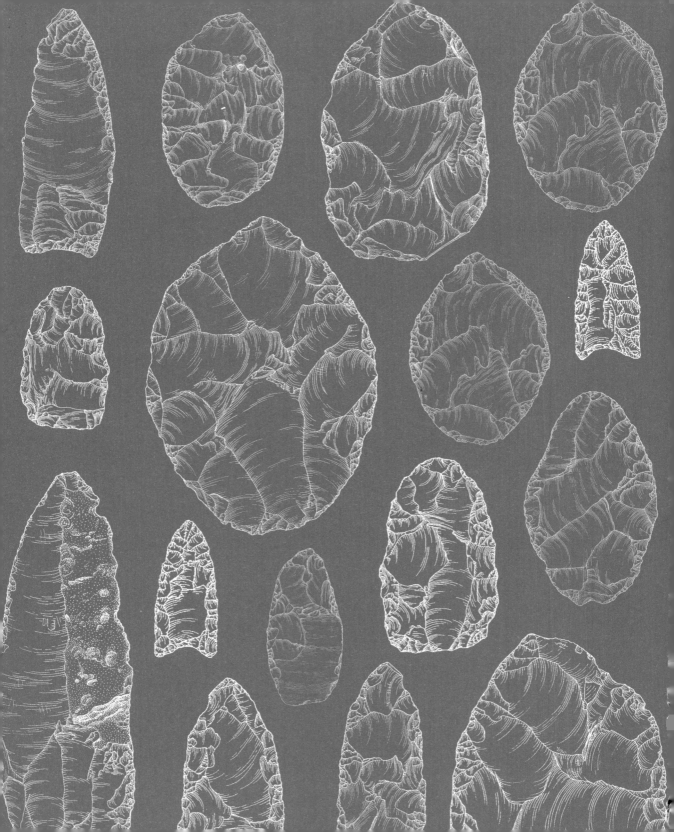